THE BUSINESS OF INCARCERATION

The Business of Modern Life Series

Series Editors: Justin Bronson Barringer and James W. McCarty

The Business of Modern Life Series explores the ways that neoliberal global capitalism has infiltrated and come to dominate virtually all spheres of modern life, including incarceration, healthcare, agriculture, technology, education, nonprofit organizations, immigration, and church, along with, of course, war. Various industrial complexes have popped up all around us, and this series will grapple with the effects that they have on our daily lives. It will be the first series of its kind—that is, one addressing a variety of theological and ethical issues of the modern world through the lens of capitalism's pervasive domination. Many books have been published on the areas we hope this series will explore, but for the most part they have neglected how finance capitalism, global markets, and economic philosophy and policy drive, or often eschew, theological and ethical concerns. Each book in this series will take on one of the industrial complexes (e.g., the military-industrial complex, the prison-industrial complex, the agricultural-industrial complex, etc.), all following the same basic format, which first addresses the biblical and theological foundations relevant to the topic, then reflects on the theological and moral state of affairs in history and in the world today, before finally closing with some uniquely Christian proposals for responding to the issues raised.

"As a theological ethicist possessing professional experience in both corrections and policing, I welcome this edited collection of essays. When I initially wrestled as a Christian with questions about classism, racism, and incarceration four decades ago while 'on the job,' there was little if any attention given to the criminal justice system and its injustices by Christian ethicists, biblical scholars, systematic and other theologians. While I do not necessarily agree with every observation or recommendation in this volume, I endorse it as a much-needed conversation partner."

—**Tobias Winright**, Professor of Moral Theology, St. Patrick's Pontifical University, Maynooth, Ireland

"This is a book that deserves to be read, shared, and discussed! It contains some of the most thorough and accessible writings on the business and practice of mass incarceration that I have read. Christians and non-Christians alike will learn from this book, including strategies for resisting mass incarceration in ways that are restorative, transformative, and abolitionist."

—**Barb Toews**, Associate Professor, School of Social Work and Criminal Justice, University of Washington, Tacoma

"The authors of this text go beyond critiquing the exploitative systems of incarceration; they do the hardest work of all—they give us hope for actual Christian resistance and ignite our imaginations for building new worlds not governed by the business of incarceration."

—**Rachelle R. Green**, Assistant Professor of Practical Theology and Education, Graduate School of Religion and Religious Education, Fordham University

"*The Business of Incarceration* is a comprehensive study of cutting-edge research addressing the pervasiveness of mass incarceration that intersects with multiple facets of life. An important argumentative arc is its claim that capitalism works together with religion to proliferate harmful systems of punishment. Still, religious communities can also challenge, and even resist, its participation in carcerality with transformative approaches oriented toward abolition. As an abolitionist and thought leader on religion and mass incarceration, I commend the curation and contributions of this significant volume."

—**Nikia Smith Robert**, Assistant Professor of Religious Ethics and Social Justice, University of Kansas

The Business of Incarceration

*Theological and Ethical Reflections
on the Prison-Industrial Complex*

Edited by
Justin Bronson Barringer,
Sarah F. Farmer,
and
James W. McCarty

CASCADE Books • Eugene, Oregon

THE BUSINESS OF INCARCERATION
Theological and Ethical Reflections on the Prison-Industrial Complex

The Business of Modern Life Series

Copyright © 2025 Wipf and Stock Publishers. All rights reserved. Except for brief quotations in critical publications or reviews, no part of this book may be reproduced in any manner without prior written permission from the publisher. Write: Permissions, Wipf and Stock Publishers, 199 W. 8th Ave., Suite 3, Eugene, OR 97401.

Cascade Books
An Imprint of Wipf and Stock Publishers
199 W. 8th Ave., Suite 3
Eugene, OR 97401

www.wipfandstock.com

PAPERBACK ISBN: 978-1-6667-5668-5
HARDCOVER ISBN: 978-1-6667-5669-2
EBOOK ISBN: 978-1-6667-5670-8

Cataloguing-in-Publication data:

Names: Barringer, Justin Bronson, editor. | Farmer, Sarah Frances, editor. | McCarty, James W., III, editor.

Title: The business of incarceration : theological and ethical reflections on the prison-industrial complex / edited by Justin Bronson Barringer, Sarah F. Farmer, and James W. McCarty.

Description: Eugene, OR : Cascade Books, 2025 | Series: The Business of Modern Life Series | Includes bibliographical references.

Identifiers: ISBN 978-1-6667-5668-5 (paperback) | ISBN 978-1-6667-5669-2 (hardcover) | ISBN 978-1-6667-5670-8 (ebook)

Subjects: LCSH: Prisons—Moral and ethical aspects—United States. | Imprisonment—United States. | Punishment—United States. | Punishment—Religious aspects—Christianity. | Christian ethics. | Corrections—Contracting out—United States. | Prisons—United States. | Privatization—United States.

Classification: HV9466 .B87 2025 (paperback) | HV9466 .B87 (ebook)

VERSION NUMBER 04/28/25

Permissions

Portions of ch. 10, s.vv. "Goals of Transformative Justice," first appeared in "Creating Safety for Ourselves," by Johonna McCants-Turner, in *Colorizing Restorative Justice: Creating Safety for Ourselves*, edited by Edward C. Valandra (Waŋbli Wapȟáha Hokšíla), 291–321 (Minneapolis: Living Justice, 2020), and are shared with the kind permission of the publisher.

Unless otherwise indicated, Scripture quotations are from the New Revised Standard Version, copyright © 1989, Division of Christian Education of the National Council of the Churches of Christ in the United States in the United States of America. Used by permission. All rights reserved.

Scripture quotations marked KJV are from the King James or Authorized Version.

Scripture quotations marked NRSVUE are from the New Revised Standard Version, Updated Edition. Copyright © 2021 National Council of Churches of Christ in the United States of America. Used by permission. All rights reserved worldwide.

Contents

Series Foreword | ix
Acknowledgments | xi
Contributors | xiii
Abbreviations | xv
Introduction | 1
  —Justin Bronson Barringer, Sarah F. Farmer, and James W. McCarty

Part One: Theological Foundations

1 The Business of Incarceration in the Bible | 9
    —Hannah Bowman

2 The Business of Incarceration and the Christian Tradition | 29
    —Kathryn Getek Soltis

3 Legal Foundations of the Business of Incarceration | 48
    —Jeffrey R. Baker

Part Two: The Business of Incarceration in History

4 Race, Racism, and Incarceration in American History | 73
    —Aaron L. Griffith

5 Reformative Impulses: Christian Theology in the History of US Carceral Institutions and Practices | 97
    —Amy Levad

Part Three: Practicing the Business of Incarceration Today

6 Mass Incarceration as the Policy Outcome of the Presumed Pathology of the Black Urban Class: A Short History | 125
    —Jermaine M. McDonald

7 Immigration and the Business of Incarceration | 137
    —Britta Meiers Carlson

Part Four: Resisting the Business of Incarceration

8 "Develop a Love for Freedom": Education and Power in Prison Systems | 163
—Elizabeth M. Bounds

9 Whole People and Communities Through Restorative Justice | 183
—Justin Bronson Barringer and Jim Buffington

10 Prison-Industrial Complex Abolition and Transformative Justice: A Primer for Christians | 200
—Johonna McCants-Turner and James W. McCarty

Bibliography | 221

Series Foreword

Over the centuries the church has been a source of guidance to many about the provision of goods and services that contribute to the common good. St. Basil started what may be considered one of the first hotels and hospitals in his Basiliad in the fourth century. Monastic communities served as a model for modern educational institutions, and sometimes served as places of sanctuary for those whose lives were in danger. And countless Christians through the centuries have sought guidance from the church about their participation in warfare or how they were going to run their businesses. To many in the modern world such a role for the church seems absurd, because we have come to believe that state actors and business leaders should dictate the what and why and how of our lives, often even letting business trends or patriotic commitments order the life of the church. However, there has also been resistance to the rise of nation-state and business logics ordering our moral lives.

In 1961 Dwight Eisenhower warned us that the ever-deepening relationship of private companies' profits to the United States' participation in war was creating a "military-industrial complex" that threatened the very practice of democracy.[1] In 1983 political philosopher Michael Walzer warned us that the moral logic of the market is imperialistic and threatens to become the dominant way we relate to each other by turning nearly every human interaction into a market transaction.[2] And Christian theologian-activists—from Martin Luther King Jr. to Dorothy Day to Desmond Tutu—have shown us ways to resist these trends through social movements and lives of radical hospitality. These phenomena—the rise of various industrial complexes, the colonialist expansion of market logics into every aspect of our lives, and the seeming completion of market expansion

---

1. Eisenhower, "Farewell Address."
2. Walzer, *Spheres of Justice*.

around the world—have become so commonplace that we rarely question them anymore.

We now speak not only of the military-industrial complex, but of the prison-industrial complex, the medical-industrial complex, and even the nonprofit-industrial complex (to name only a few). These industrial complexes are economic subsystems within the larger global market that are dependent on private actors influencing, and even shaping, public policies and practices to promote their continual expansion. Increasingly and with growing speed, sectors of our common life once considered public and shared are becoming privatized and dominated by market forces: our schools, our medical institutions, and even our churches. The books in The Business of Modern Life take these developments seriously as theological and ethical problems to be examined, critiqued, and resisted. The Christian tradition has long taught us that humans are more than consumers or commodities but bearers of God's image. The church has long reminded us that we belong not only to ourselves or our appetites but to each other and to God. And the words of Jesus have long challenged us to believe that it is the poor rather than the rich, the oppressed rather than the powerful, who are blessed by God.

In The Business of Modern Life you will find a series of books examining the social ethics of our contemporary economic life in ways that seek to resist turning everything we do into "business" and reclaiming a vision of shared life that orients us toward the business of loving God and our neighbors. The books in this series will address these topics through four primary lenses: theological foundations for understanding and addressing the industrial complex in question; the history of that particular industrial complex; the global impact of that industrial complex today; and finally, possible Christian responses to the industrial complex being addressed. Collectively, then, these volumes should be a compendium of neoliberal, global capitalism's effects on nearly the entirety of human lives. They will also suggest ways that followers of Jesus may think about and act faithfully in response to these realities, seeking out the good, the true, and the beautiful as a declaration that it is not the market and Mammon that ultimately reign, but Jesus Christ.

Acknowledgments

This book has lived many lives and been through many transitions. It began before the 2020 COVID-19 pandemic and has seen contributors and editors birth multiple children, experience professional transitions and cross-country moves, and survive severe illnesses. Some contributors had to step away, and others joined the project after it was already underway. In short, life happened. And yet people kept writing and editing, knowing the work would contribute to the disruption of the prison-industrial complex. In addition, our families and communities of support have made the time for this work to be done. For every person who has contributed to this book, directly and indirectly, we are deeply grateful.

Contributors

Jeffrey R. Baker is associate dean of clinical education and global programs and clinical professor of law at Pepperdine University School of Law.

Justin Bronson Barringer is a scholar, minister, educator, and consultant deeply involved in community outreach and development, with a PhD from Southern Methodist University. He is a co-editor of The Business of Modern Life Series with Wipf and Stock/Cascade Books.

Elizabeth M. Bounds is associate professor of Christian ethics in the Candler School of Theology at Emory University and a co-founder of the Certificate in Theological Studies at Arrendale State Prison for Women. She is the author of *Coming Together/Coming Apart: Religion, Modernity, and Community* and a co-editor of *Welfare Policy: Feminist Critiques* and *Justice in the Making: Feminist Social Ethics*.

Hannah Bowman is a literary agent, theological scholar, and the founder of Christians for the Abolition of Prisons (https://christiansforabolition.org/).

Jim Buffington is chief operating officer for the restorative justice organization Bridges to Life (https://www.bridgestolife.org/). Before coming to BTL, Jim had a thirty-year business career in financial/legal services and aerospace.

Britta Meiers Carlson is visiting assistant professor in practical theology at Sewanee: The University of the South. She researches interactions between historically white Christian churches and Latin American immigrant communities to better understand how ecclesiology is evolving in the United States.

Sarah F. Farmer is associate director at Wabash Center for Teaching and Learning. Prior to coming to Wabash, Sarah served as associate professor of practical theology and community development in the School of Theology and Ministry at Indiana Wesleyan University. She is the author of

Restorative Hope: Creating Pathways of Connection in Women's Prisons and co-author with Anne E. Streaty Wimberly of *Raising Hope: 4 Paths to Courageous Living for Black Youth*.

Aaron L. Griffith is assistant professor of American church history at Duke University Divinity School. He has also taught at Whitworth University, Sattler College, and the Prison Education Project at Washington University in St. Louis. He is the author of *God's Law and Order: The Politics of Punishment in Evangelical America*.

Amy Levad is professor of theology at the University of St. Thomas, specializing in moral theology and Christian social ethics. Her primary areas of research are mass incarceration and the ethics of criminal legal systems, which are the focus of her two books titled *Restorative Justice: Theories and Practices of Moral Imagination* and *Redeeming a Prison Society: A Liturgical and Sacramental Response to Mass Incarceration*.

Johonna McCants-Turner is associate professor of peace and conflict studies at Conrad Grebel University College at the University of Waterloo. Her current scholarship lies at the intersections of restorative and transformative justice and Black feminist and womanist theology.

James W. McCarty is clinical assistant professor of religion and conflict transformation and director of the Tom Porter Religion and Conflict Transformation Program at Boston University School of Theology. He is a co-editor of *The Business of War: Theological and Ethical Reflections on the Military-Industrial Complex* and a co-editor of The Business of Modern Life Series with Wipf and Stock/Cascade Books.

Jermaine M. McDonald is an independent scholar who lives in Philadelphia. He has published research on Martin Luther King Jr., American civil religion, and racial justice.

Kathryn Getek Soltis is director of the Center for Peace and Justice Education and associate teaching professor in the Department of Theology and Religious Studies at Villanova University.

Abbreviations

BOP	Federal Bureau of Prisons
CBP	Customs and Border Protection
CCA	Corrections Corporation of America
DACA	Deferred action for childhood arrivals
DAPA	Deferred action for parents of Americans
DHS	Department of Homeland Security
ICE	Immigration and Customs Enforcement
IIRAIRA	Illegal Immigration Reform and Immigrant Responsibility Act
INS	Immigration and Naturalization Service
NPA	National Prison Association
NSM	New Sanctuary Movement
PAC	Political action committee
PIC	Prison-industrial complex
RJ	Restorative justice
SOP	Standard operating procedure
TJ	Transformative justice

Introduction

Two of the most significant political developments in the late twentieth and early twenty-first centuries have been the rise of mass incarceration and the ever-widening economic gap between the wealthy and the poor. As the rich have gotten exorbitantly richer and the poor simultaneously poorer, those marginalized in the US by race, class, and other relevant characteristics (such as disability and immigration status) have been incarcerated at exponential rates. The US now famously incarcerates people at a higher rate than any other country even remotely close to it in population or economic standing. Reading these phenomena through the lens of this series, one might expect these developments to be related to one another. And, as the essays in this volume demonstrate, they are.

We call these related developments the prison-industrial complex. Just as the military-industrial complex has come to be shorthand for the ways that governmental and private interests are enmeshed in the ever-expanding business of war, we join with others in recognizing the increasingly intertwined ways government policy and private industry work together to police, surveille, and incarcerate growing numbers of people. In particular, this system targets poor people, people racialized in ways other than white (especially Black, Indigenous, and Latina/e/o/x), queer people (especially trans people), and disabled people. The *prison-industrial complex*, then, is a shorthand to refer to the ways that the ever-growing population of people policed, surveilled, and incarcerated in the United States is connected to the increasing profits of private industry. Public monies, that is tax revenue, are being used to increase the profits of private companies and their investors by caging, surveilling, and punishing indefinitely our neighbors.

For example, the company JPay makes its profits by managing services between incarcerated people and their families (such as money wires and transfers); multiple other companies make profits facilitating phone calls to incarcerated people; those in prisons often work at enslavement wages for major multinational corporations (for example, making clothing); companies like CoreCivic and GEO Group build and run private prisons; other companies build the products used by jails and prisons, such as jumpsuits, handcuffs, and ankle monitors, and provide private (and often insufficient) health care inside prisons. In addition, there are prisons that exploit prison labor for activities such as firefighting, farming, and the production of license plates. Incarcerated persons regularly make, after fees and the personal costs of being incarcerated, less than $1 per hour. Such cheap labor dramatically reduces costs for these companies and increases their profits. According to one report, "Incarcerated workers produce more than $2 billion a year in goods and commodities and over $9 billion a year in services for the maintenance of the prisons where they are warehoused."[1]

These institutions are not only exploiting incarcerated individuals as laborers; they are also pocketing money from taxpayers via government contracts. This double-dipping of resources ultimately creates a profit for the private prison industry at the expense of citizens and incarcerated individuals. In addition, such companies then also receive tax credits for employing incarcerated persons and, therefore, participate in a kind of triple-dipping into the basin of public monies and exploiting incarcerated people.[2] And this is just a quick survey of such profit-seeking activities connected to the ever-growing "markets" of incarcerated people and the prisons that house them.

Incarceration has taken several forms over the history of the United States. And the evolution of these forms has often been influenced, most often explicitly and sometimes implicitly, by Christian ideas and practitioners. As Amy Levad demonstrates, these evolutions have often been driven by well-intentioned spirits of mercy and redemption but have mostly succeeded in creating new ways to punish and torture those made criminal by unjust political and economic systems. And it is not only "good" Christian intentions that have had perverse results. Jermaine McDonald shows us that supposedly secular and social reform efforts, such as President Lyndon Baines Johnson's "Great Society" programs, have also contributed to the creation of the racist system of mass incarceration we have today.

This system of mass incarceration and the prison-industrial complex is having devastating effects on individuals, families, communities, and the nation. It means that millions of children spend years without a parent's regular presence in their lives; that many poor and racially oppressed communities have large percentages of their population taken and are traumatized and made to be "unproductive" in our capitalist society; and that

---

1. ACLU and GHRC, *Captive Labor*, 6.
2. Payne, "Economic Impact of Prison Labor," 16–17.

millions of citizens have their democratic rights denied them for years or even lifetimes. And it is not only those who fill jails and prisons who are so impacted. Millions more people are presently surveilled by the state while under house arrest or living under the terms of parole and probation. The tentacles of the prison-industrial complex reach into millions and millions of lives and wrap their tight grip around Black, Brown, Indigenous, queer, poor, and disabled communities from Alaska to Alabama, from the white beaches of Hawai'i to the rocky beaches of Maine.

In light of the focus of this volume, it is important to point out not only that millions of the most vulnerable citizens in the country are so marginalized but that others are making billions of dollars in profit because of or adjacent to their suffering. There are entire industries built upon a constant and growing prison population. And it is not an exaggeration to say that many incarcerated persons are sold by the prison-industrial complex as enslaved laborers to corporations that many, if not most, Americans rely upon to fund their stock portfolios and retirements. Companies as diverse as Whole Foods, McDonalds, Victoria's Secret, American Airlines, and Verizon all use prison laborers to make their profits.[3]

All of this is to say that one of the arenas in which the neoliberalization of American politics and economics is most clear is in "the business of incarceration." A system that is said to promote public goods—such as public safety, the administration of justice, the public health goals of violence reduction, or the reform of those who have committed criminal deeds—has increasingly become a system in which a primary goal for many participants is to make money for private companies and citizens. And to make that money on the backs and the suffering of some of society's most historically oppressed peoples. This is patently unjust, and Christians should witness to alternative ways of living together at every level and stage of this process.

Historically, however, Christians, especially powerful and white Christians, have been central to the creation, maintenance, and adaptation of the criminal punishment systems that have led to our present crisis. Kathryn Getek Soltis, Aaron Griffith, Amy Levad, Elizabeth Bounds, and others in this volume make clear the historical, theological, and pastoral interests that have bequeathed to us our current system. Evolving theological, pastoral, and political commitments and emphases have contributed to the creation of various models of the prison, forms of reformation and rehabilitation, and visions of just punishment. Everything from labor camps to incarceration to solitary confinement to restorative justice have had their roots, at least to some extent, in the work of Christian communities and actors. And those

---

3. McDowell and Mason, "Prisoners in the US."

intentions, whether retributive or restorative or something in between, have too often led to the entrenchment of the prison as an institution as well as the creation of new forms of punishment for those made criminal by our evolving legal systems.

This is a disheartening discovery for justice-minded Christians. Many of those we might want to look to as inspirations and guides—from Quakers in early Pennsylvania to mainline Protestants in the era of the social gospel to born-again White Evangelicals in the 1970s—have wittingly and unwittingly bequeathed to us a classed and racialized system of mass incarceration as our inheritance. This system is chewing up and spitting out our babies, often via the phenomenon that has come to be called the school-to-prison pipeline,[4] and is creating new mass traumas among communities who have already inherited the legacies of colonization and genocide, enslavement, Jim Crow, forced migration, state and interpersonal violence, structural poverty, and so much more.

So, it is with an appropriate humility, and just a bit of trepidation, that we conclude this book with three essays exploring possible Christian responses to this system of mass suffering, profit making, and exploitation. We see the ways Christians have made incarceration worse by making it bigger and newly torturous over the decades and engage this contemporary injustice, recognizing, as it were, the possibility of failure. Not to engage, however, seems fundamentally unjust and un-Christian in light of the scale of social injustice and human suffering this system is producing. So, we point to three areas in which Christians are already engaged in resisting the business of incarceration: education, especially theological education, within prisons; restorative justice as a default mode of engaging harm doing; and community-based safety and accountability processes, often called transformative justice, as ways of engaging today while moving toward the horizon of a world without prisons at all.

---

4. The school-to-prison pipeline describes the growing trend of children being put on a fast track to juvenile and/or adult incarceration via the criminalization of in-school behavior, the placement of police in schools, and the collaboration between schools and other social service agencies that have agreements with policing systems to which they refer "problem youth." In addition, increasing use of "zero-tolerance" discipline policies often results in students not being in school during disciplinary action and, therefore, more likely to get caught up in policing of their activity outside of school. Finally, because institutionalized racism and personal biases of teachers and police influence each of these phenomena, the school-to-prison pipeline disproportionately affects Black students and students with disabilities. For an in-depth account, see Hertzig, *School-to-Prison Pipeline*.

Book Summary

The book will achieve its goals of explicating the business of incarceration, uncovering the Christian legacies that undergird it, and proposing modes of resistance through a series of ten chapters in four sections. The first section examines biblical, theological, and legal foundations for understanding the business of incarceration. First, Hannah Bowman, a Christian prison abolitionist, provides an interpretation of biblical texts consistent with a hermeneutic of suspicion, if you will, of dominant visions of justice in our current system. Kathryn Getek Soltis provides an overview of the Christian theological tradition and the ways various theologies have provided foundations for different criminal justice systems across time. And Jeff Baker, a professor of law, guides us through a review of the legal tradition in the United States with an eye toward the ways it has created criminals and hints at the possibility of functioning differently going forward.

The second section analyzes historical precedents for our current system of mass incarceration. First, Aaron Griffith demonstrates the ways that race and racism, especially directed toward Indigenous and Black communities, have been intertwined with practices of incarceration in the United States from its birth. Next Amy Levad traces the ways that Christian engagement in prison reform efforts in the United States have often resulted in the expansion and entrenchment of the prison-industrial complex. This has meant a bigger and crueler prison system that functions primarily to punish rather than a more humane system that could lead to the personal and social transformation so many reformers have hoped and worked for.

The third section explores more contemporary legal, political, and social dynamics that have contributed to the rise of mass incarceration in our time. Jermaine McDonald documents the anti-Black ideologies and politics, from the 1960s to today, that have undergirded and made possible the current racialized system of mass incarceration. McDonald tells the story of how "the new Jim Crow" is such because of its intimate ties with anti-Black racism. Britta Carlson, alternatively, demonstrates the ways that anti-immigrant and anti-Latinx cultural politics has contributed to the increased criminalization of unauthorized migration and, therefore, the increasing incarceration of migrants within US borders. In these ways, racialized mass incarceration is not an anomaly of or aberration in American society. Rather, it is the necessary result of the culture, economics, and politics of contemporary America.

Finally, the fourth section of the book points toward three ways that Christians are and can be engaged in the work of resisting the business of incarceration in their own lives and communities, and how we could work toward the birth of new ways of living with one another. Elizabeth Bounds tells us stories about her years administering a theological certificate program in a women's prison in Georgia. In doing so, she provides an overview both of the complicated ways education has been related to prison reform movements *and* of the complex ways that incarcerated persons, especially women, use the opportunity to pursue education within prison walls to practice freedom. Justin Bronson Barringer and Jim Buffington describe the impact of restorative justice in their own lives, with Jim's own compelling personal story driving much of the narrative, and the possibility of restorative responses to harm and crime as the Christian way forward. And, finally, Johonna McCants-Turner and James W. McCarty reflect on practices of prison-industrial complex abolition and transformative justice as faithful Christian responses to the evils of the business of incarceration. Seeking a radical and revolutionary approach to the harms we do to one another, McCants and McCarty point us toward new worlds in which it is easier to be faithful Christians that could avoid the failures of past Christian engagements with police and prison reform.

The authors of this collection of essays show us that Christian faith has long inspired Christian social action in the sphere of criminal and social justice; that this engagement has been mixed in motivation and impact; that their engagement has often worked against even their best intentions; and, therefore, that new ways of thinking about how Christians should engage the spheres of law, policing, and incarceration are required. This mixed legacy does not, however, excuse present and future engagement to resist the business of incarceration and build new worlds in which new ways of practicing justice are possible. Racialized mass incarceration, and the business that undergirds it, is opposed to Christian justice, and in the legacy of Jesus's own ministry, the work of releasing captives and freeing the oppressed is upon us. We, the editors, pray that this book is one contribution to that necessary work of discipleship.

Part One

THEOLOGICAL FOUNDATIONS

1

The Business of Incarceration in the Bible

HANNAH BOWMAN

What relevance do biblical texts about imprisonment have today? Translating these texts to the modern context of a world structured by the interrelated systems of racism, capitalism, and mass incarceration is part of building new theologies of justice. Additionally, studying the correlations when comparing principles of prison abolition and transformative justice with Christian ethics opens up new forms of religious praxis against oppressive structures of punishment and imprisonment.

To reckon with the "business of incarceration" in the Bible means recognizing the *political* purposes and realities of incarceration as they are presented in biblical texts, while also considering how the Bible talks about retribution and reparation for harm. This chapter will explore a variety of biblical perspectives on incarceration and its relationship to politics, justice, law, economics, the land, and debt language. First, I will consider the political implications of imprisonment suggested by biblical stories. Then, I will explore key biblical texts on retribution and restitution and how these are reframed within the covenant people's relationship to the land.[1] Third, the connection to the land will point to the centrality of the biblical concept of Jubilee with its promise of freedom for prisoners and an end to systems

---

1. See Walter Brueggemann's book on the topic of Israel's relationship to land: *Land*.

of incarceration and oppression within our own economic and material realities. The final section will consider how the church, as a community built upon the proclamation of Jubilee, can conceive of and should engage in the "business of reparation" by reconceptualizing and reimagining debt language, atonement, and practices of accountability to build an alternative community that stands in opposition to the business of incarceration.

Incarceration as a Political Reality in Scripture

Regarding matters of justice, the Bible not only presents the laws and promises of God but also offers a window into the historical realities of the practice of incarceration. Christian ethics around crime and punishment often deal directly with the language in the Torah on reparation and retribution: "an eye for an eye" (Exod 21:24), the use of capital punishment, and the cities of refuge (Num 35:11–24; Deut 19:4–7). At the same time, as Lee Griffith notes, incarceration is only sometimes presented as a punishment for harm in biblical texts and probably came to Israel from foreign nations.[2] Stories of incarceration are woven through the biblical texts but mostly in ways that show the political nature of who is incarcerated versus who is not.[3] As Christopher Marshall writes,

> While prolonged imprisonment was not used in biblical times as a form of criminal punishment, it was still used for political and military ends. It was a way of silencing pesky prophets who voiced criticism of the reigning king or gave him unwelcome advice. It was a means of keeping defeated enemies under control, or detaining people accused of disloyalty. It was a way of holding individuals before selling them into slavery or putting prisoners of war into servitude. It could be used to prevent debtors from absconding, with the torments inflicted upon them in custody being an added incentive for their families to ransom them from bondage. In the New Testament, prison often serves as an instrument of religious persecution.[4]

The biblical stories about the incarceration of Daniel and his friends (Dan 3, 6), Jeremiah (Jer 37), and Joseph (Gen 39–40) illustrate this. It is important not to read these stories simply as tales of "unlawful imprisonment" for those "innocent but falsely accused." The issue is not whether

---

2. L. Griffith, *Fall of the Prison*, 91.

3. I have previously written about this, and the following argument draws on examples from my previous article, "What Does the Bible Say About Prisons?"

4. Marshall, *All Things Reconciled*, loc. 2530.

those incarcerated are innocent. Rather, as these biblical stories present, incarceration is *designed* to work in the service of power. Prison abolitionist Ruth Wilson Gilmore expresses the problem with relying on innocence to safeguard us from prison: "Innocence is not secure, and it's a mystery why it ever seemed reliable. . . . Human sacrifice rather than innocence is the central problem that organizes the carceral geographies of the prison-industrial complex. Indeed, for abolition, to insist on innocence is to surrender politically because 'innocence' evades a problem abolition is compelled to confront: how to diminish and remedy harm as against finding better forms of punishment."[5] Incarceration is better analyzed in terms of the powers that use it than in terms of whether its victims are innocent or guilty.

In the book of Daniel, two stories show this politically expedient wielding of the power of incarceration and death. The parallel stories of Daniel being cast into the lions' den (Dan 6) and Hananiah, Azariah, and Mishael being cast into the fiery furnace (Dan 3) both show Israelites in Babylon being subject to legal punishment for violating an unjust law on religious grounds. Daniel prays to God even though a law banning such prayers has been passed, while Hananiah, Azariah, and Mishael refuse to bow down to an idol built by Babylonian King Nebuchadnezzar. While both stories concern executions rather than incarceration, the connection of criminal punishment and what Griffith calls the "manifestation of death" in the form of imprisonment[6] makes these stories relevant for this study. Indeed, Griffith notes that "the identification of imprisonment with the power of death may be related to the ancient Near Eastern practice of imprisoning people in cisterns and pits and the association of these cells with the entrance to Sheol and the underworld";[7] the furnace in Dan 3 and the pit of lions in Dan 6 clearly fall into this tradition: places of death in which "criminals" are confined. Daniel and Hananiah, Azariah, and Mishael are treated as righteous in the text, but they have in fact broken Nebuchadnezzar's decree, "the law of the Medes and the Persians" (Dan 6:8). They are *guilty* of breaking the law; their righteousness is independent of legal guilt. The response of Hananiah, Azariah, and Mishael—"we have no need to present a defense to you in this matter" (Dan 3:16)—recognizes that legal punishment and incarceration have no moral force when the law does not promote real justice.[8] The law of Nebuchadnezzar functions effectively to oppress the exiles in Babylon; the

---

5. Gilmore, *Abolition Geography*, 384.
6. L. Griffith, *Fall of the Prison*, 106.
7. L. Griffith, *Fall of the Prison*, 106.
8. See H. Bowman, "What Does the Bible Say."

incarceration and attempted executions of the exiles are examples of that oppressive power.

Likewise, the incarceration of Jeremiah in Jerusalem occurs because Jeremiah speaks a threatening truth to the rulers of the city, prophesying the destruction of Jerusalem at the hands of the Babylonian army. For this, he is accused of wishing to defect to the Babylonians (Jer 37:13) and therefore imprisoned. In the book of Genesis, Joseph, after being sold into slavery, is imprisoned after a false accusation of rape by his enslaver's wife (Gen 39). In prison, he meets two servants of Pharaoh who seem to be incarcerated not because of any wrong they have done but simply upon Pharaoh's whim (Gen 40).

There is no premise of justice in the punishment doled out in these stories; prison is used as coercion to support those in power. As Griffith notes, after the fall of Jerusalem and during the Babylonian exile, this political use of incarceration turns the tables on the powers that be: "King Jehoiachin spent 37 years in a Babylonian prison (2 Kgs 25:27; Jer 52:31), King Jehoahaz died in Egyptian imprisonment, and there is no trace of King Zedekiah after he was jailed in Babylon."[9] Incarceration, then as now, is inextricable from war and domination. As per Gilmore, it is not guilt versus innocence but "human sacrifice"—the willingness to exclude from society certain populations for politically expedient ends—that is the actual underlying logic of imprisonment.

This pattern of political forces shaping how incarceration is implemented continues in the New Testament. John the Baptist is imprisoned when he criticizes King Herod (Matt 14:1–12; Mark 6:14–29). The interactions between Peter and John and the Judean authorities—which include Peter's incarceration twice, once at the hands of the Sadducees and once by King Herod (Acts 5, 12)—require careful consideration given the anti-Semitic history of the Christian perspective on the Jewish temple authorities. That said, it is clear in those stories that the incarceration is not punishment for harm done to another but instead governed by political (or theo-political) concerns: the potential political destabilization that could be caused by the claim that Jesus was the Messiah (see, for example, Gamaliel's commentary in Acts 5:38–39 comparing Jesus to previous messianic political revolts) and the threat to Herod's power presented by the church. Later, Paul and Silas are incarcerated in Philippi because they threaten the economic power of slaveholders (Acts 16:16–40).

Willie Jennings, in his commentary on Acts 5:18–42, teases out how the early church is structured as an anti-prison community:

---

9. L. Griffith, *Fall of the Prison*, 89.

> Luke shows us that the new order will challenge even the power of the prison. The prison . . . claims a God-given right to exist. It claims a right to establish order and control as a fundamental tool of worldly authorities and governments. God at this moment in the drama will again take back what God had given. The power to incarcerate will be trumped by the power to free. . . . The power to free people from bondage is of the new order just as the power to imprison is of the old order. As such, incarceration is shown in all its horror as a tool of interests—political, economic, social, religious, and deployed in the arbitrariness of law and policy, threat, and jealousy.[10]

Later, Jennings concludes about Paul and Silas's incarceration, "The prison has never been about criminals but about societies. As this story of Paul and Silas indicates, the prison is a tool for control and containment."[11] Ultimately, he writes, "the church is formed in a pedagogy of prison that we must never forget,"[12] and "the disciples of Jesus cannot escape our necessary confrontation with prisons. Arrest, incarceration, and imprisonment have never been and never are neutral processes, functioning according to basic rules of justice and human utility. Incarceration is a process at the disposal of the rich and powerful, and here we see it unleashed against the servants of Jesus."[13] The church is intended to stand in opposition to the business of incarceration that serves to preserve power and control the marginalized.

Throughout these stories, incarceration proves a method of control more than a method of justice. Perhaps it is because of this political function of incarceration that the Psalms repeatedly identify God with the freeing of prisoners (e.g., Pss 68:6; 107:14—here God seems to be responsible for the incarceration but responds nonetheless to save the prisoners when they cry out for deliverance; 146:7). Griffith notes the consistent biblical identification of prisons with the power of death. "The problem is that prisons are *identical in spirit* to the violence and murder that they pretend to combat."[14] Gilmore's definition of racism—"the state-sanctioned and/or extralegal production and exploitation of group-differentiated vulnerabilities to premature death"[15]—lends poignancy to the relationship between the prison-industrial complex's political function of racial control and its instantiation

---

10. Jennings, *Acts*, 61–62.
11. Jennings, *Acts*, 167.
12. Jennings, *Acts*, 129.
13. Jennings, *Acts*, 161.
14. L. Griffith, *Fall of the Prison*, 106; emphasis in original.
15. Gilmore, *Abolition Geography*, 17.

of the power of death. The "business of incarceration," in the Bible and still today, is the system in which political power and the power of death operate hand in hand.

It is essential to recognize that the descriptions of incarceration in biblical texts present some of the same features of a "death-dealing"[16] political system as the modern prison-industrial complex does. At the same time, grappling with incarceration and, more broadly, criminal punishment in the Bible requires us to look critically at the way it suggests the people of God should respond to harm too.

The "City of Refuge" Versus the Prison: Retribution and Reparation for Harm

To fully address what the Bible says about the prison's role (or lack thereof) in justice, we must also look at what it says about reparation and retribution. Essential to address is the *lex talionis*—"eye for eye and tooth for tooth" (Exod 21:24)—which Marshall calls "undoubtedly the best-known and perhaps most misunderstood biblical text on crime and punishment."[17] Restorative justice practitioner Howard Zehr writes, "'Eye for an eye' was a law of proportion intended to limit rather than encourage revenge. It limited destructive vengeance. In fact, this legal principle laid the basis for restitution, providing a principle of proportionality in response to wrongdoing."[18] "The *lex* [*talionis*] served the twofold purpose of limiting the destructive effects of retribution on the one hand . . . and providing an equitable basis for making restitution or reparation in personal injury cases on the other,"[19] Marshall explains, indicating that this principle probably established monetary restitution instead; and according to Richard Buck, "[The view that the *lex talionis* requires retribution] is contradicted by numerous passages in the Talmud that clearly show the text actually calls for monetary compensation of the victim."[20] For Zehr, the goal of such restitution is a return to "shalom"—justice in the form of well-being for the community.[21] "It should be no surprise that the words for 'paying back' (*shillum*) and for 'recompense' (*shillem*) have the same root word as shalom. Restitution was

16. This term, which is commonly used in abolitionist circles, derives from Gilmore, to my knowledge (*Abolition Geography*, 115).
17. Marshall, *Beyond Retribution*, 78.
18. Zehr, *Changing Lenses*, 148.
19. Marshall, *Beyond Retribution*, 80.
20. Buck, "Restorative Justice," 92.
21. Zehr, *Changing Lenses*, 134.

a way of seeking to make things right. Recompense, sometimes translated retribution but implying satisfaction rather than revenge, provided vindication. Both had to do with restoring shalom."[22]

Another key example in the Bible contrasts sanctuary with carcerality—the "cities of refuge" for unintentional killers seeking to avoid the "avenger of blood" (Num 35:11–24; Deut 19:4–7). Buck describes the cities of refuge as aimed at life rather than punishment.

> The discussion of the cities of refuge in the Talmud and various rabbinic commentaries shows that the purpose of these cities was not to punish through isolation but rather to provide for the killer a safe and easily accessible place to reflect on what had been done and to embark on a process of *teshuva* [repentance], leading, ultimately, to atonement. . . . This view of the cities of refuge can be gleaned from the end of Deuteronomy 4:42, which states that the killer should flee to the city of refuge *and live*.[23]

For this reason, those seeking refuge from vengeance could take their families and teacher to the city of refuge with them, so that "the daily life of the offender [would] resemble, as much as possible, the life he or she lived before fleeing to the city."[24] Zehr and Marshall both describe the cities of refuge as one among several "restraints on vengeance" in the Mosaic law.[25] Griffith traces this restraint back to Cain's murder of Abel, the "first crime." "Cain is guilty as sin, and yet in violation of all human 'justice,' God protects him. . . . As we deny responsibility to care for sisters and brothers ('Am I my brother's keeper?'), God intervenes to show us how. God intervenes with a mark of protection and a place of refuge."[26]

While punitive justice is nonetheless present in some parts of the Mosaic law, Marshall questions whether retribution is ever a useful category for discussing it. He writes regarding capital punishment that expiation is a more meaningful categorization, particularly for the sake of purifying the people and the land.

> The death penalty in biblical law is best understood not as an inalienable principle of state-administered retributive justice, nor even simply as a deterrent penalty, but as a cultic or religious requirement for "cleansing the land" of evil and safeguarding the

---

22. Zehr, *Changing Lenses*, 143.
23. Buck, "Restorative Justice," 93, 95; emphasis in original.
24. Buck, "Restorative Justice," 95.
25. Marshall, *Beyond Retribution*, 126; Zehr, *Changing Lenses*, 149.
26. L. Griffith, *Fall of the Prison*, 87–88.

holiness of the people of God (Num 35:33).... The way in which stoning had to take place outside the camp or city and involved the entire community helped to dramatize the ritual pollution of sin and the community's expulsion of evil from its midst.[27]

Exclusion and expulsion from community—both intrinsic to incarceration—are presented here in the context of *cleansing* the people in the land.[28] Marshall goes further to note that, instead of Scripture proposing retribution—understood as "penalties imposed from outside and as an end in themselves"[29]—as the response to evil, the "law of recompense"[30] instead often represents, as in Klaus Koch's argument, "the basic worldview conviction that deeds carry their own inherent outcome.... Every action, whether good or wicked, spreads out to affect or infect others within the covenant community, and therefore Israel's relationship with Yahweh. God proves true to his covenant commitments by purging evil from the land, and thus protecting his people, through establishing, sustaining, and symbolically dramatizing (in judicial procedures and penalties) the Deed-Consequence construct."[31] This frames punishment in the Bible within an expiatory and (ultimately) restorative framework aimed at "restoring the relational integrity of the community" and "restor[ing] the community to its covenant commitment to be a holy people."[32]

This commitment to restoration continues through the New Testament. Marshall identifies the "countertheme" to retribution found in the gospel "where the whole notion of just deserts and repayment in kind is turned on its head."[33] Ched Myers and Elaine Enns point to Matt 18 in particular as conveying principles of restorative justice including the desire that none be lost in the parable of the lost sheep (Matt 18:11–14), a description of a relational restorative-justice process in Matt 18:15–20, and an emphasis on forgiveness.[34]

Ultimately, Zehr sees the whole movement of the Bible as toward the restoration of shalom. "The real story of the Bible, from the Old Testament into the New, is this: God does not give up. It is precisely in this way that we are to imitate God, to be 'perfect': in indiscriminate love, in love that is

---

27. Marshall, *Beyond Retribution*, 220.
28. Griffith also makes this point (L. Griffith, *Fall of the Prison*, 90).
29. Marshall, *Beyond Retribution*, 121.
30. Marshall, *Beyond Retribution*, 120.
31. Marshall, *Beyond Retribution*, 121. Marshall is summarizing Koch here.
32. Marshall, *Beyond Retribution*, 124.
33. Marshall, *Beyond Retribution*, 126–27.
34. C. Myers and Enns, *New Testament Reflections*, 49–71.

undeserved, in forgiveness, in mercy."[35] The Old and New Testaments are unified in their restorative perspective:

> [The restorative] character of God's justice is demonstrated dramatically in passages such as Leviticus 26 and Deuteronomy 4. The people of Israel receive graphic descriptions of the horrible consequences of wrongdoing. Terrible things will happen. Yet the passages end by promising that God will not give up. God will not destroy them. God is faithful and compassionate.
>
> In the New Testament, Christ's focus is even more clearly on restorative responses to wrongdoing. This presents no radical break from the Old Testament direction, no rejection of the overall thrust of the old covenant. Rather, it provides an unfolding of understanding, a continued transformation of justice.[36]

Across Scripture, the emphasis is not just on communal wholeness for the people but also for the land. In the Mosaic law and Deuteronomic history, punishment is presented as necessary transformation of power for the sake of the entire people and the land. Griffith writes that "when covenantal commitments were broken, the actions of one individual stood as indicative of a corporate malady. . . . Not only all the people but the land itself was caught up in lawlessness and its consequences. . . . For Israel, the fullest response to crime was not the isolated punishment of an individual lawbreaker but the repentance of the entire nation."[37] As Walter Brueggemann puts it, from Israel's disobedience, "it is the land that is finally abused."[38] Griffith, like Marshall, turns to the language of expiation, not only for the people but for the land.

> In the Old Testament . . . capital punishment was not related to any abstract demand for justice or to any calculations regarding the potential social benefits of deterrence; rather, it was rooted in the religious demand for expiation. "Blood pollutes the land, and no expiation can be made for the land for the blood that is shed on it, except by the blood of him who shed it" (Num 35:33). If the murderer was not identified, then the city nearest the site of the murder was to offer up a sacrificial heifer to serve as a substitute in the ritual act of expiation (Deut 21:1–9).[39]

---

35. Zehr, *Changing Lenses*, 148.
36. Zehr, *Changing Lenses*, 151.
37. L. Griffith, *Fall of the Prison*, 93.
38. Brueggemann, *Land*, loc. 1848.
39. L. Griffith, *Fall of the Prison*, 90.

The law in Leviticus also promises divine judgment to secure for the land its right to rest if the Levitical laws around just land use are not followed.

> I will devastate the land, so that your enemies who come to settle in it shall be appalled at it. And you I will scatter among the nations, and I will unsheathe the sword against you; your land shall be a desolation and your cities a waste. Then the land shall enjoy its Sabbath years as long as it lies desolate, while you are in the land of your enemies; then the land shall rest and enjoy its Sabbath years. As long as it lies desolate, it shall have the rest it did not have on your Sabbaths when you were living on it. (Lev 26:32–35)

The economic realities of land and labor are implicated in the punishment of the elites among the people for injustice and lawbreaking. The punishment of Israel being given up to its enemies will give the land rest. The model remains not retribution but expiation and reparation with the land as the victim to be purified and made whole.[40]

Jubilee as a Material Reality

The need for wholeness within the land is at the heart of the Jubilee tradition, which forms the background of Jesus's proclamation of freedom for prisoners. The Sabbatical and Jubilee Years, as presented in Lev 25 and Deut 15, occur every seven years (Sabbatical) and in the fiftieth year (Jubilee). During these years, debts are forgiven, land that has been sold is returned as an inheritance to its original owners, the land is allowed to rest from cultivation, and enslaved people are set free. God promises dire punishments if Israel does not follow these laws to secure the land its Sabbath rest.

Jubilee is the basis of Griffith's prison-abolitionist reading of the Bible. Griffith refuses to equivocate on the Bible's promise of freedom for prisoners. He writes, "We must not be misled into assuming that the biblical understanding of prisoners has to do with legal ethics and calculations about what should be done by and to criminals. Rather, the Servant Song in Isa 42 is one of the earliest indications that the biblical word regarding prisoners is at once both simple and scandalous: liberty for the captives."[41] Griffith writes that the Jubilee "proclamations of liberty to the captives were concrete social responses to God's liberating activity in the exodus of Israel

---

40. L. Griffith, *Fall of the Prison*, 90; see also Brueggemann, *Land*, loc. 1848. The connection between Sabbath rest for the land and reparation—rather than simply expiation—is mine.

41. L. Griffith, *Fall of the Prison*, 97.

from Egypt."[42] He connects the freeing of enslaved people during the Jubilee as being extended to prisoners more generally during the exile: "It was from the experience of exile that Israel learned of the fundamental kinship between enslavement and imprisonment. The experience of the exile prepared the covenantal community to understand the truth of the prophets' words: the same God who frees the slaves frees the prisoners too."[43] And the proclamations of liberty to the captives in the "favorable year of the Lord" that Jesus makes in Luke 4:17–20 are "echoes of the Sabbath and Jubilee Years."[44]

Brueggemann links the restoration after the Babylonian exile to a similar sort of justice provided by Jubilee, related not only to freedom for captives but to possession of the land. "The land is redivided to prisoners and other outcasts."[45] He notes the disruptive impact of Jesus's message because it relates to an apocalyptic dispossession of land from those in power.

> This view believed that a breaking of the ages, a turning of the eons was about to occur. Among other things, those who waited patiently and faithfully would receive the inheritance of the new age, even as those who now held the land according to the norms of the old age would indeed lose it. Thus the Jesus movement is centered on the sharp and radical transformation of the human situation.[46]

> It is precisely the end of exile, with the inversion of life for those denied turf, which is recognized in the person and preaching of Jesus.[47]

Similarly, André Trocmé recognizes in the mission of Jesus the institution of a real, material Jubilee Year. He argues that Jesus, in proclaiming "the year of the Lord's favor," is calling for a Sabbatical or Jubilee Year, which was "a genuine social revolution aimed at preventing the accumulation of capital in the hands of a few."[48] This was a world-shattering threat to those in power. "By proclaiming the Jubilee, Jesus wanted to bring about a total social transformation, with an eye to the future, yet based on the vision of justice God had already set forth in the past."[49] Given what we have seen

42. L. Griffith, *Fall of the Prison*, 99.
43. L. Griffith, *Fall of the Prison*, 102.
44. L. Griffith, *Fall of the Prison*, 100.
45. Brueggemann, *Land*, loc. 2256.
46. Brueggemann, *Land*, loc. 2472.
47. Brueggemann, *Land*, locs. 2540–41.
48. Trocmé, *Jesus and Nonviolent Revolution*, 14.
49. Trocmé, *Jesus and Nonviolent Revolution*, 14.

throughout Scripture of the political powers' uses of incarceration for expedient ends, whether calculated or capricious, it is of particular interest how Trocmé contrasts this with God's will for liberation and remission of debt that is grounded in God's good and steady character. "The mercy that manifests itself during the 'year of favor' is not arbitrary. It is not the result of the king's despotic benevolence. Nor does it contradict the requirements of justice, which characterize Yahweh's will for his people. It is, rather, an expression of God's justice, which occurs at regular intervals to regularize his relations with his people."[50] God's justice seeks wholeness and is opposed to the application of power that underlies the prison.

Trocmé's assertion that Jesus proclaimed a Jubilee occurring in real, material terms right now and ushering in an "inheritance of the new age"[51] is also consistent with how scholars such as Paula Fredriksen view apocalyptic immediacy in Jesus's life and preaching as the promise that the coming reign of God is occurring now, with tangible and destabilizing political impacts.[52] Jesus's proclamation of Jubilee interrupts the business-as-usual of power, including incarceration and economic oppression.

For Griffith, Jubilee is the first strand in the story of Jesus pointing to prison abolition, and the closely related second strand is resurrection. Griffith likens the "spirit of the prison" to the "spirit of death" and proclaims that Jesus has conquered it too.[53] Jesus does not "cut loose a few captives so that the governing authorities can send in more prisoners to take their places. Rather, Jesus unmasks the powers and renders them visible. . . . The powers may pretend that captivity is based on justice, but Jesus declares that henceforth all prisoners have a right to liberty—the only possible right to liberty, based in the Word of God."[54] Many modern Christians interpret Jesus's proclamation of freedom for prisoners with spiritual freedom from the captivity of sin and death, but Griffith's connection between Jubilee and resurrection makes clear that it is both. He describes this as "an amnesty with eschatological rather than merely momentary significance."[55] Freedom for prisoners, good news to the poor, and wholeness to the land are accomplished through the overcoming of death in Jesus's resurrection. Resurrection life is Jubilee life, spiritually and materially.

---

50. Trocmé, *Jesus and Nonviolent Revolution*, 19.
51. Brueggemann, *Land*, loc. 2472.
52. See Fredriksen, *When Christians Were Jews*.
53. L. Griffith, *Fall of the Prison*, 106–7.
54. L. Griffith, *Fall of the Prison*, 109.
55. L. Griffith, *Fall of the Prison*, 109.

This relationship between liberation and land/economics spans long beyond biblical times. In modern societies structured by white supremacy, chattel slavery, and neo/colonialism, the plantation[56] and the colonial estate[57] are early paradigms of incarceration. The control of bodies (especially Black and indigenous bodies) and space for profit, intrinsic to colonialism and enslavement, is replicated in the state's control of such racialized bodies through incarceration, where incarceration also serves capitalism.[58] (Gilmore reminds us that incarceration serves to produce the difference that racial capitalism requires.[59]) Womanist theologian Nikia Smith Robert traces the history of the prison as an institution aimed at controlling oppressed, especially Black, bodies back through the plantation and the penitentiary. The prison, like the plantation, is a Christian-influenced "house of sacrifice needed to repair a breached social contract between the oppressed and dominant society by restoring law and order through the ransoming of subaltern flesh. . . . As a result, racial logic distorts Christian identity and limits the salvific power of Christ for the oppressed."[60]

According to Loida I. Martell, incarceration, particularly of undocumented immigrants, has "parallels to the colonial *encomienda* system instituted by the *conquistadores* in New Spain."[61] She characterizes the problem as the "hindrance of movement of people that leads to death"[62]—a response to controls on migration but also a fundamental feature of prison as a geographic phenomenon defined by restricting the movement of those incarcerated[63]—and insists it must be replaced for Christians with "a vision of new ways of being 'citizen' that is no longer based on exclusionary practices but based on grace . . . a new way of being, no longer based on *encomiendas*

---

56. See Robert, "Penitence, Plantation, and Penitentiary."

57. See Martell, "*Nueva Encomienda*."

58. See, for example, A. Y. Davis, *Are Prisons Obsolete?*, 84–104; Martell, "*Nueva Encomienda*," 162. On the mutual support of racialized incarceration and capitalism, see Bhandar and Toscano, "Editors' Introduction"; and Ruth Wilson Gilmore's own concise phrasing: "Capitalism requires inequality and racism enshrines it" ("Worrying State," para. 7; also in Haymarket Books, "Abolition, Cultural Freedom, Liberation," 1:23:56).

59. This is a summary of Gilmore's themes. See also her definition of racism as "the state-sanctioned and/or extralegal production and exploitation of group-differentiated vulnerabilities to premature death" (*Abolition Geography*, 17).

60. Robert, "Penitence, Plantation, and Penitentiary," 48. Robert identifies Christian theologies of sacrifice as contributing to the sacrificial logic of plantation and prison.

61. Martell, "*Nueva Encomienda*," 162.

62. Martell, "*Nueva Encomienda*," 162.

63. Gilmore is responsible for the insight of treating the prison in fundamentally geographic terms as a geographic phenomenon in this way and for popularizing the language of "death-dealing systems" (*Abolition Geography*, 115).

for profit but on communality through *vínculos*, perichoretic ties, created by the moving of the Spirit in our midst."[64] Martell is sharing a vision of community opposed to borders. "There cannot be true community, true humanity, where a people are dehumanized, enslaved (*encomendados/as*), and not allowed the freedom to move as they please."[65] The division of land, like the confinement of people in prisons, blocks the movement that supports community. Brueggemann makes a similar point: enclosure of land "images the land and one's possession of it to be unattached to and unconcerned for other social relations."[66] This "image" of the land as "unattached" mirrors the "fragmentation" of space and relationships characteristic of prisons, rather than the connections that characterize community.[67] There are echoes here of Isa 5:8: "Woe to those who join house to house, who add field to field, until there is room for no one, and you are left to live alone in the midst of the land!" Prisons break up spaces and relationships,[68] while a biblical ethic of land promotes its commonality for the community through relationship.[69] The prison is fragmentation, enclosure, sacrifice, stasis, death; Jubilee is connection, communal possession, movement, life. Jubilee, then, stands against the fragmentation of land and community that characterizes the prison and restores connection and the freedom of movement that is "foundational life"[70] both in its restructuring of relations with respect to the land and in its freeing of prisoners and those enslaved. Jubilee offers transformed material realities toward renewed communities.

Regarding this connection between Jubilee for the land and freedom for prisoners, the parable of the vineyard (Mark 12:1–12) offers a final challenge. In this parable, a wealthy landowner sends slaves and eventually his son to a vineyard he owns, all of whom are violently beaten or killed by the tenants. Typically, this parable is read through what Luise Schottroff calls the "ecclesiological" reading of this parable—which she rejects—casting the tenants as Israel and suggesting that the vineyard is taken away from Israel as punishment for their sin of rejecting God's son.[71] Yet reading the parable this way requires us to identify God with the cruel landowner. Schottroff

---

64. Martell, "*Nueva Encomienda*," 162.

65. Martell, "*Nueva Encomienda*," 179.

66. Brueggemann, *Land*, loc. 2828.

67. For the language of "fragmentation" as characteristic of the prison, see Gilmore, *Abolition Geography*, 370.

68. Gilmore, *Abolition Geography*, 316, 370.

69. See Brueggemann's discussion of this passage (*Land*, loc. 1828).

70. Martell, "*Nueva Encomienda*," 169.

71. Schottroff, *Parables of Jesus*, 19.

instead reads the parable in light of the material realities described in it, noting that "the violence of the tenants reflects the economic hopelessness of the increasingly poor agrarian population and their hatred for their new masters." In this context, the cruel landowner "acts like an opponent of God: he does the opposite of what the God of the Torah and the Lord's Prayer desires and does [remission of debts]."[72] The landowner has gained ownership over "lands that previously were cultivated in smaller parcels by subsistence farmers," enclosing and fragmenting space to the detriment of the former owners who might have become the new tenants.[73] (Schottroff's description here makes it clear that the landowner is engaging in the action of "joining house to house" condemned in Isa 5:8.[74]) This is not to support the violent response of the tenants but to make visible how the economic oppression of the landlord has led to the tenants' response of "counterviolence."[75] Schottroff reads the parable "eschatologically": "This is about Israel and its liberation (vv. 10, 11) from its suffering—violence endured and violence perpetrated, so pointedly portrayed in the narrative."[76] In this "eschatological" reading, the parable shows a cycle of violence that "sees the listening community, the people and Jesus' followers as opposite the God who is coming. God's judgment will show who are . . . the holy people of God . . . it will be the people that does not respond to Rome's exploitation with hatred and violence, but that works together and nonviolently for the future."[77] The parable calls the listeners to participate in God's work to resolve the injustice presented by the parable.[78] And Jubilee is God's nonviolent response that would return the land as an inheritance to the tenants without retaliatory violence. The just redistribution of the land overcomes the violent conflict in which both landlord and tenant are trapped.

How does this parable relate to the issue of modern incarceration? It points to the systemic causes of interpersonal violence, emphasis on which is key to "transformative justice"—a collection of practices that seek to "transform the conditions which help to create acts of violence or make them possible . . . [including] transforming harmful oppressive dynamics,

---

72. Schottroff, *Parables of Jesus*, 17.

73. Schottroff, *Parables of Jesus*, 16.

74. This is particularly interesting since Schottroff notes that the parable is in dialogue with the song of the vineyard in Isa 5:1–7 (*Parables of Jesus*, 16). See also Brueggemann's discussion of Isa 5:8 (*Land*, loc. 1828).

75. Schottroff, *Parables of Jesus*, 21.

76. Schottroff, *Parables of Jesus*, 25.

77. Schottroff, *Parables of Jesus*, 24.

78. Schottroff, *Parables of Jesus*, 19.

our relationships to each other, and our communities at large."[79] Gilmore has described these conditions in light of the prison-industrial complex perpetuating a cycle of "organized abandonment" followed by "organized violence" against marginalized communities. Economic and political powers divest from communities, then as social breakdown follows, the violent forces of police and prisons are brought in to suppress the community rather than empower community members to address and stop harm.[80] Hélder Câmara explains this in terms of the "spiral of violence": first, the violence of disinvestment, then the violence that occurs in response to this disinvestment, the countervailing violence of state power brought to restore order, and then the violence that arises against such state repression.[81] This cycle is what is portrayed in an "eschatological" reading of the parable of the tenants, in which both landlord and tenants are drawn into doing harm.

Jubilee cuts off the cycle of violence. Jubilee is God's eschatological action[82] that overcomes fragmentation and abandonment by restoring just relations, in our modern context as in biblical times. It represents "organized presence"[83] in response to organized abandonment. Jubilee, today in the form of abolitionist practices to resist incarceration and "make prisons obsolete,"[84] still brings justice instead of violence. Just as Trocmé and Griffith argue that Jesus was announcing a real material Jubilee in the expectation of an imminent apocalyptic setting right of the world by God, Jubilee has a material rather than spiritual character in our world too. A theology of embodied Jubilee calls us to the transformation of racial and economic systems in a society that seeks to organize our physical and social spaces via incarceration for the sake of maintaining capitalist power relations.

---

79. Mingus, "Transformative Justice." See also McCants-Turner and McCarty's chapter in this collection.

80. This is a common theme of Gilmore's (e.g., *Abolition Geography*, 244–48).

81. See Câmara, *Spiral of Violence*. I am indebted to Ched Myers and Elaine Enns for introducing me to this concept.

82. Schottroff, *Parables of Jesus*, 25.

83. I have previously developed the language of "organized presence" in "How to Get Beyond Punitive Thinking in a Pandemic," drawing on Gilmore's frequent description of abolition as "presence." See, e.g., her quote "Abolition is about presence, not absence" (from the conference "Making and Unmaking Mass Incarceration: The History of Mass Incarceration and the Future of Prison Abolition," University of Mississippi, Dec. 4–6, 2019; as quoted by Herskind, "Some Reflections on Prison Abolition," closing sec.).

84. See A. Y. Davis, *Are Prisons Obsolete?*

The Church Is an Anti-Prison Community of Reparation

In light of the Jubilee reality that Jesus proclaims, Christian discipleship includes opposing political systems that use the retribution of incarceration to enact social and economic control. But interpersonal harm still must be addressed within our communities. To address harm without relying on incarceration, we must also consider the "business of reparation."

Debt language is part of the conversation of retribution and reparation: dealing with the question of what is owed when harm is done.[85] Teasing apart the differences between economized debt and interpersonal obligation[86] helps provide a vision for the church as a community that rejects the "business of incarceration" via retribution while still demanding and empowering accountability and amends for harm. Andrew Sung Park recognizes the instigation of reparation in the story of Zacchaeus (Luke 19:1–10): "Jesus' staying with him evoked the repentant spirit in Zacchaeus so that he declared he would give half of his possessions to the poor and pay back four times what he defrauded anybody. Zacchaeus' offer went far beyond the requirement of the law."[87] When harm has been caused, reparation is a joyful response of repentance.

Another scriptural example of reparation is the conversion of Paul. While Paul's repentance from the harm he has done to the church—by arresting and incarcerating them!—is associated with his "promotion" to apostle, what God assures is "how much he must suffer for the sake of my name" (Acts 9:16). The point is not that God desires his suffering but that Paul's labors on behalf of the church will be difficult and perhaps function as reparation for the harm he once caused it. Paul's calling is to the work of accountability and reparation, and these are hard work indeed. His ability to engage in accountability is empowered by the supportive community around him, beginning with Ananias, who takes him in despite his doubts (9:13–17), and continuing with the support of Barnabas, who speaks for him in Jerusalem (9:27). Similarly, Zacchaeus's repentance and reparation follow Jesus's solidarity by coming to his home.[88] This presents important

---

85. Sered, *Until We Reckon*, 92. See also Ruttenberg, *On Repentance and Repair*.

86. The idea of clarifying the distinction between debt and interpersonal obligation is from Singh, "To Receive What Is Already Yours."

87. Park, *From Hurt to Healing*, 68.

88. Park, *From Hurt to Healing*, 68. Park writes here that the "respect" Jesus shows to Zacchaeus inspires his repentance and reparation, noting that "people do not change while their self-esteem is low but only when it is high" (68). I have similarly argued that Jesus's proximity and solidarity to Zacchaeus were necessary to prepare the ground for his repentance ("From Substitution to Solidarity," 376). In that article I noted Park's discussion of Zacchaeus's necessary repentance only, while I recognize here that Park also insists

insight into restorative and transformative justice: accountability for harm, including making reparation, occurs within a community of solidarity and support.[89] Rather than a community of exclusion and confinement, of borders and the restricted movement characteristic of the prison, the church provides a community of connection where accountability is possible. It is on this basis of relationship that the "debt of harm" can be addressed.

Of course, the crucifixion and the many atonement theologies surrounding it largely occupy any Christian discussion of punishment and debt.[90] Anselm's satisfaction theory of atonement with its infinite debt against God's honor has long influenced the Christian tradition. Robert identifies the satisfaction theology of atonement as a driver of systems that sacrifice people who are criminalized to punishment and incarceration. She writes:

> Applied allegorically to the contemporary social context of the Carceral State, not Christ but Black bodies become the sacrifice for human sin. This is to say, in the feudal economy as in the Carceral State there is an analogous hierarchical relationship where lords can be understood interchangeably with dominant privileged society and serfs with the criminalization of the subaltern. . . . Hence, Anselm's feudal cosmology of salvation and the US criminal justice system have this in common: both are religious, retributive, and require the sacrifice of a lower class.[91]

This is why a liberative Christian theology must resist simplistic theologies that attribute to Jesus's suffering "payment of the debt" for human sin.

At the same time, the felt need for reparations—all the way back to the biblical language of "eye for eye," encouraging not mutilation or death but monetary reparations proportional to the loss from harm[92]—suggests that debt language does have a helpful role in responding to harm, but only if carefully understood. The "debt of harm" perhaps has less to do with economized understandings than with interpersonal obligation.[93] Danielle Sered writes, "It is my belief that when we hurt people, we owe something." But what Sered identifies as paying the debt of harm is relational: "One of the

---

on the respect given to Zacchaeus as a precondition for such repentance.

89. I have previously made this point in my article "From Substitution to Solidarity," 375.

90. I have previously written on connections between debt language and atonement theology, and the argument that follows here summarizes and builds on that made in more detail in my article "From Substitution to Solidarity."

91. Robert, "Penitence, Plantation, and Penitentiary," 46–47.

92. Marshall, *Beyond Retribution*, 80; Buck, "Restorative Justice," 92.

93. Again, I'm indebted for this distinction (although not in the context of harm) to Singh, "To Receive What Is Already Yours."

things we owe is to face what we have done. In that sense, when it comes to demanding that those who have committed wrongdoing pay that debt, there is nowhere softer on crime than prison."[94] Facing truth in relationship, not just restitution, is obligatory in response to harm. Womanist theologian Kelly Brown Douglas writes about the need for more than just "compensatory reparations" for harm: for faith communities, "reparations should be directed toward building a future where all human beings are respected as the sacred creations that they are and thereby free to live into the fullness of their sacred creation. For faith communities, reparations must not be only an effort to compensate for past harms, they must also chart a pathway to a just future."[95] Payment of debt is not restricted to an economic exchange but must create new possibilities for justice to prevail over harm. Sarah Jobe writes about "living amends"—those actions taken to "commit to a whole new way of life" when "one could not actually repair and restore what was broken"—as foundational to healing from the moral injury of doing harm, as "the stuff of redemption, rehabilitation, and restoration."[96] Life-giving reparations go beyond restitution to fulfill necessary obligations after harm has occurred and to create new meaningful patterns, all founded in relationships.

Through this lens, Jesus's crucifixion can be viewed primarily as divine solidarity—rather than as vicarious punishment or sacrifice—first, with people insofar as they have *been harmed*, providing for their vindication over the powers that oppress them, including where the harm has come precisely from criminalization and imprisonment, structures that sacrifice subaltern bodies for social order;[97] and second with people insofar as they have *done harm*. For the latter case, the language of Jesus's debt bearing rejects the transfer of debt back to those who have done harm in the form of suffering or punishment. In light of divine solidarity as a fundamental reality, rather than an economized commodity that can be paid with a certain amount of suffering or imprisonment, the debt of harm is a relational, interpersonal obligation worked out in life-giving structures of transformation.[98] Instead of requiring a measured amount of suffering—the punitive "extraction" of time promised by imprisonment, in Gilmore's words,[99] or the

---

94. Sered, *Until We Reckon*, 92.

95. Kelly Douglas, "Christian Call for Reparations."

96. Jobe, "Rethinking Responsibility," 346.

97. Robert, "Penitence, Plantation, and Penitentiary," 48.

98. The above paragraph is a summary of my argument in "From Substitution to Solidarity."

99. "We are, individually and collectively, spacetime . . . and what prison is is an incapacitation that enables time to be extracted from the territory of the self" (Ruth Wilson Gilmore, in Harvard University, "Radical Commitments," 21:00).

infinite debt owed to an infinite God, in Anselm's theory—we must reframe the debt of harm in terms of ongoing, life-giving reparations lived out in communal relationships.

As restorative and transformative justice practitioners remind us, we have all done harm and been harmed. God comes to us as both victims and perpetrators of harm. It is in that context that rejection of punishment and the associated sacrifice for social order allows us to discuss accountability and reparations in constructive ways.[100] And it is in this context that the church need not be merely a community of reconciliation—understood as "forgive and forget," thereby ignoring harms done—but instead is liberated to be a community of *reparation*, a place where harm is addressed nonpunitively, a community whose faith speaks to the possibility of accountability without punishment.

God's rejection of the business of incarceration is evident from the biblical witness of Jubilee that rejects the economic and political powers that deliberately structure incarceration. God's preference for reparation over punishment is seen in the restorative structures built into the Mosaic law; the promise of restoration to Israel; and the stories of Jesus's life, death, and resurrection. And God's opposition to prisons is lived out in "Jesus the Prisoner."[101] In Matt 25:31–45, God himself identifies with those who are incarcerated as well as those who suffer from economic injustice and social marginalization. They are the same victims of the business of incarceration and the capitalist, neocolonialist production of hierarchy that it serves. "Jesus the Prisoner" makes God present to those subjected to "organized abandonment." The material practices of prison abolition allow the church to participate in living out God's divine presence here on earth and to offer, in place of the "death-dealing" business of incarceration, a community of Jubilee, a community of life.

---

100. This insight about criminal punishment as a sacrifice for social order is from Robert, "Penitence, Plantation, and Penitentiary," 48.

101. L. Griffith, *Fall of the Prison*, 126.

2

The Business of Incarceration and the Christian Tradition

KATHRYN GETEK SOLTIS

Christian reflection on being held captive—and the holding of others—is as old as Christianity itself. Yet, the tradition is of at least two minds when it comes to imprisonment. On one side is a salvation history rooted in release from captivity and return from exile. On the other is a recurring theological framework of debt and punishment that aligns captivity with justice. To some extent this tension in the Christian tradition reflects a divide over debt. Does indebtedness define the human relationship with God, or does that relationship supplant the terms of debt altogether? Centuries of Christian thought and practice suggest that imprisonment cannot be easily disentangled from such concepts of payment and owing. And yet, there are markers of the tradition that seem capable of adjudicating between these approaches. I ultimately argue for two such markers: a proactive, generative morality and the universality of the gospel's good news.

The recurring theological framework of debt and punishment has emerged from several sources. In the four sections that follow, I discuss three sources and a concrete application of them. The theological sources are the *lex talionis* ("an eye for an eye"), retributive conceptions of hell and purgatory, and the penal substitutionary theory of atonement. The application of these ideas can be detected in ecclesial practices of imprisonment intended to uphold discipline and orthodoxy. After exploring debt and punishment, I turn to other sources in the tradition that upend this framework, including Jubilee practices of debt forgiveness and the release of captives. While key markers of the tradition favor the latter trajectory of liberation and mercy, there can be little doubt of the enduring power and appeal of the debt-and-punishment framework. Indeed, any adequate narrative about the business of incarceration must include the considerable contributions of the Christian tradition. The extent to which the tradition will actually help to change that business model remains to be seen.

Three Sources for the Theological Framework of Debt and Punishment

Lex Talionis

The law of retaliation or *lex talionis* ("an eye for an eye, a tooth for a tooth") is among the most familiar accounts of punishment. While the formulation appears in the Hebrew Scriptures, it did not originate there. Scholars affirm "the virtual universality of such a 'law of retaliation' in the ancient world," pointing to evidence in the Code of Hammurabi and the Middle Assyrian laws as well as Greek, Roman, and Jewish formulations.[1] The power of the *lex talionis* has continued over time, and it appears often in both contemporary religious and secular discourse. For example, in four consecutive polls, Gallup found that "an eye for an eye" is the top reason offered by those who are in support of the death penalty in the United States.[2]

---

1. D. J. Weaver, "Transforming Nonresistance," 37.
2. Swift, "Eye for an Eye."

The law of retaliation appears three times in the Hebrew Bible: Exodus,[3] Leviticus,[4] and Deuteronomy.[5] While it is not unique to the Bible, commentators do see distinctive aspects of the biblical version. In Scripture, the *lex talionis* is widely recognized as a restraint on revenge and retaliation.[6] An offender cannot be dealt with more harshly than the offense itself. In other words, justice is *no more than* an eye for an eye. In addition, the principle's strict equivalence ensures that those with greater power or wealth receive the same treatment as the poor and vulnerable of society. The Bible's *lex talionis* sets standards of fairness and proportionate compensation. Instead of requiring vengeance, it provides a basis for settling disputes in an equitable manner, avoids excessive retaliation, and protects those who are powerless.

Of particular note is that the *lex talionis* was a guide for *economic restitution* rather than a literal mandate for physical harm. The law of retaliation was widely interpreted as allowing if not preferring financial compensation for injury. Instead of giving victims the right to vindication through equivalent injury, the majority of evidence suggests that an "eye for an eye" helped define monetary fines as repayment for victims. In the case of intentional murder, there is general agreement that "life for life" did apply in a literal manner. However, several scholars suggest that all other injuries were handled according to moral rather than physical equivalence.[7]

---

3. "When a slaveowner strikes a male or female slave with a rod and the slave dies immediately, the owner shall be punished. But if the slave survives a day or two, there is no punishment, for the slave is the owner's property. When people who are fighting injure a pregnant woman so that there is a miscarriage and yet no further harm follows, the one responsible shall be fined what the woman's husband demands, paying as much as the judges determine. If any harm follows, then you shall give life for life, eye for eye, tooth for tooth, hand for hand, foot for foot, burn for burn, wound for wound, stripe for stripe" (Exod 21:20–25).

4. "Anyone who maims another shall suffer the same injury in return: fracture for fracture, eye for eye, tooth for tooth; the injury inflicted is the injury to be suffered. One who kills an animal shall make restitution for it, but one who kills a human being shall be put to death. You shall have one law for the alien and for the native-born, for I am the Lord your God" (Lev 24:19–22).

5. "If the witness is a false witness, having testified falsely against another, then you shall do to the false witness just as the false witness had meant to do to the other. So you shall purge the evil from your midst. The rest shall hear and be afraid, and a crime such as this shall never again be committed among you. Show no pity: life for life, eye for eye, tooth for tooth, hand for hand, foot for foot" (Deut 19:18–21).

6. See, for example, Marshall, *Beyond Retribution*, 79–84.

7. For example, Mikliszanski, "Law of Retaliation." See also Marshall, *Beyond Retribution*, 80–84. A comprehensive study of the issue by James Davis surveys sixteen recent interpreters of the *lex talionis* and suggests that a literal application was a viable, though perhaps not majority, view in first century CE during a time of intense debate on the matter (J. Davis, *Lex Talionis*).

Interpretation of the *lex talionis* is complicated by its apparent rejection in the New Testament in Jesus's Sermon on the Mount: "You have heard that it was said, 'An eye for an eye and a tooth for a tooth.' But I say to you: Do not resist an evildoer. But if anyone strikes you on the right cheek, turn the other also" (Matt 5:38–39). Scholars vary on how to interpret this passage. Some suggest that Jesus leaves the law of retaliation intact for legal settings and renounces it only within the sphere of private action.[8] Others see this as a repudiation of the law itself.[9] Still others interpret the Sermon on the Mount as transcending the *lex talionis*. In this view, Jesus's commands to turn the other cheek and to surrender one's cloak constitute a new standard of righteousness modeled after divine justice and appropriate to the eschatological kingdom.[10] This suggests Jesus is not abolishing the *lex talionis* but advocating for "a different starting point in human relationships."[11] Regardless, there are elements of compatibility between the Pentateuch's *lex talionis* and the Sermon on the Mount, namely those related to conflict resolution and restraint on punishment. James Davis notes that the law of retaliation "sought to prevent personal acts of revenge by taking matters of justice out of individual hands and placing them in a court context. Jesus sought to prevent such acts by calling for positive actions of excelling love, which would help diffuse situations of conflict."[12]

Despite questions about the status of the *lex talionis* in the New Testament, it remains a powerful approach to justice and punishment in the Christian imagination. It affirms the moral order in God's world and does so with heavily economic terminology. Harm swings the balance to the advantage of the offender. Order is restored and the balance is righted when punishment inflicts equal harm on that offender. Victims can look forward to a moment when the books are closed on their suffering, suggesting a zero-sum game in which their deliverance hinges upon the punishment of those who have harmed them. None of this requires the literal, imitative injuries of "an eye for an eye." Instead, this approach to punishment is better understood with the interpretation offered by Pinchas Lapide: "eye-compensation for eye, tooth-compensation for tooth."[13] Ultimately, the *lex talionis* aligns punishment with repayment, suggesting that justice is quantifiable.

8. See, for example, Barton and Muddiman, *Oxford Bible Commentary*, 140, 855.

9. For example, Richard Hays describes "a paradigm shift that effectually undermines the Torah's teaching about just punishment for offender" (*Moral Vision of New Testament*, 325).

10. See Marshall, *Beyond Retribution*, 85; J. Davis, *Lex Talionis*, 149.

11. Marshall, *Beyond Retribution*, 88.

12. J. Davis, *Lex Talionis*, 168.

13. See Lapide, *Sermon on the Mount*, 128–30.

Atonement Theories

The themes of debt and payment are central for Christian thought on atonement. The atonement theories of ransom, satisfaction, and penal substitution are particularly significant in this regard, and they reveal another key intersection between economics and punishment in the Christian tradition. Ransom theory was the dominant view of the early church and can be found in the work of Origen and Gregory of Nyssa, among others.[14] In this view, humanity had sold itself into slavery to the devil. To release humanity from its bondage, God offered Christ as a ransom payment. The theory utilizes powerful imagery of slavery and imprisonment as well as an economic framework through the payment of ransom. For example, Gregory of Nyssa explained that the devil "recognized in Christ a bargain which offered him more than he held. For this reason he chose him as the ransom for those he had shut up in death's prison."[15]

In the eleventh century, Anselm of Canterbury introduced the satisfaction theory of atonement, influenced by the church's practice of penance as well as the feudal system. In this theory, Christ again functions as payment. However, instead of the devil receiving the payment, it is now God. In short, humanity, by its nature, owes a debt of obedience to God. With sin, humanity dishonors God and fails to give what is owed. Since God's justice requires that this debt be paid, God becomes human and pays on humanity's behalf. Anselm's satisfaction theory is related to—and yet distinct from—penal substitutionary theory. Both their points of connection and divergence are noteworthy.

In his treatise *Cur Deus Homo* (Why God became man), Anselm is clear that every sin must be followed by *either* satisfaction or punishment, and it is significant that Anselm presents these as alternative possibilities. Satisfaction, a restoration of God's ordering of things, is offered through obedience and maintaining justice.[16] Thus, satisfaction comes about through the infinitely just will of Christ. This pathway to atonement is entirely separate from the option of punishment, which denotes a penalty endured against one's will. Since it was the infinitely just will of Christ that carried out the atonement, Anselm claims that God opted for satisfaction *rather* than punishment. It is obedience, not suffering, that pays the debt. In fact, Anselm suggests that punishment is not an actual option for God since

---

14. For further discussion of the ransom theory, see, for example, Kotsko, "Persistence of the Ransom Theory."

15. Gregory of Nyssa, "Address on Religious Instruction," 300.

16. Anselm, "Why God Became Man," 1.9.

it is God's nature to bring to perfection what God began.[17] Despite Anselm's dismissal of punishment, it did not take long for the satisfaction theory to become aligned with the idea of a punitive, vicarious sacrifice made to appease the wrath of God.

Mere decades after Anselm, both Hugh and Richard of St. Victor taught that Christ satisfied divine justice through the suffering of a substitutionary punishment.[18] In the thirteenth century, Thomas Aquinas also maintained a close association of satisfaction and punishment.[19] However, the theory of penal substitution is most often associated with the Reformers, and it is typically in the work of John Calvin that scholars identify the first full account of the theory.[20] Penal substitution is anchored in law and punishment. Divine law is understood to require that sin is punished. Thus, the punishment that is owed by sinful humanity is paid by the suffering and death of the God-man Christ. God's justice, in this view, consists in upholding the law that God has established for creation, a law that demands punishment to repay the debt of sin.

Two key presumptions are shared by the theories of satisfaction and penal substitution. First, both operate within a paradigm of debt repayment that is directed toward God. Second, both consider it absolutely necessary that God collect on that debt; simply forgiving it is out of the question. For Anselm, who lived amid a feudal economy of honor, it is a violation of God's honor and the just ordering of creation to forgive the debt without satisfaction. For Calvin, who lived amid a justice determined by criminal law, it is a violation of God's law to forgive the debt without punishment. Timothy Gorringe summarizes it thus: "In Anselm Christ pays our debts; in Calvin he bears our punishment."[21]

Satisfaction and penal substitution take different stances on the need for punishment, but they agree upon the imperative for repayment. Gorringe argues that these theological frameworks of satisfaction and penal substitution "provided one of the subtlest and most profound" justifications

---

17. Southern, *Saint Anselm*, 207.

18. Gorringe, *God's Just Vengeance*, 115–16.

19. Aquinas, *Summa Theologica*, 1-2.87.6. Aquinas does make a distinction between satisfactory punishment and punishment simply. Satisfactory punishment is that which is voluntarily accepted (although it is still punishment and, absolutely speaking, it is against the person's will). Satisfaction, for Aquinas, designates punishment that is endured with consent (since the person wills to be reunited with God); the term also applies to those who willingly endure punishment on behalf of another (e.g., Christ who bore a satisfactory punishment for our sins). See 1-2.87.7 for additional explanation of this distinction.

20. Holmes, "Penal Substitution," 307.

21. Gorringe, *God's Just Vengeance*, 139.

for retributive justice.[22] They reinforced legal retributive thinking by demonstrating that sin and crime must be punished without exception. As the criminal law became identified as an instrument of God's justice, a "mysticism of pain" emerged, which offered redemption to those who paid in suffering.[23] Despite Anselm's clear separation between the options of satisfaction and punishment (and despite his conclusion that punishment is not a conceivable option for God), the forces of law and suffering seem to control the legacy. In the penal substitution theory, the Christian imagination found a particularly compelling account of punishment necessitated by the justice of God.

Still, in observing the differences between satisfaction and penal substitution, one can detect something more than a punitive model at work here. The metaphor of debt looms large. Indeed, it unites not only satisfaction and penal substation but ransom theory as well. These theories place debt at the center of the relationship between God and humanity. While some scholars attempt to rewrite atonement to remove its support for abuse and violence, Devin Singh warns that they fail to challenge the problematic logic of debt that fundamentally structures atonement theory.[24] He calls for a soteriology that resists the notion of Christ as repayment, one in which God throws out debt and refuses to be bound by debt's terms. Singh's warning underscores the powerful legacy of these theories of atonement. They center debt as a key structuring principle of the Christian tradition, and, as noted above, punishment emerges as the favored means to pay such debt.

Hell and Purgatory

A relationship between debt and punishment is found not only in atonement theory but also within eschatology, specifically in accounts of hell and purgatory. The concept of hell has emerged in the Christian tradition in a manner that largely legitimizes imprisonment and that aligns such captivity with God's justice. Eternal punishment has been associated with debts that a sinner cannot (or will not) pay. On the other hand, purgatorial economies have offered temporary captivity and far more transactional potential.

The prisonlike character of hell can be traced to one of its earliest progenitors: Tartarus from ancient Greece. Unlike the house of Hades—a shadowy, neutral place for all the dead—Tarturus was a netherworld prison where the wicked were punished. In fact, the mythic prison Tarturus is the

---

22. Gorringe, *God's Just Vengeance*, 12.
23. Gorringe, *God's Just Vengeance*, 102.
24. Singh, "Sovereign Debt."

first example of eternal punishment.[25] In ancient Judaism, the dominant account of the afterlife was the neutral underworld of Sheol, a concept parallel to the Greek house of Hades. Indications of postmortem punishment along the lines of Tarturus were only minimally present in the Hebrew Bible (e.g., "the depths of the Pit" in Isa 14:15), and were eventually translated into the Greek Hebrew Bible as Gehenna. This idea of punishment after death appeared more clearly in Jewish apocryphal literature, including the First Book of Enoch where heavenly beings, "after committing abominations, end up in subterranean prisons, subjected to fire and brimstone."[26]

The writers of the New Testament continued the distinction between a neutral Hades and the punitive, prisonlike Gehenna/Tarturus. However, as the biblical text was translated from Greek into Latin, there was a tendency to "shade Hades into hell."[27] The eternal punishment denoted by Gehenna/hell also received powerful descriptions in the New Testament regarding the physical suffering of the wicked. Hell is depicted as the place "where their worm never dies, and the fire is never quenched" (Mark 9:48, referencing Isa 66:24); "the outer darkness, where there will be weeping and gnashing of teeth" (Matt 8:12); "the eternal fire prepared for the devil and his angels" (Matt 25:41); and the place of torment "with fire and sulfur" (Rev 14:10). A significant and more detailed description of hell emerged later with the second-century apocryphal Apocalypse of Peter. This text has been credited as the main source for Dante's nine circles of hell, John Milton's *Paradise Lost*, and Angelus Silesius's "Physical Description of the Four Last Things."[28] In the Apocalypse of Peter, the punishments of hell are carefully and directly linked to the particular sins: blasphemers hang by their tongues, idolators are burned with their idols, etc.[29] In this highly analytical account of sin and punishment, the victims sometimes even participate in punishing the guilty and those who have been saved from hell are able to see the punishment of the condemned. In short, the Apocalypse of Peter and its legacy align God's justice with punitive vengeance. In the text, the damned themselves acknowledge the rightness of their fate since they are punished according to their deeds. Historian Alan Bernstein captures the powerful account found in the Apocalypse of Peter:

> This combination—matching the punishment to the sin, the victim to the offender, and placing like offenders together—demonstrates

25. Bernstein, *Hell and Its Rivals*, 8.
26. Bernstein, *Hell and Its Rivals*, 11.
27. Bernstein, *Hell and Its Rivals*, 21.
28. Küng, *Eternal Life?*, 133.
29. Bernstein, *Formation of Hell*, 285.

even to hardened sinners that God's design is equitable. They sing praise of his plan, acknowledge his justice, and beg for mercy, but the attendant angel only taunts them for not mending their ways in life, while there was still time.[30]

In this way, hell and its punishments reveal the nuances of God's moral order and provide an eschatological blueprint for justice.

Retributive accounts of hell do not simply create a vision for postmortem punishment; they also reinforce and legitimize punishments imposed in life. Thus, the prisonlike hell helps to justify incarceration itself. Both Augustine and Aquinas make these lines of connection explicit in their writings. Augustine contrasts hell, the city of the devil, with heaven as the city of God; he argues that eternal suffering awaits those condemned to the former. Augustine vigorously defends this notion of eternity, especially against the objection that it is out of proportion with human sin (i.e., offenses that are limited in duration). To do so, he turns to the nature of earthly punishments (e.g., fines, imprisonment, flogging, slavery, exile, death) and concludes that the "only reason why they cannot be everlasting is that this life, in which the punishment is inflicted, is itself not extended into eternity." For Augustine, the earthly punishments of imprisonment, exile, and death are of one and the same character as the punishment after death: "Thus the removal of men from this mortal community by the punishment of the first death answers to their removal from that Immortal City by the punishment of the second death."[31] In both human life and beyond it, Augustine affirms the need for an equivalence of evil, and he explicitly identifies such retribution as an act of justice.

Similarly, Aquinas finds the punishment of the damned in hell to be fitting for divine justice.[32] Citing Augustine's argument quoted above, Aquinas defends the idea of everlasting punishment with an appeal to the continuity between God's law and human law. The punishment inflicted by the earthly state would be as everlasting as hell were it not for the fact that the person's life or the state itself will come to an end first.[33] The natural law theology of Aquinas provides the foundation for his vision of a universe governed by God's law and order. The human law is derived from natural law, which is itself a participation in God's eternal law.[34] Thus, punishment is a fitting and necessary activity for the earthly state, which receives its

30. Bernstein, *Formation of Hell*, 290.
31. Augustine, *City of God* 21.11.
32. Aquinas, *Summa Theologiae*, suppl. q. 97, a. 1.
33. Aquinas, *Summa Theologiae*, suppl. q. 99, a. 1.
34. Aquinas, *Summa Theologiae*, 1–2 q. 93, a.3ad2.

authority from a God who punishes the wicked eternally. The preservation of order is key.[35] For Aquinas, the sinner commits an offense against an order; therefore, the sinner is "put down . . . by that same order, which repression is punishment."[36] Significantly, Aquinas also speaks of sin as incurring a "debt of punishment."[37] As a transgression of the order of divine justice, the one who sins "cannot return except he pay some sort of penal compensation, which restores him to the equality of justice."[38] A belief in the eternal punishment of hell poses no problem for the framework of debt and payment. For Aquinas, the punishment of the damned is intended for those who sin mortally and therefore reveal a willingness to remain in sin.[39] In other words, all sinners are debtors, but some are unwilling to pay their debts. The latter face eternal punishment as a result.

The economic power of a retributive afterlife is clearest in the notion of purgatory, a place of purification for those who—though in a state of grace—are unworthy of direct entrance to heaven. There is no explicit reference in the Bible to the concept of purgatory, and the noun form *purgatorium* did not even emerge until the middle of the twelfth century.[40] The idea of purgatory was largely established through the works of the church fathers and in the liturgy.[41] Tertullian noted the possibility of "compensatory discipline" for some of the elect, and Clement of Alexandria suggested there could be a discriminating fire that purifies the souls of those who are not beyond correction.[42] Augustine similarly entertained the possibility that some of the saved might require purification after death.[43] For these and other patristic authors, the idea of purgatorial suffering was speculative and considered with caution. However, the medieval concept of purgatory introduced more certainty and specificity, beginning with Gregory the Great. Gregory reflects Western theology's "perennial concern with merit" along with an increasingly ordered penitential system that differentiated between

---

35. For further discussion of Augustine, Anselm, and Aquinas—along with the Christian tradition's interest in order—see Soltis and Grimes, "Order, Reform, and Abolition."

36. Aquinas, *Summa Theologiae*, 1–2 q. 87, a.1.

37. Aquinas, *Summa Theologiae*, 1–2 q. 87, a.3.

38. Aquinas, *Summa Theologiae*, 1–2 q. 87, a.6.

39. Aquinas, *Summa Theologiae*, suppl. q. 99, a. 1.

40. Salkeld, *Catholics and Evangelicals*, 33.

41. Küng, *Eternal Life?*, 137.

42. Atwell, "From Augustine to Gregory the Great," 174.

43. For example, Augustine comments on purgation in his *Enchiridion* 18.69; *City of God* 21.26.

mortal and venial sin.[44] Written at the end of the sixth century, book 4 of Gregory's *Dialogues* recounts a semi-geographical state where the suffering of departed souls could be relieved by prayers of the faithful, especially the offering of Mass. Gregory's vivid portrayal of purgatory was a model throughout the Middle Ages and provided an understanding of purgatory that "would later be abused for economic gain."[45]

In subsequent centuries, accounts of purgatory became even further systematized and lucrative. Concerns soon arose that the wealthy had greater access to relief in purgatory by funding Masses on their behalf. In response, the abbot of Cluny introduced the Feast of All Souls in 997.[46] In the thirteenth century, Hugh of Saint-Cher based the idea of indulgences on the notion "that a 'treasury of merits' from Christ, the Virgin Mary, and the saints is available to the Church to dispense to the faithful under certain prescribed conditions."[47] The sale of indulgences was closely tied to the doctrine of purgatory and became a source of great scandal. In 1518 at the University of Paris, indulgence vendors were described as "false, ridiculous, scandalous and dangerous preachers who extort from the poor."[48] Indeed, the abusive practice of indulgence sales led Martin Luther to compose his *Ninety-Five Theses*, which ultimately resulted in the division of Western Christianity. One example of the growing "purgatory industry" comes from the English Austin Friars in the century leading up to the Reformation. Initially, the friars would mostly offer letters of confraternity, a form of indulgence that provided participation in the spiritual merit of the Augustinian Order. These letters were local and small scale, issued to married couples who were patrons of particular convents. Yet, in the beginning of the sixteenth century, the English Austin Friars turned toward larger-scale enterprises like plenary indulgences and the *scala coeli* indulgence, marking "a vast increase in their participation in and profit from the penitential economy."[49] Despite the criticism of Reformers, the Council of Trent affirmed "that there is a purgatory and that the souls detained there are helped by the acts of intercession of the faithful, and especially by the acceptable sacrifice of the altar." Even so, the council states that popular sermons should avoid "those things that belong to the realm of curiosity or superstition, or *smack of dishonorable*

---

44. Atwell, "From Augustine to Gregory the Great," 177.
45. Salkeld, *Catholics and Evangelicals*, 43.
46. Salkeld, *Catholics and Evangelicals*, 45.
47. Walls, *Purgatory*, 23.
48. Salkeld, *Catholics and Evangelicals*, 48.
49. Laferrière, "Peddlers of Paradise," 32. Laferrière explains that the *scala coeli* indulgence was a "popular devotion, widely perceived as immediately effective in the salvation of a soul from the pains of Purgatory" (44).

gain."⁵⁰ Scholars note that the Council of Trent was relatively restrained in its affirmation of purgatory, deliberately leaving open numerous questions. Even so, the strong language of penal satisfaction and expiation continued to dominate popular understandings of purgatory until at least the Second Vatican Council in the twentieth century.⁵¹ Ultimately, purgatory has served to reinforce a debt economy for God's justice, just as hell has affirmed the righteous horrors of prison—in eternity and in the present.

Ecclesial Prisons

From the *lex talionis* to atonement to hell/purgatory, prominent theological resources of the Christian tradition point to a divine justice anchored in debt, repayment, captivity, and punishment. These images and concepts have influenced current realities of incarceration, with the price of redemption in the eyes of the secular state bearing out a clear theological legacy. Even so, the contributions have not been limited to abstract ideas. The Christian tradition innovated many carceral practices and thus has itself been directly involved in the business of incarceration.

Numerous carceral developments from recent centuries have emerged out of penal reform efforts. Michael Ignatieff, in his study of the penitentiary in England, examines the influence of evangelical, Methodist, and Quaker reformers.⁵² In a similar study of American penal development, Andrew Skotnicki focuses on two prototypical American penitentiaries that emerged in the early nineteenth century: Eastern State Penitentiary in Pennsylvania and Auburn Penitentiary in New York. Skotnicki shows that religious beliefs were defining influences for both, with the separate system of Eastern State reflecting Quaker theology and the silent system at Auburn reflecting its Presbyterian and Calvinist roots.⁵³ However, Christianity's most significant contributions to incarceration come a great deal earlier than these examples—and largely without reformist associations.⁵⁴

Despite instances found over time and as far back as ancient records,⁵⁵ the regular use of imprisonment as punishment is a recent phenomenon.⁵⁶

---

50. From the decree on purgatory from the Council of Trent (1563), as quoted in Salkeld, *Catholics and Evangelicals*, 50; emphasis added.
51. Salkeld, *Catholics and Evangelicals*, 51.
52. Ignatieff, *Just Measure of Pain*.
53. Skotnicki, *Religion and the Development*, 6.
54. For more on these institutions, see Amy Levad's chapter in this volume.
55. Johnston, "Evolving Function."
56. Foucault, *Discipline and Punish*.

It was the medieval European church that actually led the way in establishing incarceration as the default means of punishment. Three key manifestations of the Christian prison are worthy of note: monastic, ecclesiastical, and inquisitorial.

Monastic prison practice has a long history. A fourth-century papal letter states that delinquent monks and nuns should be confined in a disciplinary cell. From the sixth century on, a number of monastic constitutions used the Latin term *carcer* to identify penitential confinement, the length of which would be determined by the abbot and in some cases was for life.[57] Megan Cassidy-Welch takes up the example of the Cistercian order, noting its first formal statute for optional monastic prisons in 1206. In 1229, the Cistercian General Chapter declared that all abbeys that were able must build a strong prison to hold their criminals. The sentences could be severe. For example, in 1226, one monk was sentenced to perpetual incarceration for threatening to kill his abbot with a razor.[58]

While monastics had already chosen a life of relative solitude and separation, the experience of confinement spread more broadly in the medieval church through the use of ecclesiastical prisons. A primary reason for the development of such prisons was canon law, which prohibited punishments that involved the shedding of blood. As secular punishments of the time became more severe, there was increasing pressure to hold clerics accountable for the serious crimes that they committed. As Jean Dunbabin has shown, imprisonment seemed "the only option" for the church.[59] While previously the use of prisons was typically only for custody and not for punishment, Pope Boniface VIII formally introduced imprisonment into canon law as a fitting punishment in 1298.[60] Penal techniques developed by the medieval church were later employed by secular states. Sociologist David Garland has noted that the Vatican prison served as a model for prison design in Europe and America as late as the end of the eighteenth century. According to Garland, the Protestant Reformation also contributed to secular imprisonment, especially with the sixteenth-century Dutch houses of correction and the early nineteenth-century Quaker penitentiaries. These models helped "to formulate a combination of solitary cellular confinement and productive work which was supposed to produce spiritual redemption as well as painful bodily punishment."[61]

57. Peters, "Prison Before the Prison," 26.
58. Cassidy-Welch, *Imprisonment in Medieval Religious Imagination*, 28–29.
59. Dunbabin, *Captivity and Imprisonment*, 144.
60. Dunbabin, *Captivity and Imprisonment*, 151.
61. Garland, *Punishment and Modern Society*, 204.

Christian incarceration also developed through the fight against heresy by way of inquisitorial prisons. Initially, there was no thought that it would be of any benefit to those suspected or convicted of heresy. The positive impact of incarceration was its ability to prevent serious damage to society. Only later, when inquisitorial confinement became more common, was its use justified along the penitential lines of the monastic model.[62] These prisons were used to detain suspected heretics, encourage confession, and punish those convicted. Canon law actually prohibited coercion of heretics, but the "social need for suppression eventually triumphed."[63] Torture and sentences of perpetual imprisonment were permitted, and the church became newly involved in the legal process as both prosecutors and judges. The church had made its calculations, and it was simply too costly not to imprison. The justification was the protection of souls and the Christian faith. Accordingly, the inquisitors of thirteenth- and fourteenth-century France were inclined to see the prison as a "productive" space.[64] The prison generated truth and knowledge, and it prevented corruption of Christian communities. Thus, the medieval church not only developed model penal practices but demonstrated them to be a most beneficial enterprise.

Not far beneath the surface of contemporary systems of incarceration are resources of the Christian tradition on punishment and the debt economy. It is a theological vision in which suffering is currency and the moral order is a balanced ledger. It is a religious imagination in which captivity begins with indebtedness and ends with ransom. Lines blur between sin, debt, and crime—and for good linguistic and historical reasons. Ched Myers and Elaine Enns note that, in Aramaic, the central metaphor for sin was debt. In Greek, the words are closely related such that the terms are sometimes interchangeable in the New Testament. In first-century Roman Palestine, the consequence of debt was often crime, and so an early association was forged in Christianity between the debtor class and sinfulness.[65] This alignment of debt with sin resonates well with a contemporary carceral system in which the economically vulnerable are a key demographic. And yet, the Christian tradition also possesses resources to challenge this entire framework of punishment and debt.

---

62. Dunbabin, *Captivity and Imprisonment*, 144–45.
63. Dunbabin, *Captivity and Imprisonment*, 152.
64. Cassidy-Welch, *Imprisonment in Medieval Religious Imagination*, 77.
65. C. Myers and Enns, *New Testament Reflections*, 73.

Jubilee Debt Forgiveness and Release of the Imprisoned

The Jubilee and Sabbath Year proclamations exemplify resources of the Christian tradition that are anchored in liberation and debt forgiveness.[66] The Hebrew Bible decrees that every seventh year (the Sabbatical Year), debts are to be forgiven and those who have sold themselves into bondage are to be released (Deut 15). The Jubilee occurs after seven Sabbatical Years (Lev 25) and entails the return of land and, again, the release of those who had been enslaved for their debts. At the heart of the institution of Jubilee are the themes of liberty (from debt and bondage) and return (to the land and to family that might have been scattered out of economic need).[67]

Historical evidence does not suggest that these proclamations were regularly practiced. Noncompliance is even scripturally affirmed. The prophet Jeremiah blames the Babylonian exile on the failure to free slaves in the seventh year (Jer 34). While some commentators consider Jubilee and Sabbath Years to be utopian concepts that were never practiced, others suggest they were implemented but fell into disuse. Regardless, it is clear that Sabbath and Jubilee Year proclamations created a powerful grammar for prophetic eschatology and pronouncements about the reign of God.[68] The economic significance of these proclamations remains relevant even in their metaphorical usage.

The economic dynamics of the Jubilee are especially noteworthy. As Christopher Wright observes, the Jubilee intended to prevent the inequitable accumulation of wealth, which led to oppression and alienation. Rather than redistribution of land, it involved a *restoration* to God's "broadly equitable distribution of the resources of the earth."[69] In particular, Wright claims that the Jubilee was directed at family units, enabling them once again to provide for their own needs rather than labor out of indebtedness to others. In this light, the Jubilee was a force for dignity, agency, and social inclusion; it was a mechanism for "restoring people to the capacity to

---

66. For an extended and constructive interpretation of the biblical Jubilee tradition, see Hannah Bowman's chapter in this volume.

67. C. Wright, "Theology of Jubilee," 9.

68. Lee Griffith notes that Sabbath and Jubilee were important themes in Judaism, including extensive commentary in the Talmud (*Fall of the Prison*, 98n22).

69. C. Wright, "Theology of Jubilee," 12. Michael Barram, on the other hand, emphasizes *redistribution* of wealth in his discussion of Jubilee, noting that land often changed hands "through exploitation and poverty-induced selloffs (often catalyzed by drought, crop failure, and insurmountable indebtedness)" ("Economic and Social Reparations," 82).

participate in the economic life of the community, for their own viability and society's benefit."[70]

In the experience of exile, Israel discovered a "fundamental kinship" between enslavement and imprisonment.[71] Thus, the Jubilee and Sabbath Year proclamations to free those in debt bondage became a broad call for liberation, including the release of prisoners. This association is clearly present in the prophet Isaiah: "The spirit of the Lord God is upon me, because the Lord has anointed me; he has sent me to bring good news to the oppressed, to bind up the brokenhearted, to proclaim liberty to the captives, and release to the prisoners; to proclaim the year of the Lord's favor, and the day of vengeance of our God; to comfort all who mourn" (Isa 61:1–2). The "year of the Lord's favor" is a clear echo of the Sabbath and Jubilee Years, and freedom here is for captives and prisoners alike. As Lee Griffith notes, this proclamation of liberty was neither intended as charity nor based on any special righteousness of those in bondage. Instead, it was a direct response to God's prior liberating action in the exodus of Israel from Egypt. God interceded as the *go'el* for Israel. The *go'el* was a kinsperson who paid ransom in order to free a family member who had been enslaved through indebtedness. With the liberation of Israel, and as reflected in Isa 61, God has paid the ransom for all future captives.[72] The Jubilee and Sabbath Year themes—release and return—are located at the very heart of the narrative of salvation.

The Christian tradition centers these same themes in the person of Jesus Christ and the witness of the New Testament. In Luke 4, Jesus establishes the platform for his ministry, directly quoting from Isa 61 and stating, "Today this scripture has been fulfilled in your hearing" (Luke 4:21). Jesus proclaimed "good news to the poor," "release to the captives," and "the year of the Lord's favor" (Luke 4:18–19). The latter reference, alluding to Jubilee and Sabbath Years, would have made clear to Jesus's hearers that his intentions were for material and not simply spiritual liberation. Further echoes of the Jubilee and Sabbath Years occur throughout the New Testament.

The forgiveness of debts is explored in the parable of the unforgiving servant (Matt 18:21–35). Peter's opening question to Jesus about the extent of forgiveness due for sins is answered through the economics of debt. The parable suggests that forgiveness of sin/debt is not simply a moral imperative but "an expression of God's reign in the very fabric of human

---

70. C. Wright, "Theology of Jubilee," 12.

71. L. Griffith, *Fall of the Prison*, 102.

72. L. Griffith, *Fall of the Prison*, 99–100.

community and social relationships."⁷³ In the servant's refusal to forgive the much smaller debts of his fellow servants, despite having received the king's forgiveness for his truly enormous debt, a tension emerges between an old and new order. Sharon Ringe suggests that the servant's actions constitute a denial of "the new economy of mercy in favor of the old one in which the bonds and obligations leading to indebtedness still hold sway."⁷⁴ While the parable concludes with the servant's imprisonment, it is not a captivity that arose, in the first place, from debt. Instead, Ringe suggests it is a result of the self-exclusion from God's reign of mercy and liberation.⁷⁵ It seems the only prisoners who cannot partake of Jubilee release may be those who stand opposed to Jubilee itself.

Echoes of the Jubilee and Sabbath Year proclamations can also be found in the Lord's Prayer and in similar Gospel statements about the advent of God's reign. In the Lord's Prayer, the petition for the forgiveness of debts (Matt 6:12; Luke 11:4) recalls the tradition of Jubilee and reveals that the typical patterns and structures of indebtedness have been upended. Allusions to Jubilee and Sabbath are found in the writings of St. Paul as well. In the Second Letter to the Corinthians, Paul suggests an alternative economy in which God provides unlimited abundance: "All this is from God, who reconciled us to himself through Christ, and has given us the ministry of reconciliation; that is, in Christ God was reconciling the world to himself, not counting their trespasses against them, and entrusting the message of reconciliation to us" (2 Cor 5:18–19). Myers and Enns note that the verb "to reconcile" has an economic meaning here, along the lines of reconciling a bank statement, and they identify a Jubilee allusion in the phrase "not counting their trespasses against them." Once again, a new order comes into view here. Paul celebrates the passing away of the old debt system and the divine economy of grace that has replaced it.⁷⁶

Release from debt and imprisonment is not mere imagery for the Christian tradition; it is also established practice. In the first century, Clement of Rome recounts that Christians offered themselves as ransom in exchange for persons in captivity.⁷⁷ Historical records are clear that efforts to attend to those imprisoned were not limited to visitation and food but also included financial means in an attempt to secure liberation. Such material support was provided not only to Christians but to all those who

---

73. Ringe, *Jesus, Liberation, and Biblical Jubilee*, 75.
74. Ringe, *Jesus, Liberation, and Biblical Jubilee*, 76.
75. Ringe, *Jesus, Liberation, and Biblical Jubilee*, 77.
76. C. Myers and Enns, *New Testament Reflections*, 11–12.
77. Keenan, *Works of Mercy*, 17.

were imprisoned. Even when funds were not able to secure freedom, they were used in an attempt to achieve better conditions for the ones imprisoned. An example of this can be found in the *Martyrdom of Perpetua and Felicitas* in which two deacons are described as bribing the soldiers to allow Perpetua and her companions to move to a less miserable part of the prison. It appears that early Christian care and intervention for prisoners were so widely recognized that they were even a source of ridicule. In Lucian's late second-century *Death of Peregrinos*, Christians are mocked for bribing prison officials and offering round-the-clock care to a disingenuous convert to the faith.[78] In his treatment of the works of mercy, James Keenan notes that a number of charitable Christian institutions were established in the twelfth century in order to release prisoners. For example, the Trinitarians were "singularly dedicated to ransoming prisoners and laboring to alleviate the conditions of those who remained in slavery."[79] Similarly, a number of Jesuit communities in the sixteenth century raised funds through begging in order to pay off the creditors of prisoners and to ransom back those taken captive by the Turks.

While there are ample Christian sources that uphold a framework of debt and punishment, there are also foundational concepts of the tradition that upend this framework. On one hand, salvation and divine justice demand paying one's debts and enduring just imprisonment. On the other hand, God's justice and salvation are synonymous with the cancellation of debts and release from captivity. At least one place of agreement seems to be the long-standing proximity between economics and punishment in the Christian tradition. Theologically, incarceration has always been something of a business matter. What remains to be determined here is how one trajectory of the tradition can be prioritized over the other.

Conclusion

Within the theology and history of the Christian tradition is part of the origin story of the carceral system. The *lex talionis*, atonement theories, hell/purgatory, and ecclesial prisons reveal a powerful account of divine justice at the intersection of sin, debt, and punishment. Yet, the Christian tradition simultaneously offers a vision at odds with this account, foregrounding the forgiveness of debts and the release of prisoners. The mixed legacy should neither be hidden nor denied. Even so, it is worthwhile to pursue markers

---

78. Nicklas, "Ancient Christian Care for Prisoners."
79. Keenan, *Works of Mercy*, 17–18.

of the tradition that could adjudicate between these approaches. I suggest two such markers.

First, the Christian tradition ought to be characterized by a proactive rather than reactive morality. At the heart of Christianity should be generative action that lovingly creates and sustains, not action generated in response to evil that precedes it. If God's actions are fundamentally understood by the response to evil, then evil is prior to God. Similarly, justice cannot be contingent on the presence of injustice if the telos of humanity is justice itself. This marker significantly challenges the centrality of the debt economy in our relationship with God and prefers instead the economy of grace. Likewise, this marker regards incarceration as a deviation from the plan of salvation rather than the necessary path to it.

The second marker is the nature of the "good news" of the gospel. For it to be truly good, it ought to be good news to all, not only for a portion. This marker casts doubt upon the enterprise of punishment itself. Punishment requires suffering and is therefore not received as good news by all. It may be argued that, once corrected, a person will be grateful for the suffering that has brought about that correction. Yet, this confuses punishment with accountability. Accountability, while difficult, can be good news for all. Punishment is no guarantee for accountability, however, and often works against it. A framework of debt and punishment may provide order, but it is not the universally good news of liberation that we receive from the practices of Jubilee and mercy.

Key markers of the Christian tradition favor liberation over imprisonment and the economy of grace over the economy of debt. Even so, the framework of debt and punishment has had enduring power and appeal. The fact is that the Christian tradition has long been implicated in the business of incarceration. It remains to be seen whether that same tradition can make it its business to do otherwise.

3

Legal Foundations of the Business of Incarceration

JEFFREY R. BAKER

The business of incarceration in the United States arises from long practices and policies that rest on constitutional, statutory, and common law and depend on the vast discretion of police, prosecutors, and courts. These practices and policies reflect popular political trends that favor incarceration as a response to social and cultural problems and that rely on the economic and corporate interests that profit from it. Mass incarceration and its business interests result from policy choices, but they are not the only possible policy choices. The same legal scaffolds that sustain a prison-industrial complex can also support more just, humane, and redemptive systems, when the people and their representatives choose them.

In the United States, incarceration is the dominant form—but not the only form—of lawful, state-sanctioned punishment for the commission of certain crimes. In this system, incarceration is physical detention, forcible restriction of individual liberty, institutional confinement, and isolation. In the first half of the twenty-first century, the US incarcerates a higher percentage of its population than any other nation on earth.[1] In 2022, the federal and state governments incarcerated over 1.9 million people. At this

---

1. Walmsley, *World Prison Population List*; see also Weisberg, "Reality-Challenged Philosophies of Punishment," 1203.

time, approximately 600,000 people enter prison each year, and people go to jail about 10 million times per year, with about 25 percent of people in jail being arrested again in the same year.[2] Within this huge population, the incarceration of Black and Brown people is radically disproportionate to the general population; racism and white supremacy are endemic to the history of criminal justice in the United States.[3]

Whether as intentional strategy or attendant consequence of other policies, the phenomenon of mass incarceration rests on bases of law and law enforcement. Federal and state laws provide for various forms of incarceration for certain people convicted of certain crimes. The means and length of incarceration and the crimes for which the state incarcerates people evolve over time. These changes are subject to shifting political interests, social values, and assumptions about the nature of crime, punishment, vengeance, deterrence, rehabilitation, public safety, and restoration.[4]

The business of incarceration has evolved with shifting philosophies of punishment, rehabilitation, and correction. Throughout history, the state has seen fit to seek profit from incarceration, invest in incarceration as economic development, and permit private enterprises to enrich themselves by imprisoning people. The business of incarceration extends from public facilities for the detention of people convicted of crime to private enterprises that contract with the state to detain people for profit. In many iterations of carceral law enforcement, the state has profited or defrayed its costs through the labor of the people it incarcerates, sometimes through their direct labor or through leasing their labor to private actors. Prisons and other detention facilities become centers for economic activity for the people they employ and the communities that host them. These financial incentives often drive policing and policies that expand incarceration for economic gain, not for public safety or correction.

Mass incarceration is not inevitable, and profit from the business of incarceration is not endemic to criminal law systems. Concurrent racism and racial disparities are not unavoidable, collateral accidents. Incarceration and the means of incarceration are deliberate choices in law and policy, and political communities may choose other paths. Other paths, policies, laws, and systems are available and viable under the US Constitution. In a constitutional republic, politics and economics drive these decisions in law and policy, and the choices reflect public and political priorities.

2. Sawyer and Wagner, "Mass Incarceration."
3. Alexander, *New Jim Crow*; Butler, "One Hundred Years."
4. See generally Dyszlewski et al., "Mass Incarceration"; see also United States Sentencing Commission, "Annotated 2021 Chapter 1," A.1.

The constitutional structure of criminal law permits alternatives that reflect popular values and social commitments. However intransigent they may be, if the policies and consequences of incarceration run counter to the people's morals and virtues, priorities and objectives, the people may elect alternative legal and policy approaches to punishment, rehabilitation, deterrence, and restoration. But if dominant power structures and their attendant business interests insist on propping up racist incarceration practices and private profit off the labor of prisoners, they will continue to defend them as they have throughout American history.

Crime and Punishment in US Law

In the United States, the legal bases for incarceration arise first from the US Constitution (1789). The Constitution assumes a system of criminal law that includes incarceration.[5] It enumerates certain negative rights that provide basic standards and limits on criminal law and procedure, policing and enforcement, prosecutions and convictions, sentences and punishments. Within these limits, legislatures adopt statutory laws to define crimes and prescribe sentences for their violation. Police and prosecutors then exercise their discretion to determine how to enforce the laws and whom to prosecute. Courts render judgment, then sentence the convicted.

Constitutional Rights and Limits on Criminal Law, Procedure, and Punishment

The Bill of Rights includes amendments limiting the government's power and jurisdiction in matters of criminal law and punishment. The Fourth, Fifth, Sixth, and Eighth Amendments provide the principal constitutional rights addressing policing, prosecution, trial, and punishment.

The Fourth Amendment describes the "right of the people to be secure in their persons, houses, papers, and effects, against unreasonable searches and seizures." The Fifth Amendment recognizes the right to a grand jury and protects the people from double jeopardy, self-incrimination, and the deprivation of life, liberty, or property without due process of law. The Sixth Amendment guarantees the right of a defendant to a speedy, public trial by jury; to be informed of the charges; to confront adverse witnesses; to compel witness testimony; and to assistance of counsel. Regarding incarceration after conviction, the Eighth Amendment provides the Constitution's principal

---

5. See, e.g., U.S. Const., art. I, §8, cl. 6, 10, 18; art. II, §3, cl. 3; art. IV, §2.

guidance on the nature of punishment: "Excessive bail shall not be required, nor excessive fines imposed, nor cruel and unusual punishments inflicted."

The Fourteenth Amendment incorporates the rights to due process and equal protection to the states: "No State shall make or enforce any law which shall abridge the privileges or immunities of citizens of the United States; nor shall any State deprive any person of life, liberty, or property, without due process of law; nor deny to any person within its jurisdiction the equal protection of the laws" (§1).

The Thirteenth Amendment is crucial to understanding the trajectory of incarceration and mass incarceration in the US. It is one of the Reconstruction Amendments addressing slavery and civil rights in the aftermath of the Civil War. The Thirteenth Amendment made slavery unconstitutional in most forms: "Neither slavery nor involuntary servitude, *except as a punishment for crime whereof the party shall have been duly convicted*, shall exist within the United States, or any place subject to their jurisdiction" (§1; emphasis added). Although policies and practices have changed through the decades, often in response to Eighth Amendment litigation over what may be "cruel and unusual," the Thirteenth Amendment permits slavery or involuntary servitude for people convicted of crimes.

Within these constitutional boundaries, federal and state governments have enormous discretion when defining and prosecuting crimes and imposing sentences. Legislatures may define crimes and establish attendant punishments so long as they do not violate these constitutional and civil rights, but the interpretation and application of these constitutional principles have evolved over time to address new political and philosophical thresholds for acceptable policing and punishment.

US Criminal Law and Procedure

Typically, but not always, penal incarceration follows conviction in a trial or a guilty plea for committing a crime defined by statute and sentencing by a judge to punishment prescribed by law for that crime.[6] This procedural path to incarceration is common and methodical, based on rules, and driven by the statutory authority and discretion of police and prosecutors to investigate, arrest, and try people for committing crimes defined by statute. Each of these steps is a creature of laws and rules established by legislatures and courts.

---

6. See generally Committee on the Judiciary, *Federal Rules of Criminal Procedure* (2021).

Theories of Incarceration

Within these legal and procedural systems, policies of incarceration advance multiple, important societal goals, like public safety, punishment, deterrence, incapacitation, retribution, restitution, and rehabilitation.[7] These interests shift through long, cyclical debates over the conception, philosophies, and purposes of prisons and penalties.[8] Historically, there are other goals, too, like vengeance, shame, profit, and the subjugation of Black people.[9]

Criminal law has assumed a form of exceptionalism in the US, with an implicit claim that criminal law enforcement is the best way to order society, a catch-all for community and cultural problems that often dodges serious criticism.[10] The formal law itself rarely articulates these purposes expressly, but the politics and policies are evident in public discourse, critical observation, and legislative histories.

Policy Decisions and Discretion in US Law

For policies of incarcerations, the first major choice is the decision to define a given action as a crime. Once lawmakers have designated a certain action or omission to be a crime, then they determine the range of punishments to impose on the commission of that crime. Lawmakers, prosecutors, and courts determine whether and whom to prosecute, then decide whether and how to punish them. If that sentence is incarceration, then the state chooses the nature, form, and length of the incarceration.

Defining Crimes

During the colonial era and the early days of the United States, substantive criminal law arose in the common law, but soon after independence, legislatures increasingly undertook to define crimes by statute.[11] Throughout most

---

7. See, e.g., Weisberg, "Reality-Challenged Philosophies of Punishment"; Ashe, "Prison-House of Prison-Houses"; Jouet, "Mass Incarceration Paradigm Shift?"; Bronsteen et al., "Retribution and the Experience"; Ulen, "Skepticism About Deterrence"; Chiao, "Mass Incarceration."

8. See, e.g., Avio, "On Private Prisons."

9. See, e.g., Ajunwa, "Modern Day Scarlet Letter"; Ghoshray, "America the Prison Nation"; Bronsther, "Long-Term Incarceration"; Mulch, "Crime and Punishment"; Halladay, "Thirteenth Amendment."

10. See Levin, "Criminal Law Exceptionalism."

11. Common law is court-made law that evolves over time as courts compare cases to cases and develop laws, rules, and standards through deliberative processes. Statutes

of US history, legislatures define and refine actions and behaviors prohibited as crimes, and courts largely defer to legislatures' definitions.[12] These definitions change over time.[13]

For example, from the founding until the 1900s, federal and state governments did not regulate hemp, cannabis, and marijuana; governments began defining their use as crimes only in the 1930s, with penalties increasing throughout the 1950s. The political movement to criminalize cannabis appealed to racism and anti-immigrant sentiments.[14] During the 1960s, the public perception of marijuana began to change within the larger social upheavals of the day. The National Commission on Marihuana and Drug Abuse recommended decriminalizing marijuana in 1972, but it took until the 1990s and early 2000s for states to begin legalizing medicinal and recreational use.[15] Between the 1930s and 2000s, police arrested hundreds of millions of people for the use or possession of marijuana, with all the collateral consequences of an arrest or conviction. Black Americans were almost four times more likely to be arrested than white people despite common use.[16] By 2021, a majority of states had decriminalized marijuana, but its use and possession remained a crime in federal law.

The criminalization and decriminalization of marijuana were public policy choices in response to evolving social, political, and economic forces. For a relatively short period of US history, governments created crimes and expended fortunes on the enforcement, prosecution, trial, and incarceration for actions later made legal again. Even as the marked legal and political trend is toward the decriminalization of marijuana, police arrested over six million people on marijuana charges between 2010 and 2018, and police arrest Black people far more than white people for the same crimes, although Black and white people use marijuana at comparable rates.[17]

The overwhelming trend throughout the twentieth century and continuing into this century is an acceleration of criminalization.[18] This expan-

---

are laws created by legislatures, like Congress, through political processes by elected representatives. See Hessick, "Myth of Common Law Crimes"; cf. Rosenberg, "Growth of Federal Common Law."

12. See, e.g., United States v. Wiltberger, 18 U.S. 76, 95 (1820).
13. See, e.g., Dervana and Podgor, "'White Collar Crime.'"
14. Vitiello, "Marijuana Legalization."
15. Bonnie, "Surprising Collapse of Marijuana Prohibition."
16. See Ahrens, "Retroactive Legality," citing Edwards et al., *War on Marijuana*. See also R. King and Mauer, "War on Marijuana," 6.
17. Edwards et al., *Tale of Two Countries*.
18. "On average, Congress created fifty-seven new crimes every year between 2000 and 2007, roughly the same rate of criminalization from the two prior decades, resulting

sive growth of new crimes is primarily around regulatory crimes, but it also springs from broad judicial interpretation of ambiguous drafting, especially when prosecutors choose to pursue aggressive applications.[19] This trend has not necessarily arisen from a broad policy consensus that more defined crimes are better for society. Rather, the results of over criminalization meet with broad consensus that the trend is destructive. Over criminalization results in more statutory crimes, excessive incarceration, and perhaps more criminal behavior itself from rationalization through too many poorly defined crimes.[20] The expansion of criminalization has also served to marginalize vulnerable communities and perpetuate inequalities; it creates more stumbling blocks, traps, and small catastrophes that drive inequity in law and society.[21]

Choosing Punishments

After lawmakers define crimes, the next major choice becomes adopting preferred forms of punishment. These punishments, often even for the same crimes, may differ and evolve over time. For example, Congress passed the Sarbanes-Oxley Act in 2002 in response to a record number of massive, disruptive bankruptcies.[22] Sarbanes-Oxley included the White-Collar Crime Penalty Enhancement Act (WCCPA) that imposed increased mandatory incarceration for mail and wire fraud.[23] This policy choice prompted intense debate over the nature and purpose of incarceration, including from critics who suggested that incarceration for these "nonviolent" crimes did little to protect the public from harm.[24] The new sentences for white-collar crimes resulted, as usual, in marked racial disparities in sentencing, with Black and Hispanic defendants receiving significantly longer prison sentences than white defendants, often connected to the inability to pay a fine.[25] These

---

today in some 4,500 federal laws that carry criminal penalties" (S. Smith, "Overcoming Overcriminalization," 537).

19. S. Smith, "Overcoming Overcriminalization"; Parker, "Developing Consensus Solutions."

20. For more on these arguments, see Levin, "Consensus Myth"; Haugh, "Overcriminalization's New Harm Paradigm."

21. Levin, "Consensus Myth"; Karakatsanis, "Punishment Bureaucracy."

22. Sarbanes-Oxley Act of 2002, Pub. L. No. 107–204, 116 Stat. 804 (2002).

23. See Recine, "White Collar Crime Penalty."

24. See, e.g., Green, "Moral Ambiguity"; Podgor, "Challenge of White Collar Sentencing"; Weissmann and Block, "White Collar Defendants"; Gunn and Sun, "Sometimes Cure Is Worse"; Diamantis, "White-Collar Showdown."

25. See Schanzenbacha and Yaeger, "Prison Time, Fines."

consequences and their attendant debates illuminate a confused national understanding of the purposes of incarceration, whether incarceration is for punishing offenders, protecting the public, rehabilitating wayward people, or something else.

One of the most notorious examples is the federal policy to incarcerate convicted defendants more harshly for the possession of crack cocaine than for powder cocaine. In 1986, again reacting to a perceived new threat and public attention, Congress passed the Anti-Drug Abuse Act of 1986.[26] This law imposed significantly longer prison sentences for the possession of crack cocaine. Yet within a decade, the US Sentencing Commission reported to Congress that the policy rested on misunderstanding about the chemistry of crack cocaine and misapprehensions about the people most likely to use it.[27]

The Sentencing Commission and others noted profound racial disparities in sentencing.[28] At the height of the "war on drugs" under the Anti-Drug Abuse Act, Black people accounted for 85 percent of defendants incarcerated in federal prisons on crack convictions, even though white people were the majority of dealers and at least half the users of crack cocaine.[29] Whether intentional or merely correlated, the effect of imposing heightened prison sentences for particularly disfavored drugs was the incarceration of vastly more Black people, far out of proportion to the commission of specific crimes. Twenty-five years later, Congress addressed these problems with the Fair Sentencing Act of 2010. These reforms sparked confusion and controversy over whether and how the new sentencing regime should apply retroactively to people serving vastly longer prison sentences.[30]

These examples demonstrate a tendency in the US for lawmakers to react to perceived crises by criminalizing more activities and increasing carceral penalties. Both policies had consequences beyond deterrence, punishment, and rehabilitation, and both resulted in increased incarceration and pronounced racial disparities in arrest and sentencing.[31]

---

26. Anti-Drug Abuse Act of 1986, Pub. L. No. 99–570, 100 Stat. 3207 (codified as amended at 21 U.S.C. §§841–904 [2012]).

27. See Kilty and Joseph, "Institutional Racism and Sentencing Disparities"; Fabens-Lassen, "Cracked Remedy."

28. See U.S. Sentencing Commission, *Preliminary Crack Cocaine Retroactivity*; Coyle, "Race and Class Penalties."

29. See LaJuana Davis, "Rock, Powder, Sentencing," 375, 388.

30. LaJuana Davis, "Rock, Powder, Sentencing"; Brungard, "Finally, Crack Sentencing Reform."

31. See Berry, "Eighth Amendment Presumptions."

The Discretion of Police, Prosecutors, and Courts

Discretion is central to the criminal legal system in the United States. Police have significant discretion in the activities they investigate and the people they arrest. Prosecutors have expansive discretion in the people they charge and the charges they bring against them. Courts have significant discretion in sentencing after conviction. Their respective discretions inform each other and serve important policies, and they contribute to trends of mass incarceration and racial disparities in arrests, prosecution, and sentencing.

Police Discretion

American police have extraordinary discretion to arrest, investigate, and charge people under criminal laws. This discretion may be necessary to some degree, but it contributes dramatically to current modes of incarceration.[32]

The United States Supreme Court affirmed and entrenched this discretion in *Town of Castle Rock v. Gonzales*.[33] Jessica Gonzales, now Lenahan, received a civil protection order against her husband; he violated it and took their three children without her consent.[34] She contacted the police several times, showed them the court order, and pled for them to enforce it; the court order instructed the police to "use every reasonable means to enforce this restraining order."[35] The police refused repeatedly to enforce the order.[36] Within hours, her husband arrived at a police station and opened fire on police, who killed him. The police found the three children murdered in the back seat of his car.[37] Lenahan sued the town of Castle Rock, arguing that the police's refusal to enforce the order violated her civil rights.[38] The Supreme Court, in a majority opinion by Justice Scalia, found that the protection order did not give Lenahan a personal property interest in its enforcement and recognized that a "well established tradition of police discretion has long coexisted with apparently mandatory arrest statutes."[39]

32. See, e.g., Beckett, "Uses and Abuses of Police Discretion."
33. Town of Castle Rock v. Gonzales, 125 S. Ct. 2796 (2005).
34. Town of Castle Rock v. Gonzales, 125 S. Ct. 2796 (2005), 2800.
35. Town of Castle Rock v. Gonzales, 125 S. Ct. 2796 (2005), 2801.
36. Town of Castle Rock v. Gonzales, 125 S. Ct. 2796 (2005), 2801.
37. Town of Castle Rock v. Gonzales, 125 S. Ct. 2796 (2005), 2802.
38. Town of Castle Rock v. Gonzales, 125 S. Ct. 2796 (2005), 2802.
39. Town of Castle Rock v. Gonzales, 125 S. Ct. 2796 (2005), 2806–7. In a later petition to the Inter-American Commission on Human Rights, the commission found that the police's refusal to enforce her protection order was a violation of international human rights law: Jessica Lenahan (Gonzales) v. United States, Report No. 80/11, Case

In Castle Rock, the Supreme Court found that even statutes requiring mandatory police action did not overcome the long tradition of police discretion. Thus, police have all the more discretion when statutes do not require them to act. Whether by correlation, causation, or other effect, this discretion produces profound racial disparities in the people the police arrest. In a 2021 report, the Bureau of Justice Statistics within the Department of Justice reported on arrests from 2018 and noted significant disproportions for arrests of Black and Hispanic men relative to their share of the population.[40] This is consistent with long trends in the US.[41]

Prosecutorial Discretion

Prosecutorial discretion is a hallmark of the American criminal law system.[42] Prosecutors represent the state in legal actions against people accused of violating criminal laws. In this role, prosecutors enjoy vast discretion to evaluate evidence, analyze charges, negotiate guilty pleas, bring cases to trial, and seek sentences upon conviction. The essential, vaunted, yet theoretical role of prosecutors is not to win at any cost but should be to serve justice on behalf of the people.[43]

Toward this end, within constitutional limits, prosecutors exercise strategic and tactical discretion in investigation, charging, negotiating, and trying cases. Prosecutors' roles in the criminal legal system are essential and undeniable, but the responsibilities of prosecutors in the modern era of mass incarceration and the business of incarceration are subject to pointed debate.[44]

Prosecutorial discretion is a factor in mass incarceration, whether by correlation, causation, or active contribution.[45] An increase in prosecutorial discretion under federal sentencing guidelines likely incentivized more severe sentencing in a system that promotes increased convictions.[46] Nearly 90 percent of all federal criminal cases involve guilty pleas, and most of

---

12.626, Inter-American Commission on Human Rights (July 21, 2011).

40. See Beck, "Race and Ethnicity of Violent Crime."

41. See, e.g., Langan, "Racial Disparity"; NAACP, "Criminal Justice Fact Sheet"; Sentencing Project, "Report to the United Nations."

42. See Krauss, "Theory of Prosecutorial Discretion"; Pizzi, "Understanding Prosecutorial Discretion."

43. See Berger v. U.S., 295 U.S. 78, 88 (1935).

44. See, e.g., Griffin and Yaroshefsky, "Ministers of Justice"; Bellin, "Reassessing Prosecutorial Power"; Leonetti, "Speaking of Prosecutors."

45. See Pfaff, *Locked In*; cf. Bellin, "Reassessing Prosecutorial Power."

46. See Boerner, "Sentencing Guidelines."

these involve plea bargains.[47] The disposition of these cases depends almost entirely on prosecutorial discretion, even if judges ultimately will accept them and impose sentences.

Most prosecutors are elected officials subject to local, electoral politics, so sentencing can be a significant means to signaling to constituents and responding to political incentives. This can work to exacerbate mass incarceration, but prosecutorial discretion may also be a means of promoting creative, even progressive, approaches to criminal justice.[48] But these possibilities and factors still depend on individual and institutional discretion largely unfettered by judicial or legislative review so may bend with politics and public pressure.[49] Even so, several reforms may be effective to confront mass incarceration while conserving prosecutorial discretion. Lisa Griffin and Ellen Yaroshefsky suggest reforms that are possible within existing frameworks of prosecutorial discretion to acknowledge and address mass incarceration: adjusting prosecutors' conceptual roles in recognition of the current mass incarceration crisis; promoting disciplined independence from law enforcement in charging; collecting data on charging decisions and their consequences; and establishing charging policies based on that data.[50]

Cynthia Alkon proposes limitations and cultural shifts in the use of coercive plea bargains.[51] Carissa Byrne Hessick argues that plea bargaining has become the central procedure of the US criminal justice system with catastrophic results for deliberative justice. Hessick demonstrates that prosecutors often leverage the threat of excessive charges for plea bargains on cases that would be questionable at trial, and that these practices have become widespread and common. "It has caused lawmakers to make sentences longer and allowed prosecutors to evade all sorts of rights and protections for defendants. Perhaps most important, it has made it far too easy to punish people, and because it is so easy to do that, our jails and prisons are bursting at the seams."[52] To address this, she calls for public disclosure of the additional charges that prosecutors threatened to coerce a guilty plea; defendants' rights to see the evidence against them before accepting a deal; prohibition on the waiver of counsel before accepting a plea bargain; and judicial refusal to accept fictitious guilty pleas.

---

47. Devers, *Plea and Charge Bargaining*, 1, s.v. "Background."
48. See Wadhia, "Immigration Enforcement"; Lee and Ashar, "DACA, Government Lawyers."
49. See J. Baker and Timm, "Zero-Tolerance."
50. Griffin and Yaroshefsky, "Ministers of Justice," 301.
51. See Alkon, "Overlooked Key to Reversing."
52. Hessick, *Punishment Without Trial*, 221.

In the current system, with scant judicial review or legislative restrictions, prosecutorial discretion is largely subject only to executive priorities and the self-policing of professional ethics.[53] These are the effective floor for prosecutorial ethics, but creative, engaged prosecutors could engage in constructive, intrinsic, ethical responses to improve these systems, advance justice, and inspire trust.[54] Discretion could be a ratchet that drives the criminal legal system toward liberty and restoration instead of incarceration and destruction.[55] Tamara F. Lawson teaches that the criminal legal system and prosecutors should center the moral imperatives of human dignity in their discretion, as an elemental factor in seeking justice.[56] Angela Davis argues that prosecutors have an outright ethical obligation to confront and reduce mass incarceration as they exercise their extraordinary power and influence on charging and sentencing.[57]

Judicial Discretion

Once prosecutors bring a case to a conviction or plea bargain, judges enjoy significant discretion to determine the means and length of incarceration or other penalties and consequences. These options typically include incarceration, fines, probation, and restitution, although recent movements include alternatives for therapeutic and restorative justice.

State and federal statutes prescribe ranges for permissible sentences. For example, the state of Tennessee has established classes of felonies with ranges for sentences of incarceration: at least fifteen years in prison for a Class A felony, eight years for a Class B felony, four years for a Class C or D felony, or two years for a Class E felony.[58] Prosecutors bring charges against a defendant at trial, and if the court convicts the defendant of the crime, the judge considers the ranges and minimum penalties when sentencing the defendant.[59]

In the 1980s, Congress empowered the United States Sentencing Commission to craft sentencing guidelines to "further the basic purposes of criminal punishment: deterrence, incapacitation, just punishment, and

53. American Bar Association, "Rule 3.8: Special Responsibilities of a Prosecutor."
54. See Podgor, "Ethics and Professionalism of Prosecutors."
55. See Markowitz, "Prosecutorial Discretion Power"; Levin, "Imagining the Progressive Prosecutor."
56. See Lawson, "Human Dignity."
57. See A. J. Davis, "Prosecutor's Ethical Duty."
58. See Tenn. Code Ann. §40-42-101.
59. See, e.g., Tenn. Code Ann. §40-28-101.

rehabilitation."[60] Congress had three objectives. The first, basic objective "was to enhance the ability of the criminal justice system to combat crime through an effective, fair sentencing system."[61] Second, the guidelines should promote "reasonable uniformity in sentencing by narrowing the wide disparity in sentences imposed for similar criminal offenses committed by similar offenders."[62] Third, the guidelines should effect "proportionality in sentencing through a system that imposes appropriately different sentences for criminal conduct of differing severity."[63] The guidelines recognize tension between uniformity and proportionality. The guidelines include judicial discretion for unusual cases, but they err against broad discretion on the idea that it may undermine the basic purposes of national guidelines. The history of these guidelines is fraught with controversy over whether they are rigid requirements or general guidelines, and courts now enjoy greater discretion to depart from them.

In the age of mass incarceration, however, William Berry argues for more individualized sentencing for all felonies. Noting that the Supreme Court has proscribed mandatory death sentences and extended increased discretion to juvenile life-without-parole cases, Berry argues that individualized sentencing could ameliorate the dehumanizing effects of felony convictions and would return real sentencing discretion to courts with constitutional authority and away from prosecutors.[64]

In federal systems, police and prosecutors are further removed from direct political accountability than their counterparts in state systems. In the states, police leadership, prosecutors, and most judges are subject to local elections. This suggests that state and local criminal law systems ought to be more responsive and accountable to the values of their communities and may be more responsive to alternatives to incarceration that may better promote public safety, rehabilitation, and restoration, but they may also be more vulnerable to reactionary political and economic pressures to sustain and expand the carceral state.

---

60. United States Sentencing Commission, "Annotated 2021 Chapter 1," A.1.2, "The Statutory Mission." See United States v. Booker, 543 U.S. 220 (2005); Berry, "Discretion Without Guidance."

61. United States Sentencing Commission, "Annotated 2021 Chapter 1," A.1.3, "The Basic Approach," para. 1.

62. United States Sentencing Commission, "Annotated 2021 Chapter 1," A.1.3, "The Basic Approach," para. 2.

63. United States Sentencing Commission, "Annotated 2021 Chapter 1," A.1.3, "The Basic Approach," para. 2.

64. Berry, "Individualized Sentencing."

An extreme example of judicial discretion was the practice of judicial override in Alabama capital punishment cases. Alabama was the last state to permit judges to override jury sentences in capital cases, either to impose a death sentence when the jury recommended life in prison or vice versa. It ended the practice in 2017.[65] Although judges could override jury recommendations for life or death sentences, judges imposed death sentences over jury recommendations in 92 percent of cases from 1976 to 2011, sentencing 107 defendants to die when juries had recommended life in prison. In Alabama, judicial elections are partisan, and in election years, judicial overrides in favor of the death penalty increased significantly. Judges imposing death sentences in override cases demonstrated significant racial disparities in their discretion as well, imposing death more often for Black defendants and more often when victims were white.[66]

Profit from Incarceration

Systems of criminal law and law enforcement in the US arise from certain constitutional constraints. These systems accommodate competing and conflicting philosophies of criminal justice and fix immense discretion in individual state actors. The field of policy possibilities is vast, but in a capitalist economy during de jure white supremacy, systems of law enforcement and incarceration reflected the prevailing interests of power and influence. As de jure white supremacy slowly gave way to de facto forms after the Civil War, then as the civil rights movement gained traction a century later, the systems reacted accordingly.

In various forms at different times, that state has chosen to permit and encourage private profit from public incarceration. From peonage to labor leasing to private prisons, some systems of incarceration in the United States permit private actors to exploit incarcerated people for private gain. This creates markets, producers and consumers, lobbies, and economic incentives to perpetuate and prolong incarceration.

When prisons and jails are public, the institutions generate their own economic incentives and inertia, as sites of local industry, revenue, and jobs in economically vulnerable regions. Public spending for incarceration often deprives other policy options of funding they need to be successful, so without sufficient investment in alternatives, incarceration can appear to be the only effective option, thus perpetuating more incarceration. These

65. See Ala. Code Ann. §§13A-5-45, 13A-5-46, 13A-5-47, amended by Senate Bill 16 (2017).
66. Equal Justice Initiative, *Death Penalty in Alabama*, 4.

economic forces can entrench and perpetuate immoral and destructive practices that place profit and economics over human dignity, public safety, and rehabilitation.

The following examples illustrate these cycles. Some were explicitly racist and rooted in white supremacy. Others are later manifestations of policies that are racially neutral on their face but have racially discriminatory effect. All of these examples perpetuate incarceration as a solution to crime and entrench economic incentives toward policies of incarceration.

Peonage and Labor Leasing

After the constitutional abolition of slavery, many in the South concocted new ways to ensure access to cheap Black labor. Peonage was the practice of compelling free labor as a means of repaying debts manufactured to entrap people in intractable cycles of servitude.[67] These legally actionable debts arose from interest, loans, or fines associated with coercive employment contracts; police would arrest people for the debts, then deliver them into forced labor to repay creditors. This amounted to enslavement by another name. Private employers would impose exploitative contracts on vulnerable laborers who could be charged with vagrancy if they did not have a job. The contracts themselves could create usurious conditions that would lock a worker into perpetual labor, and the criminal codes would impose hard labor and impossible fines for violating employment contracts. The US Supreme Court found that the criminal statute violated the Thirteenth Amendment: "The state may impose involuntary servitude as a punishment for crime, but it may not compel one man to labor for another in payment of a debt, by punishing him as a criminal if he does not perform the service or pay the debt."[68]

While the bonded labor of peonage suffered legal setbacks, the practice of convict leasing persisted and thrived under that notorious exception in the Thirteenth Amendment.[69] Convict leasing began in the South after the Civil War when economies and governments were bankrupt. The practice was a means to return extremely cheap labor to plantations and other hard labor while generating public revenue. States would lease convicts as laborers to private actors or put them to work on chain gangs for public works. In many Southern states, the legislature and police propped up these markets with Black codes and "pig laws," minor crimes enforced only against Black

---

67. See Schmidt, "Principle and Prejudice."
68. Bailey v. Alabama, 219 U.S. 219 (1911), 244.
69. See Schmidt, "Principle and Prejudice," 646.

men that created sustainable pipelines of profitable Black labor.[70] These laws enriched private industry and generated revenue for the state.

Funding Courts and Systems by Fees and Fines

After the landmark 1963 case of *Gideon v. Wainwright* recognized the right to counsel in criminal cases, every state adapted to provide defense counsel to indigent defendants and established various forms of public defense.[71] In Louisiana, for decades before Hurricane Katrina in 2005, the state erected a unique user-pays system for funding its system of public criminal defense. That is, the state of Louisiana funded public defense through fines and fees generated by people moving through the system. This is a massive, systemic conflict of interest, in which the state funds defenders by imposing criminal fines and penalties on the people they are defending. With massive caseloads, traumatic wait times in detention, and stark short-staffing, the New Orleans indigent defense system came under sharp scrutiny and reform efforts for years, but the Hurricane Katrina crisis laid bare its unsustainability. Although defenders achieved significant reforms and increased funding, the user-pays system persists, and the system remains inundated with too many clients and too few lawyers.[72]

The reality of a user-pays system means that the court system, and in Louisiana the defenders themselves, depends on people grinding through the system, being found guilty or pleading guilty, and racking up fines. Louisiana is not unique in funding its courts through fines and fees. Courts, prosecutors, police, and defenders often rely on the revenue from the people they are adjudicating, perpetuating conflicts of interest and impeding reform.[73]

Although peonage and convict leasing do not survive in their Jim Crow modes, Tamar Birckhead makes a compelling argument that contemporary systems of misdemeanor fines, court costs, fees, restitutions, assessments, attachments, and forfeitures still create insurmountable debt burdens that perpetuate cycles of incarceration. These debt burdens can lead to incarceration, loss of parental rights, suspended licenses, intractable barriers to reentry, and increased recidivism, which leads to further debt burdens.[74] For many poor people, the criminal law systems can create and

---

70. Lipman, "Mississippi's Prison Experience," 685, 688.
71. See Gideon v. Wainwright, 372 U.S. 335 (1963).
72. Bunton, "Rising from Katrina's Ashes."
73. See, e.g., McDonald and Carpenter, *Frustrating, Corrupt, Unfair*.
74. Birckhead, "New Peonage."

sustain oppressive cycles of financial indebtedness, creating revenue for the state necessary to sustain these systems.[75]

In Washington State, a single defendant with one conviction may be subject to up to twenty-eight financial sanctions; these are not the sentence for the crime but the fees imposed for defending against the charge brought by the state. Bryan Adamson critiques the practice of Washington courts that refer these financial obligations to private debt collectors. The Washington statute allows courts to transfer a non-incarcerated debtor's obligations to a private debt collector if the debtor is thirty days delinquent and allows the debt collector to impose a collection fee up to 50 percent of the outstanding debt under $100,000 and 35 percent of the unpaid debt over $100,000, plus a 12-percent per annum charge on its collection fee. Since most defendants in Washington are indigent and since most people have difficulty finding good work after incarceration, these terms make repayment extraordinarily difficult. Adamson argues that these penalties are excessive fines that violate the Eighth Amendment and that referring them to debt collectors violates the due process and equal protection clauses of the Fourteenth Amendment.[76]

In 2022, John Archibald reported on the town of Brookside, Alabama. In 2022, Brookside had a population of about 1,253. Between 2011 and 2018, Brookside reported fifty-five serious crimes in its city limits. In 2018, revenue from traffic tickets constituted about 14 percent of the city budget. Beginning in 2018, however, Brookside began a new campaign of policing; in two years, its municipal revenue from criminal fines and forfeitures exploded to make up more than half the city's budget. By 2020, total arrests rose 1,109 percent. Brookside's spending on police increased by 560 percent. It bought a riot control military vehicle; it hired vastly more police than the national average for a town its size. This police force patrolled six miles of road with no traffic lights and a short stretch of an interstate highway. The town's total income more than doubled in two years through fines and forfeitures. Archibald reported the Brookside police chief's response to these numbers: "I see a 600% increase—that's a failure. If you had more officers and more productivity you'd have more.... I think it could be more."[77]

---

75. See, e.g., Richards and Cohen, "Price Kids Pay."
76. Adamson, "Debt Bondage."
77. Archibald, "Police," para. 24.

Direct Profit from Prisons

The Mississippi State Penitentiary, most commonly known as Parchman Prison or Parchman Farm, in the Mississippi Delta is one of the most notorious prisons in the United States and one of the most profitable. Parchman is a plantation, a working farm, relying on prisoners for labor. Parchman's economic model relies on free or extremely cheap human labor to work a farm that profits the state of Mississippi. Mississippi is no stranger to the economic model.[78]

The Thirteenth Amendment permits involuntary servitude upon conviction of a crime, so the legal structure of a penal plantation like Parchman does not violate the Constitution. It was a deliberate means of re-enslaving Black men after Reconstruction when political power returned to the white planter classes in the Deep South. In his history of criminal justice reform in Mississippi in the 1830s, David M. Lipman explains that lawmakers were concerned even then with whether a prison could be self-supporting and profitable for the state. The state recognized financial value in prison farms during and after Reconstruction and invested in building Parchman in 1900. Almost immediately, it earned a reputation of brutality that shocked many in Mississippi, but "the criminal treatment of inmates which has plagued Parchman since its early years has been habitually accepted as necessary for efficiency, productivity, and profit."[79]

In 1965, Parchman came under withering scrutiny when civil rights activists were arrested at a demonstration in Natchez, Mississippi, and detained at Parchman. In a civil rights lawsuit, the Fifth Circuit Court of Appeals found that the conditions and protocols of detention at Parchman violated the Eighth Amendment's prohibition against cruel and unusual punishment.[80] In the 1972 case of *Gates v. Collier*, a federal district court again found that practices at Parchman were violations of the Eighth Amendment and began a decade of court-supervised reform.[81]

While there might have been improvements in conditions, corporal punishment, and prison policies, the economic model persists. The Mississippi Department of Corrections prominently features its model relying on free labor to profit the state: "MSP offenders provide more than 100,000 hours of free offender labor each year to adjacent municipalities

---

78. See Oshinsky, *"Worse Than Slavery."*

79. Lipman, "Mississippi's Prison Experience," 686.

80. See Anderson v. Nosser, 456 F.2d 835 (5th Cir. 1972).

81. See Gates v. Collier, 349 F. Supp. 881 (N.D. Miss 1972); 548 F. 2d 1241 (5th Cir. 1977); 423 F. Supp. 732 (N.D. Miss. 1976).

and counties, as well as assisting other state agencies."[82] In 2020, Mississippi legislators opened an inquiry into a transfer of prisoners from Parchman to a for-profit prison in the Delta operated by CoreCivic.[83] The inquiry was into the basis of the contract award, not the relative policy merits of prisons for profit.

Private Prisons and Capitalist Enterprises

Private prisons are a relatively new phenomenon in the United States, arising as major projects in the 1980s.[84] They are part of a trend toward privatizing public functions through for-profit contractors. The legality of delegating public functions to private industry is fairly well settled, even if the wisdom is not.[85] The rise of private prisons tracks the history of the rapid criminalization of drugs and consequential explosion of people sentenced to prison.

The logic of privatization suggests that private contractors can operate more efficiently and with fewer bureaucratic and economic barriers than government agencies, so it serves the public interest while generating economic profit and growth in the private sector. By 2010, at least thirty-five states and the District of Columbia incarcerated people in private prisons, and the federal government contracted with private prisons for criminal and immigration detentions.[86]

Laura Appleman illuminates the grave risks to society, offenders, and the hope of rehabilitation when the people delegate the fraught burden of punishment to private corporations: "When offenders are punished by private entities, it lessens the expressive, restorative, retributive message normally sent by the community, since the offender is punished by a for-profit, private entity. The community loses both its voice and its means of participation."[87] Mary Sigler argues that this is a risk to democratic accountability in private prisons and undermines the nature of punishment itself.[88]

Commercial interests have largely outweighed such moral concerns with the advancing trend of private prisons. The political decision to use private prisons creates inertia in their use. Most private prisons contract for revenue from the state based on per capita occupancy, with guaranteed

---

82. Mississippi Department of Corrections, "Mississippi State Penitentiary," para. 4.
83. Ganucheau et al., "State Inked a Deal."
84. See Gold, "Privatization of Prisons"; Fulcher, "Hustle and Flow."
85. See Robbins, "Legal Dimensions of Private Incarceration."
86. See Sigler, "Private Prisons, Public Functions."
87. Appleman, "Cashing In on Convicts," 581.
88. White, "Rule of Law," 151.

minimum prisoners to ensure sufficient revenues and profit margins to justify the enterprise.[89] Thus, to ensure the viability of the contracts, both the state and the prison have stark financial incentives to incarcerate a certain number of people, without regard to actual rates of crimes or justifiable convictions. Private prisons also operate like the capitalist enterprises they are, seeking to maximize profit and cut costs. Business pressures to cut costs pull against investments in physical conditions, rehabilitation, mental health, education, or other costs toward humane and constructive policies.[90]

This extends to services and ancillary businesses that attach themselves to profit from prisoners, families, and the prison-industrial complex. Systems of cash bail are ancient markets for bail bondsmen who profit by fronting money for people awaiting trial, fueling systemic incentives for more arrests and plea bargains and sustaining cycles of tricky debt.[91] More recently, companies like JPay, a for-profit corporation owned and operated through several layers of private equity firms, offer communication, financial transfers, and transactions for people in prison and families seeking to support them and generate capital and revenue for shareholders.[92]

Of course, this is true of public prisons, too; private prisons may merely extend the public pathologies of incarceration.[93] Sharon Dolovich assesses private prisons through a lens of liberal legitimacy and observes that private prisons are a phenomenon of larger, systemic features of criminal law systems in the United States, not a separate category.[94] Hadar Aviram suggests that shifting the economic incentives away from per capita occupation toward rehabilitation standards and outcomes could leverage the market forces for good, if private enterprise could envision models to profit from moral and therapeutic outcomes rather than volume incarceration.[95]

Michelle Alexander observes that, like every capitalist enterprise, any investment in an industry demands growth, so the businesses themselves look toward an increasing market. In *The New Jim Crow*, she quotes directly from the 2005 annual report from the Corrections Corporation of America: "The demand for our facilities and services could be adversely affected by the relaxation of enforcement efforts, leniency in conviction and sentencing

89. See Anderson, "If You've Got the Money."
90. See Aviram, "Are Private Prisons to Blame."
91. Wiseman, "Bail and Mass Incarceration."
92. See https://www.jpay.com/; Weinberger, "Inmate Families Face Cash-Transfer Fees."
93. See Pfaff, "Incentives of Private Prisons."
94. See Dolovich, "State Punishment and Private Prisons."
95. See Dolovich, "State Punishment and Private Prisons," 447–88. See also Anderson, "If You've Got the Money," 43.

practices or through the decriminalization of certain activities that are currently proscribed by our criminal laws."[96] This is big business, and corporate and political interests often align with stakes in the market expansion of mass incarceration.[97]

In a signal of a movement away from private prisons, in 2016 the US attorney general instructed the Federal Bureau of Prisons to decline to renew contracts with private prisons as they end. In the memo, Deputy Attorney General Sally Yates noted that the federal prison population had grown 800 percent between 1980 and 2013, but that the population was declining in light of sentencing reforms. She acknowledged that private prisons had been useful but do not provide the same level of correctional services, do not save substantially on costs, do not maintain safety and security, and do not reduce recidivism.[98] Attorney General Jeff Sessions rescinded Yates's directive in 2017,[99] but in 2021, President Joe Biden issued an executive order that the federal government would not renew Department of Justice contracts with private prisons. President Biden wrote that the system should prioritize "rehabilitation and redemption," giving people "a fair chance to fully reintegrate into their communities."[100]

Public Investments and Community Economies

For decades, public investment in prisons has been a signature of rural economic development, building prisons for jobs.[101] This has been a long practice of federal and state governments attempting to prop up lagging economies in rural areas as once-dominant industries wane.[102] Building and operating prisons in rural areas may generate economic activity, but these projects may well have adverse fiscal consequences and likely create gravitational pull for greater levels of incarceration.[103]

---

96. Alexander, *New Jim Crow*, 287–88; quoting U.S. Securities and Exchange Commission, Corrections Corporation of America, Form 10K for the fiscal year ending Dec. 31, 2005.

97. See Brickner and Diaz, "Prisons for Profit"; Cummings et al., "Private Prisons."

98. Yates, "Phasing Out Our Use."

99. Federal Bureau of Prisons, "Memorandum on Use."

100. Biden, "Executive Order," s.vv. "Section 1. Policy."

101. See Hamilton, "Rural Lands," 179, 190; Bassett, "Ruralism," 273, 326–27; Russell, "Cruel and Unusual Construction."

102. See Beale, "Prisons, Population, and Jobs."

103. See Beckett and Beach, "Place of Punishment," 1, 18–19; Besser and Hanson, "Development of Last Resort."

The story of Susanville, California, illuminates the cycles and traps when an industry declines and a prison arrives, then leaves as sentencing and carceral policies change.[104] Susanville is a small town in rural, northeast California near the Nevada state line. Since 1963, it was home to the California Correctional Center. In the late 1800s and early 1900s, timber and lumber mills were the heart of the Susanville and Lassen County economy, but by the 1950s, the mills began to close in an economic downturn for the region. When the prison opened, the local businesses that had grown to serve those in the lumber mills began serving those who worked in the prison. The Susanville prison was one of thirty-five in California and housed about 2,300 inmates. In 2021, the prison provided nearly 1,100 jobs in a town of just over 8,000 residents. When the state of California announced that it would close the prison to save nearly $122 million per year, it caused great anxiety about the economic life of the community.[105] The town relied on the prison for most of its better-paying jobs, and businesses and local government depended on the employees who work there, even as the overall population has been in steady decline. This is especially true when funding of public schools and other services depend on population.

In closing the Susanville prison, the state of California was responding to shifting priorities and declining inmate populations, but the effect on Susanville's non-prison economy demonstrates the economic pressures and incentives to maintain and expand penal incarceration. The economic dependence on prisons as centers for employment and markets for local businesses can deepen inertia and reluctance to address crime, corrections, and rehabilitation in ways other than mass incarceration.[106] They also harm local economies rather than bolstering communities in economic decline.[107]

Conclusion

While incarceration, even mass incarceration, may be legal within constitutional limits in the United States, it is not inevitable or necessary. The business of incarceration is profitable and deeply entrenched in American economies and politics. The American people and their government could choose other means and methods of defining crimes, enforcing the law, caring for victims, and responding to people who violate the law. As the

104. See Branson-Potts, "California's Prison Boom."
105. California Department of Corrections and Rehabilitation, "CDCR Announces Deactivation."
106. See French, "Future for Susanville."
107. See Genter et al., "Prisons, Jobs, and Privatization."

law often favors punishment, retribution, and isolation, so it could also promote restoration, reparations, and true rehabilitation. The state could serve public safety with creative investments in human development and care more effectively than it can with violent detention. It may choose from many options that respond to diverse people in complex situations rather than further entrenching the very limited policies of penal incarceration.[108] The catastrophe of racist mass incarceration reflects the values and policies favored by lawmakers, police, prosecutors, courts, and the people, but the people and their government could choose to advance the higher values of rehabilitation, restoration, and imagination.

The nation's policies reflect the moral vision of the people. If the people will tolerate brutal, racist, humiliating, destructive, and expensive forms of carceral punishment, they may have them. If the people would prefer more humane, disciplined, restorative, and efficient means of safety, deterrence, rehabilitation, and punishment, those options are available under the law, even if they would disrupt the business of incarceration.

---

108. See generally Bradley, *Ending Overcriminalization and Mass Incarceration*.

Part Two

THE BUSINESS OF INCARCERATION IN HISTORY

4

Race, Racism, and Incarceration in American History

AARON L. GRIFFITH

Introduction

Race and racism have been integral to the American experience, and they have also profoundly shaped American systems of crime and punishment. The role of race in shaping the post-1970s carceral state has received a great deal of attention by scholars, activists, and the general public in recent years, in no small part because of works like Michelle Alexander's *The New Jim Crow*. This chapter takes a longer view by synthesizing a number of recent scholarly works to showcase the ways race and racism have influenced carceral policies, cultures, and modes of resistance from early America to the present.

The stakes: throughout American history, people of color have borne the brunt of American systems of punishment. This is still true today. As of 2022, the United States' incarceration rate per capita is the highest in the world, with around 1.9 million people confined in local jails, state and federal prisons, and immigration detention facilities. This alone is a shocking number, but racial disparities are even more glaring. Black Americans are 38 percent of this incarcerated population, though making up only 12 percent of the total US population. Around one in twelve Black men in their thirties are incarcerated in the United States. Native Americans and Latinos are also overrepresented in American prisons. For example, Latino men are 2.5 times more likely than white men to spent time in prison. Across all racial and ethnic categories, those who are incarcerated are typically poor, and their future economic prospects are further damaged by the disruption of imprisonment. American prisons themselves are overcrowded, brutal places, and high recidivism rates indicate the complete failure of prisons' ostensibly corrective goals.[1]

It is crucial to note that the history of punishment in the United States is best understood as disconnected from that of crime.[2] Similarly, the expansion of prisons does not always correlate with rising crime. Indeed, incarceration often destabilizes communities, creating conditions for crime, while prisons themselves are spaces that encourage violent behavior.[3] Racialized conceptions of crime have often led Americans to believe certain minority communities harbor criminal propensities because of their race and have blinded outsiders to these communities' needs and to solutions that might better address their problems beyond punitive measures. Whereas public investment through governmental, economic, or educational interventions have often benefited white communities (sometimes under the misleading guise of the free market), racial minorities have routinely faced the more brutal, violent edge of governmental intervention through state-sponsored surveillance, violence, and imprisonment. We might extend Naomi Murakawa's claim concerning federal crime politics in the twentieth century to a wider historical scale: "The United States did not face a crime problem that was racialized; it faced a race problem that was criminalized."[4]

This chapter explores the history of several experiences of racialized minorities with American carceral systems, including Native Americans, Asian Americans, and Latinos. However, most of the focus will be on Black Americans, the criminalization of whom, as Elizabeth Hinton and DeAnza Cook have written, "has been, and continues to be, the canary in the coal mine for underserved and hyperpoliced communities caught within the ever-expanding web of American law and order."[5] This chapter also examines how incarcerating forces drew upon notions of racial superiority to advance their agendas. Finally, this chapter discusses some ways racial

---

1. Sawyer and Wagner, "Mass Incarceration."
2. The connection is "tenuous at best," as Simon Balto and Max Felker-Kantor have recently argued ("Police and Crime").
3. Thompson, "Inner-City Violence."
4. Murakawa, *First Civil Right*, 3.
5. Hinton and Cook, "Mass Criminalization of Black Americans," 262–63.

solidarity mattered for resistance and reform movements that attempted to challenge such forces.

Three general themes mark this history. First, and perhaps most obviously, race served as a clear dividing line between the people groups who bore the brunt of incarceration practices and those who benefited from it or simply found it far less burdensome. To be sure, it was not the only dividing line. Class and economic status have likewise proved important (and indeed, each has intersected with race in important ways throughout the history of American criminal justice, as will be discussed later in this chapter). However, from the colonial period to the present, race has proven central in determining who ended up surveilled, policed, incarcerated, and punished.[6] Second, race served as a dividing line between perceptions of need, with minorities being perceived as needy and whites as benevolent, believing they could offer assistance.[7] From the origins of the penitentiary system to today, prisons have routinely been idealized as benevolent institutions, spaces that can remake, rehabilitate, or redeem criminals' bodies and souls. They often fail in this mission, but even when they seemingly succeed, race has been shown a determining marker of whose life is in need of reformation and what ideals of rehabilitation one might strive for. Third, race sometimes operates in carceral systems without acknowledgment, within a seemingly colorblind frame. This was particularly true of the post–civil rights era, but there were important antecedents in earlier periods.

Early America

Precontact Native American life was exceedingly diverse, as were Native conceptions of crime and practices of punishment. However, one major theme connecting many such Native conceptions and practices was an emphasis on social cohesion and restoration following commission of an offense. Sometimes this occurred through the compensation of victims by an offending party. Other times punishment might require ostracism or retribution through corporal punishment.[8]

European colonizers arrived in the Americas in increasingly greater numbers from the late fifteenth century on, seeking riches, converts, and an advantage over rival neighboring powers. Settler colonial violence followed as Europeans enslaved and destroyed native communities and transmitted

---

6. S. Bowman, "How Did We Get Here?," 2.

7. S. Ryan, *Grammar of Good Intentions*. See also Graber, "Natives Need Prison," discussed below.

8. Traisman, "Native Law"; Nielsen, "Context of Native American," 6.

diseases. Colonizers also implemented new systems of punishment that dramatically altered Native life, routinely ignoring or destroying long-standing Native systems of punishment and restoration that had been present for generations.[9] For example, Spanish Franciscan missionaries to present-day Southern California punished the Tongva peoples who refused to cooperate with their religious, civilizing mission. In response to offenses like Tongvas' breaking of Franciscans' gender-segregation rules, missionaries would lock away women and girls. As Kelly Lytle Hernández put it, this was "the first experiment in human caging in Tongva territory."[10] However, the predominant Spanish punishment of Natives were corporal penalties like beatings and shackling, not incarceration. These punishments were often instituted in service of colonists' economic aims. Spanish officials prohibited Natives from utilizing traditional practices that undercut agricultural production, such as burning fields, and punished those who refused to work. Whatever the mode or rationale of punishment, establishing and reinforcing a clear hierarchy over Natives was the overarching goal. Punishment via violence, threatened or realized, helped build the settler colonial order.[11]

Colonial New England

Criminal justice in colonial New England was pessimistic. Reflecting Calvinist belief in original sin and humanity's propensity to depravity, colonists believed human beings would not be reformed through punishment. Instead, harsh penalties might simply deter criminal behavior. Punishment in colonial New England was financially demanding (fines), humiliating (confinement in stocks or banishment), violent (whippings), or sometimes lethal (hanging). Jails might be used to hold offenders awaiting punishment, but rarely was imprisonment meted out as the punishment itself.[12]

As English colonists grappled with distance from their home country, the presence of outsiders, whether Native Americans, Africans, or non-English Europeans, was seen as a threat. Race proved a convenient framework to contrast insider from outsider, friend from foe. Their conceptions of crime and criminal behavior fit within this frame, with crimes by Africans often serving as a symbol of both the threat that non-English posed and the likely chaotic conclusion to which a disorderly colonial society might devolve.[13]

9. Lujan and Adams, "U.S. Colonization," 11.
10. Hernández, *City of Inmates*, 25.
11. Hernández, *City of Inmates*, 25, 28–29.
12. Morris and Rothman, *Oxford History of the Prison*, 112.
13. Slotkin, "Narratives of Negro Crime," 4.

Sermons preached by Puritan ministers at executions expressed colonial religious conceptions of crime and punishment. Such sermons explained how the rightful wages of sin was death while urging the criminal and crowd alike to confess their sins and repent of their wicked ways. Execution sermons for Black criminals showed the entanglement of colonial concepts of race, religion, and punishment. One purpose of famed Puritan clergyman Cotton Mather's sermon at the execution of Hanno, a formerly enslaved Black man convicted of murder, was to showcase the problems of freedom and the blessings of servitude for "the Ethiopian and other slaves among us." "If you were Free," Mather preached, "many of you would not Live near so well as you do."[14] For Mather, Hanno's crime was the logical outcome of Black slaves' ungodly ambitions for temporal freedom. Mather's sermon was a theological defense not only of retributive justice but also of Black peoples' subservient place in the New England economy. Though this subjugation materially benefited white slaveholding elites like Mather, it could be flexibly rendered as humane and uplifting for enslaved people as well.

The Rise of the Penitentiary

Northern reformers in the early republic saw punishment practices of the past as problematic, both for their brutality and for how they forsook the prospect of changing criminals. Reformers' optimism that human beings might improve their spiritual and moral lot matched their hopes for the new nation and its realization of the blessings of liberty. Self-determination and the prospect of change, of the polity and offender alike, was the new ideal.

This ideal's institutional manifestation was the penitentiary, a model that originated in England but quickly found supporters among Northern reformers in America. As its name suggests, these prisons were envisioned as spaces of confinement where offenders could do penance for crimes and through disciplined reflection be remade into virtuous subjects. Some reformers, particularly Quakers, promoted the notion of the prison as a "garden" where incarcerated people could find solace apart from criminogenic social ills and brutal corporal punishment. Other prisons operated as "furnaces" where disorderly people's bad behavior could be burned away through reformative labor. Both ideals were difficult to realize in practice, and these underfunded and overcrowded penitentiaries soon devolved into hells on earth with little to show in prisoner reformation and tremendous evidence of their suffering.[15]

14. Ringer, *Necropolitics*, 23. See also Weiner, *Black Trials*, 48.
15. Graber, *Furnace of Affliction*.

These institutions came to serve as warehouses for marginalized people groups, disproportionately immigrants and Black Americans.[16] For example, the jail and penitentiary house at Walnut Street in Philadelphia, the nation's first state penitentiary, was built in 1790 as part of the reforming push away from corporal and capital punishment. A decade earlier, Pennsylvania had abolished slavery and had eliminated its race-specific penal codes. And yet, though officially race neutral, the Philadelphia prison disproportionately incarcerated Black people. According to one contemporary account, African Americans comprised 2.3 percent of the Pennsylvania population in 1790 and 4.6 percent of Philadelphia, but they comprised 14.9 percent of the incarcerated population at Walnut Street around the same time.[17] These disproportionate Black incarceration rates persisted throughout much of the nation for the rest of the nineteenth century.[18]

Early American reformers and general public proffered various explanations for such disparities. Occasionally, observers acknowledged the challenging economic conditions African Americans faced, with some even noting white discrimination as a causal factor. Others simply offered justifications based on their belief in Blacks' inherent criminality or political danger.[19] African Americans were frequently targeted for prosecution because of their race and received disproportionately harsh sentences, particularly for crimes that had associations with resistance against white supremacy. Whereas arson by whites was individualized in the court of law, seen as simply the result of personal immorality, African American arsonists raised the specter of Black rebellion and endured far harsher sentences. Though "the rebellion of white girls, whether American or foreign born, was never seen to represent their race . . . when [Black] women and girls set fires, they were seen to be representative of the summary rebellion of the entire race."[20] As Mark Kann has shown, this racial logic justified Blacks' harsh punishments within prisons. Despite the original humanitarian hopes reformers had for the penitentiary, "prison officials expressed no desire to redeem black souls."[21]

Recent immigrants were likewise overrepresented in American prisons in the early republic and antebellum periods, and many faced nativist

---

16. Kann, *Punishment, Prisons, and Patriarchy*, 192–211.

17. Patrick-Stamp, "Numbers That Are Not New," 100–102.

18. Kann, *Punishment, Prisons, and Patriarchy*, 15–16, 75; Western and Pettit, "Incarceration and Social Inequality," 9.

19. Kann, *Punishment, Prisons, and Patriarchy*, 77–78.

20. Manion, *Liberty's Prisoners*, 132.

21. Kann, *Punishment, Prisons, and Patriarchy*, 206.

prejudices regarding their inherent criminality and predisposition to crime.[22] Luke Ritter documented that in 1850 foreign-born immigrants made up around 36 percent of prisoners, though only 10 percent of the total population. Ten years later, 47 percent of prisoners were foreign born though only 13 percent of the total population. As with Black Americans, immigrants' punishment justifications and practices intersected with realities of their deprivation. Many immigrants were economically desperate, and other Americans resented their drain on public institutions and threat to social order. Labels and logics of punishment coded economic need as criminal, as arrests of recent immigrants were more often than not for crimes associated with poverty such as vagrancy, prostitution, and public drunkenness. Nativist observers labeled those immigrants arrested as "leeches," their poverty evidence of their unfitness for American virtue and liberty.[23]

Racial and ethnic minorities' experiences of incarceration were both difficult. For example, Irish immigrants and African Americans both encountered discrimination in their interactions with the legal system and their experiences inside the penitentiary. Jennifer Manion writes, "In the first twenty years of the penitentiary, Irish and African American women shared a status as the poorest, most reviled, most highly incarcerated women in the young nation."[24] However, over the first few decades of the nineteenth century, whiteness gradually proved to be a flexible category that recent European immigrants increasingly proved adept at negotiating. Though Irish women had been regarded as foreign and loathed, they became "white" as "black" consolidated into a linguistic category to describe African Americans. Prisoners of European descent had previously been identified by birthplace, but around 1810, they began to be identified as white. And this whiteness carried with it the assumption of belonging in the new nation, as Irish immigrants were gradually welcomed into the growing industrial economy.[25] African Americans, by contrast, would be criminalized all the more.

Paralleling the rise of the penitentiary system was the growing practice of imprisonment in the American West, often linked to the settler colonial expansion of US empire. After Los Angeles came under US control in 1847 in the aftermath of the Mexican-American War, imprisonment emerged as a powerful act of Anglo-American dominance of the local Native population in an attempt to realize manifest destiny. "The local jail," Kelly Lytle

22. Kann, *Punishment, Prisons, and Patriarchy*, 72–73.
23. Ritter, "Immigration, Crime," 64, 66–67, 75–77.
24. Manion, *Liberty's Prisoners*, 139.
25. Manion, *Liberty's Prisoners*, 139–40.

Hernández writes, "represented the foundational structure of US conquest in Los Angeles." To be sure, authorities saw incarceration as a valid response for dealing with social disorder such as the violence, gambling, and theft that characterized growing settlements that had not established the rule of law. But the Native population bore the brunt of the law, as they were routinely targeted by law enforcement for vagrancy while white violators of public order remained free. For example, on a single summer night in 1860, the city marshal arrested forty-one Natives, around 20 percent of the local Indigenous population. Convicts were subjected to chain gang labor and horrific conditions inside the jail that fostered transmission of disease. Indigenous people who had inhabited the region for thousands of years were now subjected to a "carceral assault" that was part of a larger campaign of outright eradication.[26]

Slavery and Its Successors

Race-based chattel slavery in the American South relied on the threat of punishment, typically from owners themselves, although the law usually allowed for any white person to punish an enslaved person. The cruelty of these punishments knew no bounds. Most often, owners administered physical punishment through whippings and beatings, but brandings or other forms of bodily pain would be used as well. Enslaved people were generally not incarcerated as this would deprive owners of labor, but occasionally they would be executed as a warning to others.[27]

Slavery also provided an important context for the development of American policing. In much of colonial America and well into the nineteenth century, most policing was relatively informal or ad hoc. A sheriff or constable might have official status, but they relied on community members to monitor neighborhoods and respond to offenses. Major Northern cities resisted the development of permanent police forces until the 1840s. By contrast, colonies with large slave populations saw policing as an essential institution for control. South Carolina founded its first slave patrol in 1639, and the ongoing fear of slave revolts motivated Charleston's development of militarized forces with arresting powers in 1783. By the eve of the Civil War, Charleston's department had one hundred officers, its own investigative arm, and systems for classifying and identifying suspects (including a picture gallery).[28] Patrols had three primary duties: searching slave quarters,

26. Hernández, *City of Inmates*, 34–37, 39–42.
27. Friedman, *Crime and Punishment*, 84–93.
28. Dale, *Criminal Justice*, 36–37, 50–51.

whether for weapons, books, or persons of interest; dispersing slave gatherings (including unsanctioned religious meetings); and surveillance of roads, looking for potential runaways.[29] Unlike the penitentiary system, these patrols were a uniquely American institution.[30]

Since chattel slavery was a powerful form of racial control and because masters had little desire to relinquish free labor, Southern prisons were overwhelmingly white leading up to the Civil War. After emancipation, however, Southern laws targeting African Americans became increasingly common, and with them, a growing Black population caught up within Southern systems of criminal justice. These laws, known as "Black codes," criminalized Black behavior, and those who were arrested often found themselves leased to wealthy whites as cheap labor.

Black codes were challenged during Reconstruction as African American political power expanded and Congress passed the Fourteenth Amendment to the Constitution (which declares "equal protection of the laws" for any person born or naturalized in the United States) and the voting protections of the Fifteenth Amendment. The Thirteenth Amendment had abolished slavery, but it had a provision that insulated a particularly devastating form of Southern white supremacist punishment: convict leasing. The amendment states, "Neither slavery nor involuntary servitude, except as a punishment for crime whereof the party shall have been duly convicted, shall exist within the United States, or any place subject to their jurisdiction." The clause "except as a punishment for crime" allowed states to continue to force African Americans to labor in the aftermath of their arrests, typically in industrial sites or mines. This work was backbreaking and dangerous, with annual mortality rates as high as 15 percent. As with slavery, economic incentives drove the racialized carceral control of Black bodies. Though whites were sentenced to convict labor as well, it was an overwhelmingly Black institution; approximately 90 percent of those in convict leasing camps were African American. It was both a system of racial control and of economic prosperity for wealthy industrialists and the states who leased convicts to them (for instance, in 1890 in Alabama, leasing accounted for 6 percent of the state's income).[31] In both respects, it was "slavery by another name."[32]

Though the relationship of religion to convict leasing remains understudied, Brad Stoddard notes how Protestantism was "an integral part" of

29. Hadden, *Slave Patrols*, 106–10.
30. Hadden, *Slave Patrols*, 4.
31. Pruitt, "Convict Lease System."
32. Blackmon, *Slavery by Another Name*.

the system and was utilized by camp administrators "to create more disciplined and obedient laborers in the short term and more law-abiding citizens in the long term."[33] Laborers rarely had other options for diversion and so potentially saw the camp chaplains, volunteer ministers, and Bible studies as a welcome presence. But the Christian message was nonetheless a source of both "comfort and control, consciously deployed to help the convict laborers accept their status as slaves of the states."[34]

In addition to the brutality of the convict leasing system, the policing of Black lives continued through the ongoing terror of white supremacist violence and lynching. In its first iteration from 1866 to 1870, the Klan was a powerful force in the American South as they resisted Reconstruction's gains through violent terror campaigns against African Americans and whites sympathetic to their advancement. They drew upon the example of slave patrols in years past, regulating the movement, gatherings, and property ownership of Black Americans with the threat of violence. As one white Southern defender of the Klan's violent behavior wrote, "The Ku-Klux Klan with its night visits and whippings and murders was the legitimate offspring of the patrol. Every Southern gentleman used to serve on the night patrol, the chief duty of which was to whip severely any negro found away from home without a pass from his master." Violent policing of Black life was deemed crucial by the Southern white establishment before and after emancipation.[35]

The Klan again became a powerful force in the early twentieth century, sparked in no small part by the wildly popular 1915 film *Birth of a Nation*, which depicted Black men's criminal predations of white women and hailed the Klan as the saviors of womanhood and Southern virtue. The new Klan defenders combined these racist sentiments with nativism and Protestant nationalism and found their religiously infused white supremacist vision had mainstream cultural resonance beyond the South. *Birth of a Nation* was screened in Woodrow Wilson's White House while the Klan boasted a nationwide membership of four million members in 1948.[36]

Lynching, the extralegal punishment of a person outside the formal justice system, was a powerful form of white supremacist terror against African Americans in the late nineteenth and early twentieth centuries. Lynch mobs saw the practice as a necessary form of justice for Black crimes

33. Stoddard, "'Slaves of the State,'" abstract, para. 6.
34. Stoddard, "'Slaves of the State,'" s.vv. "2. Religion and/in Convict Lease Camps," para. 4.
35. Hadden, *Slave Patrols*, 212–13.
36. K. Baker, "Artifacts of White Supremacy."

or violations of the racist social order, a way to punish individual African Americans and to reclaim the sacred character of a white supremacist land through the destruction of Black victims as a scapegoat for sin. Despite being illegal, the practice was often ignored by authorities and sometimes even had their blessing or participation.[37] Recent European immigrants and religious minorities also faced the prospect of lynching in the late nineteenth and early twentieth centuries, demonstrating how extralegal systems of justice targeted anyone of racial or ethnic differentiation in a white supremacist social order.[38]

Resistance to lynching took a variety of forms. Most famously, the journalist and activist Ida B. Wells wrote and spoke extensively on the matter, challenging stereotypes of Black criminality and mobilizing lynching statistics to show how pervasive the crime was throughout the nation. "When the Christian world knows the alarming growth and extent of outlawry in our land, some means will be found to stop it."[39] Other African Americans linked lynchings to the crucifixion of Christ. To see Jesus as a lynching victim (as W. E. B. Du Bois, Gwendolyn Brooks, and, much later, James Cone, did) raised the possibility that in the similarity between the cross and the lynching tree was hope for crucified bodies and God's judgment upon perpetrators.[40]

American systems of punishment (official and unofficial) in the nineteenth century not only allowed for brutal, discriminatory penalties for racial and ethnic minorities; they also failed to serve these same people groups, leaving them victimized by whites and lacking protection under the law. For example, accompanying Chinese migrants' experiences of discrimination and white mob violence was the legal declaration from the California Supreme Court in *People v. Hall* (1854) that the Chinese were "a people whom nature has marked as inferior." Therefore, a Chinese person had no right to testify in court against a white person even in cases of white violence against Chinese (at issue in this particular case). In justifying this position, the court linked the identities of Chinese with that of Native and African Americans, all of whom were deemed inferior racial stock in comparison to whites. California state law stated that "no Black or Mulatto person, or Indian, shall be allowed to give evidence in favor of, or against a white man," and the court upheld the law by indicating that Chinese fell within these racial categories

---

37. Mathews, *At the Altar of Lynching*; A. Griffith, "Real Victim of Lynch Law."

38. Jacobson, *Whiteness of a Different Color*, 41–42.

39. Wells-Barnett, *Red Record*, ch. 10, s.vv. "A Field for Practical Work," para. 1.

40. Du Bois, *Darkwater*; Brooks, "*Chicago Defender*"; Cone, *Cross and Lynching Tree*.

as well since "the word 'white' has a distinct signification, which *ex vi termini*, excludes black, yellow, and all other colors."[41] Racial exclusion in legal systems and economic exploitation fed upon each other. It was policies and rulings like these targeting Asians, Simeon Man has argued, that "ensured the maximisation of their labour, and not their lives . . . the law buttressed lawless violence; the two worked in tandem to discipline Chinese labor."[42]

As white settlers sought out new lands in the American West in the late nineteenth century, they subjected Native communities not only to ejection from their homelands but also to incarceration. In 1875, seventy-two Native men from the Great Plains who had resisted unfair treaties and continued settler encroachment were arrested and sent to the Fort Marion military prison in Florida. This mode of incarceration was different than the earlier use of imprisonment as a method of Native removal, as in eighteenth-century Los Angeles. Instead of outright destruction, white elites hoped this experience of incarceration would transform the Native men, deemed "savages in dress, in behavior, and in instinct," into peaceful, civilized, Christian subjects.[43] The incarcerated Natives' souls were shaped through religious instruction and sermons. Their appearances were transformed as their hair was cut and their traditional clothes were exchanged for uniforms. They were forced to labor in service and agricultural jobs, a remaking of economic life that had previously been focused on hunting and trading. The effect, as the novelist Harriet Beecher Stowe marveled, was the Native men were "savages" no more but endowed with "use of a new set of faculties."[44] Of course, this transformation depended upon coercion and force. But prison officials saw this carceral work as a mode of benevolence: "needy" natives would benefit from prison spaces and become more civilized and amenable to the American way of life.

Native prisoners at Fort Marion recorded their perception of their identity and incarceration through artistic production. One Kiowa man named Chêthâidè (White Horse) drew pictures of himself not as a prisoner but as a warrior and strong leader. As Jennifer Graber puts it, though "benevolent reformers understood him to be a potent symbol of racialized need, Chêthâidè depicted himself as a man of dignity and power." Through their artistic renderings, Natives proclaimed their pride and worth and, by

---

41. People v. Hall, No. 4 Cal. 399 (Supreme Court of California 1854). See also Lyman, "Chinese Before the Courts."

42. Man, "Anti-Asian Violence and US Imperialism," 26.

43. Graber, "Natives Need Prison," s.vv. "1. Introduction," para. 8.

44. Graber, "Natives Need Prison," s.vv. "1. Introduction," para. 9.

contrast, illuminated the destructive problem of the racialized prison space and its ostensibly civilizing project.[45]

Other forms of resistance by racialized minorities around this time included working within the criminal justice system itself. Amid the colonial expansion of the United States in the New Mexico Territory during the late nineteenth century and the accompanying extensive anti-Mexican racism, Mexicans regularly collaborated with the region's justice system. As Laura E. Gómez has shown, they served as jurors, witnesses, and law enforcement officials, "roles virtually unprecedented for members of a racially subordinated group in American history."[46] This enabled Mexicans to contest the power of European-American judges and prosecutors. This "racial-power sharing" served colonial interests in that it built respect for the emerging state apparatus.[47] But it also "gave Mexicans a measure of self-determination, group power, and perhaps even the basis for future organizing as a racially distinctive group in opposition to European-American elites."[48]

Though routinely victimized by the criminal justice system during Jim Crow, African Americans in the South advanced similar strategies aimed at obtaining some measure of power in a system set up against them. They pushed for police protection against violent crimes and even managed to exploit police practices for their own benefit. In Memphis, for instance, Black residents endured racist violence from officers, yet they also worked with police. They reported homicides, served as witnesses, and helped to identify suspects, showing they were willing to use an oppressive system to address threats of violence to their communities.[49]

Other African Americans sought to remake the racist criminal justice system itself. In the face of routine police brutality, forced confessions, and courts that proved unwilling to convict officers for misconduct, Black activists lobbied for legal accountability. In the early twentieth century, the NAACP Legal Department successfully pushed for sentence reversals for Black defendants who had allegedly endured coercion by law enforcement (and in doing so, established important legal precedents regarding the use of confessions in trials). Though police brutality against African Americans remained common, these efforts were part of a broad freedom struggle that

---

45. Graber, "Natives Need Prison," s.vv. "3. Drawing Other Worlds at Fort Marion," para. 3.
46. Gómez, "Race, Colonialism, and Criminal Law," 1138.
47. Gómez, "Race, Colonialism, and Criminal Law," 1132.
48. Gómez, "Race, Colonialism, and Criminal Law," 1166.
49. Jett, "'Many People "Colored" Have Come.'"

helped lay the foundation for the mass movement for civil rights in the 1950s and sixties.[50]

Making Justice Modern

In the late nineteenth century, politicians, academics, and law enforcement officials, particularly in the urban North, sought to modernize and remake the criminal justice system. Many looked to the emerging discipline of criminology and used the tools of statistical analysis to reconceptualize the relationship of blackness to crime. Using data from sources like the 1890 census, white observers believed they had identified clear sources of criminality among African Americans (who were increasingly migrating to northern cities). For example, in his popular book *Race Traits and Tendencies of the American Negro*, German immigrant and insurance statistician Frederick Hoffman argued that Northern Black communities were rife with crime, to him clear evidence of their "downward grade" from their past enslavement. Unlike slaves, free Black Americans had rejected the educational and moral offerings of white society and had "failed to develop a higher appreciation of the stern and uncompromising virtues of the Aryan race."[51]

Hoffman and like-minded observers also reconceptualized whiteness, beginning the process of explaining away European immigrants' criminal behavior with reference to their social dislocation and the trials of adjusting to a new land. Yet the existence of African Americans was linked with criminality, a "condemnation of blackness" that in turn increased discriminatory forms of surveillance and policing of Black neighborhoods. Despite the racial biases of observers and their misuse of crime data, these statistical analyses and the accompanying prescriptions maintained an air of objectivity and, crucially, racial neutrality and colorblindness. As Khalil Gibran Muhammad put it, "Neither the dark color of southern chain gangs nor the pale hue of northern police mattered to the truth of black crime statistics."[52]

Lynching, mob violence, and racial injustice in the criminal legal system eventually drew the condemnation of key federal authorities, particularly liberals. Politicians such as Harry Truman argued for a "right to safety" as a part of a broader civil rights agenda with the hope that improved procedures and policies would reduce discrimination and inequality in the justice system and better protect racial minorities from violence. Naomi Murakawa points out that this was a distinctly liberal law-and-order mandate, one

50. Niedermeier, "Forced Confessions," 59–60, 63, 72.

51. A. Griffith, *God's Law and Order*, 22.

52. Muhammad, *Condemnation of Blackness*, 4.

that assumed racism was an irrational aberration in the smooth operation of criminal justice and that it "could be corrected with 'state building' . . . the replacement of the personalized power of government officials with codified, standardized, and formalized authority."[53] However, this approach helped lay the foundation for the modern carceral state by overlooking (or even accommodating) the ongoing linkage of criminality to blackness and by reinforcing the reformed, "neutral" power of the state to enact coercive violence on vulnerable populations.[54]

Liberal appeals for streamlined justice were likewise made by white Americans on the local level who were aware of problems but who saw the answer in reformist terms. For example, white Protestant ministers often blasted lynchings and mob violence but typically focused on how each crime portended anarchy, not white supremacy. The real victim of lynching, one Virginia minister argued in his analysis of the miscarriage of justice in the trial and execution of Jesus, was the *government*, not Black Americans. "All who would be lovers of law and order must be lovers of Jesus," he wrote, signaling the connection of religious fervor with confidence in a streamlined, effective justice system.[55]

Professionalizing, modernizing impulses, combined with a growing concern with crime in the years around World War II, helped transform American criminal justice. Government officials and civic leaders routinely called for a new "war on crime," while law enforcement adopted sterner strategies for punishing offenders. Amid this surge, Jeffrey Adler has written, "race control became embedded in the crime-control crusade, shifting the enforcement of a racialized definition of law and order from popular justice and white mobs to legal institutions and the police."[56] In interwar Louisiana, for example, even though violent crime rates were down, the prison population grew 50 percent, and the incarcerated population of African Americans grew by 143 percent compared to only 39-percent growth of whites. These rates paralleled national developments in incarceration as well as those related to the death penalty. Over the course of the 1930s, the number of executions rose 50 percent and went from 60-percent white to 60-percent African American. This war on crime, with pronounced effects on Black communities, was expanding while crime rates were going down.

---

53. Murakawa, *First Civil Right*, 11.

54. Murakawa, *First Civil Right*, 12–19.

55. Wellford, *Lynching of Jesus*, 101–2; repeated in *Crime and Cure*, 77. See also A. Griffith, "Real Victim of Lynch Law."

56. Adler, "Less Crime, More Punishment," 43.

"Crime and punishment moved in opposite directions, with race mediating the disjuncture."[57]

Heightened concern about crime persisted in the following decades and with it a disproportionate focus on nonwhite, urban communities. From the 1930s to the 1960s, American anxiety was pronounced around juvenile delinquency and the apparent threat unruly teenagers posed. Black youths were deemed to be a particular threat, often missing out on the sympathy for white delinquents that government, civic, and religious leaders were willing to provide. There was a common presumption, as Carl Suddler points out, "that black youths elicit a less essential conception of childhood and the presumption of criminality."[58] In New York City, this presumption drove media crime reporting and in turn, justified expanded surveillance and policing of Black youths.

During World War II, the criminalization of Asians continued apace with the massive incarceration campaign of over one hundred thousand Japanese Americans on the West Coast. In Franklin Roosevelt's words, the stated purpose of this imprisonment campaign was to secure "every possible protection against espionage and against sabotage," though no evidence of real danger was present. Many Japanese American families lost their property and found their lives completely disrupted as they were forced into prison camps across the western United States.[59]

In the 1960s, liberal politicians linked anti-poverty and anti-crime efforts. As part of his broader Great Society and civil rights social agenda, President Lyndon Johnson proposed, in Elizabeth Hinton's words, "punitive legislation" that established "a direct role for the federal government in local police operations, court systems, and state prisons for the first time in American history." The "capstone" of this push by Johnson was the Safe Streets Act of 1968, which created the Law Enforcement Assistance Administration to disperse $400 million to states for law enforcement modernization and expansion. Over the next eighteen years, the LEAA would disperse $10 billion to states to fund around eighty thousand crime control projects, approximately three-quarters of which would go to police departments. The overall result, Hinton concludes, "was a significant expansion of America's carceral state."[60]

The 1960s also saw the climax of the civil rights revolution for Black Americans and, with it, growing frustration over the continued neglect of

57. Adler, "Less Crime, More Punishment," 45.
58. Suddler, *Presumed Criminal*, 12; see also 68–95, 124–50.
59. National Archives, "Executive Order 9066," transcript, para. 1.
60. Hinton, *From War on Poverty*, 1–2.

Black citizens' economic needs and their experiences of racism and brutality from law enforcement. Civil rights leaders did not limit their challenge of Jim Crow segregation to racial discrimination. In their calls for equality, leaders like Martin Luther King Jr. also had in mind the problems of policing that burdened Black communities. In his famous "I Have a Dream" speech at the 1963 March on Washington for Jobs and Freedom, King decried not only the destructive forces of segregation but also the "unspeakable horrors of police brutality."[61] And some Black Americans, frustrated with the slow pace of change, led rebellions throughout American cities, often as a response to law enforcement brutality and over policing, part of "a broader system that had entrenched unequal conditions and anti-Black violence over generations."[62]

Though the civil rights movement secured important victories, conservative politicians advanced punitive policy as a stand-alone solution to what they saw as the problems of crime in the streets and the unruly excesses of this riotous revolution. Most famously, Barry Goldwater and later Richard Nixon repeatedly declared that America's streets lacked "law and order," an appeal that resonated with an emerging "Silent Majority" of voters who remained suspicious of black civil rights advancement. Though officially race neutral, "law and order" language was often a cover for race and was frequently mobilized by segregationists. H. R. Haldeman, Nixon's chief of staff, quoted the president's declaration of his strategy in a diary entry from 1969: "You have to face the fact that the whole problem is really the blacks. The key is to devise a system that recognizes this while not appearing to."[63] What was unfolding here was "frontlash," as Vesla M. Weaver termed it, "the process by which formerly defeated groups may become dominant issue entrepreneurs." Politicians who had lost the fight on civil rights found crime and disorder convenient new stand-ins that energized their constituencies.[64] Federal policymakers also undercut or retreated from Johnson's social programs, leaving a focus on the crime war as the priority for poor and minority communities.

Mass Incarceration

From the 1970s into the early twenty-first century, the carceral state expanded exponentially. Minority populations were affected dramatically, and their

61. Martin Luther King Jr., in NPR, "Read," para. 15.
62. Hinton, *America on Fire*, 7.
63. Hinton, *From War on Poverty*, 142.
64. V. Weaver, "Frontlash," 230.

disparate nature grew over the course of these decades. From 1970 to 2006, the incarceration rate exploded from 161 to 789 per 100,000. Around one-third of these prisoners were Black in the mid-1950s, rising to around 40 percent in 1970. By the mid-1990s, half of all state and federal prisoners were Black, and by the first decade of the twenty-first century, at any given time, one-third of Black men in their twenties were in jail, in prison, or on probation or parole. These rates are around five to seven times higher than those of white men and even more disparate when considering life sentences.[65]

The particular reasons for this growth are complicated, and scholars have pointed to a number of factors shaping the emergence of the modern carceral state and its associated inequalities. A national "war on drugs" was announced by Ronald Reagan early in his presidency despite the fact that drug use was decreasing. Politicians pointed to a "crack epidemic," directed funding to anti-drug law enforcement, and passed harsh drug sentencing laws. Most famously, the 1986 Anti-Drug Abuse Act created mandatory sentences that had racially disparate effects: crack cocaine (a drug used more often by Black people) and powder cocaine (used more by whites) had a one-hundred-to-one ratio of comparison with a five-year penalty given to possession of five grams of crack compared to five hundred grams of powder cocaine.[66] Rates of drug use and drug selling vary little by race, but arrest rates for Black Americans were substantially higher than that of whites (nearly 6 times higher in the late 1980s and 3.5 times higher in 2008).[67] Though the war on drugs was almost always defended in race-neutral terms, its prosecution strategy (focus on street-level dealers in cities) disproportionately affected Black communities. And the motivating decision to sell drugs in these communities was directly linked to the lack of job opportunities and to low wages, products of discriminatory housing and economic policies that stretched back decades.[68] The intersection of race and class proved a powerful indicator for how anti-drug enforcement would be mobilized, as poor neighborhoods (which in urban areas were disproportionately Black) saw dramatically higher drug arrest rates. One retired police major-turned-justice reformer described American drug enforcement strategy in precisely these terms: "We had our officers go out and make as many drug arrests as they could. Where did we do that? We did that in communities of color. . . . Most of the people in these impoverished communities are always in the streets. They sell on the street corner. They

65. Tonry, *Punishing Race*, ix, 15, 31–32, 37.
66. Totenberg, "Race, Drugs and Sentencing."
67. Tonry, *Punishing Race*, 54, 58, 61–62.
68. Tonry, *Punishing Race*, 53–56.

have no political power or capital and no financial power, so there's also very little pushback."[69]

Changes in sentencing and policing practices from the 1970s onward also resulted in growing prisons and growing numbers of incarcerated minority populations. On the state level, voters and politicians alike welcomed more punitive sentencing policies, such as "three strikes" and "ten-twenty-life" laws. As Heather Schoenfeld has shown in her study of mass incarceration in Florida, a "carceral ethos" dominated state politics, with Republican policymakers welcoming laws that pushed prison time for low-level offenses; mandatory minimum sentences; increased requirements for serving time before parole; and the reintroduction of harsh, humiliating punishments within prisons, like chain gangs. The result, despite crime rates going down between 1998 and 2010, was an increase in incarceration rates, from 442 to 538 per 100,000.[70] At the beginning of the twenty-first century, though Florida's general population was only 14.6 percent Black, Black people made up 48.1 percent of its incarcerated population.[71] By 2017, Black people in the state were incarcerated at 3.6 times the rate of whites.[72] On the federal level, throughout the 1980s and 1990s, Democrats routinely worked to match Republican law-and-order ferocity, "reclaiming what Nixon stole" by championing tougher sentences and the expanded funding of police departments.[73] These departments implemented new programs to expand their reach into poor and minority communities while militarizing their tactics and equipment.[74]

Recently, some observers of American criminal justice have argued that more attention must be paid to prosecutors in the creation and maintenance of mass incarceration, even more important than harsh sentencing and anti-crime campaigns like the war on drugs. Prosecutors have a great deal of power in the justice system but with little to no oversight or review. Most are elected to their office and, following the lead of other "law and order" politicians, run campaigns pledging to be tough on crime. As Emily Bazelon put it, "American prosecutors have breathtaking power . . . and when black defendants are punished more severely than white defendants for similar crimes, the choices of prosecutors are largely to blame."[75]

69. Lopez, "These Maps Show the War," paras 5–6.
70. Schoenfeld, *Building the Prison State*, 188.
71. Human Rights Watch, "Incarcerated America."
72. Vera Institute of Justice, *Incarceration Trends in Florida*.
73. Murakawa, *First Civil Right*, 115.
74. Felker-Kantor, *Policing Los Angeles*.
75. Bazelon, *Charged*, xxv. See also Pfaff, *Locked In*.

At the same time, criminal defense in the United States is highly stratified. Though all defendants are constitutionally ensured an attorney if they cannot afford one, there is no guarantee that a public defense attorney will be able to represent them adequately given the tremendous demands and lack of funding of public defender offices (particularly in comparison to prosecutors). Criminal defense is demanding work, and there is a tremendous gap in the quality of defense work that is linked to a client's ability to afford representation and the high numbers of clients public defenders must serve.[76] Given the link between economic and racial inequalities, it is no surprise that those who have been the least able to afford quality representation are poor people of color. Court-appointed defense lawyers often urge their clients (whom they have likely spent very little time with) to plea bargain with prosecutors (the vast majority of criminal convictions are resolved by plea bargain), accepting guilty pleas with lower penalties to avoid the higher sentence that is possible if a case were to go to trial. The result is a dramatic number of minority defendants incarcerated through plea bargains for crimes that wealthier defendants can more easily avoid.[77] As with the war on drugs, the overlap of race and class determine not only who is most likely to be surveilled and arrested in the modern United States, but also who receives a fair trial (or who is given a trial at all).

What emerged as a result of these shifts was the rise, in Michelle Alexander's words, of a "new Jim Crow," a massive prison population with highly disproportionate numbers of racial minorities inside its walls that served as an instrument of social control and civic exclusion. The particular challenge of this new racial caste system is colorblindness; whereas the "old" Jim Crow facilitated discrimination overtly, mass incarceration does so without direct reference to race. And, as Alexander stresses, this system's primary targets are *poor* Black Americans. Indeed, she critiques the "'awkward silence' of the civil rights community" stemming from the emergence of professional legal activists who are disconnected from affected communities and the strategies that focus energies on solving racial disparities affecting the Black middle class (affirmative action initiatives designed to diversify elite colleges and corporate America being obvious examples). All too often, wealthier Americans (even those with strong civil rights sympathies) have ignored the plight of what is in effect a lower caste that has emerged: poor Black citizens

---

76. For a broader discussion of criminal defense and the ironic inequalities that stem from the Warren Court's criminal procedure rulings (designed to make criminal defense more egalitarian), see Stuntz, *Collapse of American Criminal Justice*.

77. For a description of this "broken system" of prosecution and a few modest proposals to address it, see Stuntz, *Collapse of American Criminal Justice*, 298–305.

who face the profound harms of over policing and mass imprisonment, and who have little economic or political recourse.[78]

Alexander's book *The New Jim Crow* is a powerful account and has been profoundly influential in raising awareness of the problems of race and mass incarceration in the United States. There are a number of complications of this account, however, that have each been raised by critics (some sympathetic) of Alexander's book and the larger activist push that has accompanied it. Two are discussed here.

The first concerns violent crime. Alexander's focus on the war on drugs and the accompanying reformist policy thrust to address disparities around nonviolent offenses has often downplayed the fact that Black people are still overrepresented in arrests for murder and robbery and that, more generally, incarceration rates for violent offenses outpace those for nonviolent ones.[79] The second concerns Black and minority support for tough-on-crime politics and law enforcement. As scholars have noted in the years after the publication of *The New Jim Crow*, some Black Americans routinely exhibit similar punitive sentiments as whites and have supported a number of tough-on-crime policies.[80]

Both these challenges must be read alongside the widespread protest of police violence in the post–civil rights era by everyday Black Americans (often youth) and must take economic status and class considerations into account.[81] James Forman Jr., who has meticulously documented Black support for punitive policies in Washington, DC, argues that the challenge actually undercuts the regular claim by defenders of law-and-order politics that Black Americans don't care about lawbreaking. Black Americans have long been concerned with public safety, but their concerns have also encompassed calls for civil rights, jobs, public investment, better schools, and political inclusion. These were pleas often denied. "African Americans never got the Marshall plan—just the tough on crime laws."[82] Similarly, to recognize Black support for tougher criminal justice should not "minimize the role of whites or of racism in the development of mass incarceration," the clear biases and criminalization of blackness that have been a part of American systems of punishment from the start.[83] The fact that violent crime is a

---

78. Alexander, *New Jim Crow*, 275–325.

79. For a discussion of this point and other criticisms of Alexander, see Forman, "Racial Critiques of Mass Incarceration." See also Pfaff, *Locked In*.

80. Forman, *Locking Up Our Own*; Fortner, *Black Silent Majority*.

81. Hinton, *America on Fire*, 7, 12–14.

82. Forman, *Locking Up Our Own*, 13.

83. Forman, *Locking Up Our Own*, 11.

major problem facing Black communities is evidence not of the criminality of blackness but of a nation that has repeatedly limited the opportunities for Black Americans both in and outside the criminal justice system.

The Jim Crow analogy also should not blind us to the ongoing criminalization of non-Black minorities. In particular, immigrant criminalization has intensified with repeated public and policy attacks on Central American migrants since the 1980s. These migrants often left their home countries because of devastating economic conditions or to flee drug-related violence (both of which have clear links to US policies), but they have been met with clear anti-Latino racial animus and nativist sentiment that characterizes their presence as an "invasion." Since 2006, those who crossed the border illegally risked not only deportation but incarceration as the Office of Homeland Security adjusted its policy for non-Mexican immigrants from "catch and release" to "catch and detain" (Mexican immigrants already faced the prospect of detention).[84] The result has been a burgeoning system of immigrant detention centers, some operated by private corporations. Those undocumented Latino migrants who avoid arrest typically find themselves limited to low-wage labor and avoiding vital social and health services that might expose their legal status. The constant threat of detention and the accompanying marginalization produces, in Roberto Lovato's words, a "Juan Crow" caste system with detrimental economic, cultural, and psychological effects on migrants.[85] The underlying "immigration-industrial complex," conceptualized by Tanya Golash-Boza, depends upon viewing migrants in racialized terms as "others" and "illegals" that are undesirable and threatening to economic and national security in a manner analogous to common views of crime and Black Americans and the corresponding carceral logic of the prison-industrial complex.[86]

In the era of mass incarceration, with its accompanying racial inequalities, a number of different challenges have emerged to contest the punitive status quo. First of all, prisoners themselves have resisted, documenting and protesting horrific conditions and unfair procedures and demanding public recognition of their rights as citizens and human beings. Incarcerated people of color have been particularly vocal in resisting the racism that characterizes the carceral state.[87] Proximity to incarcerated and system-impacted

---

84. Karen Douglas and Sáenz, "Criminalization of Immigrants," 203, 206.
85. Lovato, "Juan Crow in Georgia."
86. Golash-Boza, "Immigration Industrial Complex."
87. Berger and Losier, *Rethinking the American Prison Movement*.

people has given scholars and activists on the outside necessary insights into both problems and solutions needed for lasting change.[88]

Second, prison and criminal justice reform movements have emerged, often pushing specific policies that target racial injustices, such as the crack/cocaine sentencing disparities originally formulated in the war on drugs. Christian criminal justice reform organizations have proven particularly adept at navigating complex political terrain in Washington and on the state level, helping to secure important policy victories in recent years such as 2018's First Step Act.[89]

Third, prison abolitionists have made the case for the complete dismantling of America's justice system. Often concerned that the reformist approach is too modest, piecemeal, or accepting of the presence of the prison as a given in American life, abolitionists argue that Americans must move beyond the carceral state entirely to a place, as abolitionist Angela Davis puts it, where "prison no longer serves as our major anchor."[90] Abolitionist ideas have been mobilized in contemporary debates about policing (with the call to "defund the police," popularized in the wake of highly publicized police killings of Black people in 2020) and animated networks of activists who urge alternatives to incarceration for dealing with violence and crime.[91]

Crucially, proponents argue, the abolition of prisons entails both the absence of racialized state systems of control through their dismantling and the presence of new systems of accountability and economic well-being. As scholar and abolitionist Ruth Wilson Gilmore argued, abolition is about presence—not only the closing of prisons but the creation of supportive ways of life that eliminate inequality and offer people new alternatives to resolve their problems other than policing and prisons.[92]

Conclusion

Certainly, there are any number of strategies we should consider for addressing the inequalities (several of which are taken up in this volume),

---

88. On the importance of proximity, see Stevenson, *Just Mercy*. See also R. Miller, *Halfway Home*, 283–97.

89. See Dagan and Teles, *Prison Break*. See also ch. 6 of A. Griffith, *God's Law and Order*.

90. A. Y. Davis, *Are Prisons Obsolete?*, 21.

91. For an account of the importance of religious presence in abolitionist work, see Dubler and Lloyd, *Break Every Yoke*.

92. Kushner, "Is Prison Necessary?"

racial and otherwise, that make up the modern carceral state. But given the deep history of racism in American systems of punishment, it seems we might consider how the abolitionist work of dismantling and presence offers real, substantive, and needed hope. This is hope for those Americans wanting to break from the destructive systems and structures of the past. It is also hope for a future without prisons, one where we might work to build new lives that are bound together in relationships of trust and care.

5

Reformative Impulses

Christian Theology in the History of US Carceral Institutions and Practices

AMY LEVAD

Carceral institutions and practices in the United States are, from their inception, an outgrowth of reformative impulses. The history of incarceration here is marked by a pattern of dissatisfaction with the current ways of responding to criminal behavior and ensuring public safety, resulting in efforts to innovate more effective ways. In most (but not all) instances, reformers also hope the innovations will be more humane. Yet new ways eventually fail (if ever actually fully implemented), leading to renewed efforts for reform. Historian Edgardo Rotman observes, "The cycle seems never ending: exposés, reports, proposals, then more exposés."[1] In this cycle, idealism about the potential of incarceration to redeem individuals and restore social order repeatedly comes into conflict with the realities of operating prisons: limited budgets, overcrowding, security concerns, political posturing, and prioritization of obedience and domination over rehabilitation and redemption. These realities tend to win out, and carceral institutions—despite reforms—remain impervious to meaningful and substantive transformation. As realities override ideals, reform rhetoric and ideology often offer ethical

---

1. Rotman, "Failure of Reform," 151.

cover for some of the worst abuses of these institutions, from corporal punishments in nineteenth-century penitentiaries to excessive sentences and solitary confinement in correctional institutions today.

Throughout the history of incarceration in the United States, Christian theology has informed idealism about carcerality and thus helped legitimate incarceration. Christians repeatedly sought to create more humane and effective responses to criminal behavior, and thus they hoped to foster conditions for a stable and redeemed social order. Conceptions of crime and sin, punishment and forgiveness provided rhetoric and ideology that spurred reformative impulses. If carceral innovations are supposed to be more humane and effective, inspired by moral and religious convictions, then it can be difficult to discern the harm that they cause despite benevolent intentions. Furthermore, it can be hard to recognize that innovation and reform of carceral institutions has repeatedly and seemingly inevitably fed a downward spiral of coercion, violence, and corruption. And so, Christians often have not recognized the fault of providing moral and religious cover for the inhumanity and ineffectiveness of carcerality.

Another historical cycle, running alongside that of prison reform, impacts these challenges. The pattern of creating and recreating prisons has occurred in a society marked by racialized oppression, especially (but not exclusively) against Black people.[2] The forms of this oppression have changed since the end of chattel slavery, but it has nonetheless endured due to what legal scholar Reva Siegel describes as "preservation-through-transformation."[3] According to Siegel's framework, when forms of oppression (for example, chattel slavery or segregation) are increasingly recognized as unjust and illegitimate and then successfully contested (for example, through abolition or civil rights legislation), new forms emerge that maintain status privileges of the groups who benefited from the previous forms (white people) through shifting ideologies, rhetoric, institutions, and practices that are more contemporary and less overtly controversial than those of the past (chattel slavery shifts into segregation, segregation into mass incarceration). Oppression is preserved but transformed into a more palatable—but still harmful—form. Siegel's conclusions indicate that

---

2. I capitalize "Black" when referencing Black or African American people. Where not capitalized, I follow the practice of quoted authors. See Chicago Manual, "Black and White." In addition, I refer to people who are incarcerated always as people, avoiding terms that erase their humanity. Where "inmate," "offender," "felon," or other terms that reduce the humanity of people in prison appear, I quote other authors.

3. Siegel, "Why Equal Protection." See also Alexander's discussion of Siegel's argument (Alexander, *New Jim Crow*, 21).

we cannot grasp the repetitive failures of prison reform apart from the endurance of racialized oppression.

Throughout the history of racialized oppression in the United States, Christian theology has informed white supremacy and legitimated racialized oppression. Sociologist Robert Jones defines "white supremacy" by its plain meaning:

> The continued prevalence of the idea that white people are superior to, or more valuable than, black and other nonwhite people . . . [which] thus *entitles* them to hold positions of power over black and other nonwhite people.[4]

White Christians have deployed their faith to maintain myriad forms of racialized oppression. Biblical interpretations held that Black people descended from Cain, the first murderer, and so they continue to bear his violence and criminality. Churches segregated congregations and pews. Sermons taught that God chose white people to subdue the earth and all its nonwhite inhabitants.[5] Jones continues,

> Perhaps the most powerful role white Christianity has played in the gruesome drama of slavery, lynchings, Jim Crow, and massive resistance to racial equality is to maintain an unassailable sense of religious purity that protects white racial innocence. Through every chapter, white Christianity has been at the ready to ensure white Christians that they are alternatively—and sometimes simultaneously—the noble protagonists and the blameless victims.[6]

These tropes have also shaped the efforts of Christians, especially white Christians, to reform—repeatedly—carceral institutions, which have always incarcerated a disproportionate number of people deemed nonwhite.[7] Often

---

4. Jones, *White Too Long*, 16; emphasis in original.

5. While these specific teachings and practices may not be widely or explicitly held by white Christians today, and while many (if not most) white Christians may overtly reject them, Jones documents how these teachings and practices have been preserved through transformation and their legacy among white Christians endures (*White Too Long*). See also Kelly Douglas, *Stand Your Ground*; Fletcher, *Sin of White Supremacy*; Jennings, *Christian Imagination*.

6. Jones, *White Too Long*, 20–21.

7. Whiteness, of course, is a social and cultural construct, and the groups deemed nonwhite have changed. Irish immigrants, for instance, in the nineteenth century were not readily accepted as white—a view that impacted carceral institutions and practices. While these categories have fluctuated, whiteness has always been constructed in opposition to Black people, who have borne the brunt of racialized oppression, and groups (such as Irish immigrants) have "become" white by defining themselves in contrast to Black people. See Garner, *Whiteness*.

white Christians have been the "noble protagonists" and "blameless victims" in the cultural narratives surrounding criminal legal reform, in contrast to nonwhite people, who are portrayed as ignoble victimizers.

With mass incarceration today, we are now witnessing the intersection of these two historical patterns. Reform after reform has not prevented (and perhaps has furthered) unprecedented and unequaled incarceration rates in the United States, especially of Black people. The effort to make prisons more humane has largely been lost, while concern with their effectiveness in ensuring *this* social order remains. Reforms of carceral institutions and practices that do not address their fundamental and repeated failures, as well as their embeddedness in a white supremacist society, will recreate and uphold racialized oppression. And with such high rates of incarceration among Black people, racialized oppression has not only informed carceral institutions and practices; it has *transformed into* mass incarceration. A central motif of white supremacy, theologian Kelly Brown Douglas documents, is the portrayal of the "free black body" as dangerous, violent, and criminal because "it presumably threatens the very social order" and because "it contests the notion that the world as it is is the way God ordained it to be [that is, with Black people subordinated to white people]."[8] This motif, with its theological undertones, serves to justify the incarceration of Black people, and people of color more generally (especially Latinx, Native and Indigenous, and Southeast Asian American people), as their freedom seems to constitute a threat to social order, where "order" is understood as white supremacy.

Together, these cycles indicate that reform of carceral institutions and practices will not likely result in individual redemption or a *just* social order and that reform alone will likely contribute to the reconstitution of systems of racialized oppression in new forms. Increasingly, critics of our current ways of responding to criminal behavior and ensuring public safety are recognizing the need for more radical responses, such as "non-reformative reforms," transformative justice, or even prison abolition.[9] At the same time, these responses require reassessment of Christian theology, especially as preached and practiced by white Christians. This reassessment ought to attend to how Christian conceptions of crime and sin, punishment and redemption contributed to the creation and recreation of prisons in US history. It also ought to attend to how these conceptions overlap with racialized oppression. To get out of these patterns, we will need to deconstruct (white)

---

8. Kelly Douglas, *Stand Your Ground*, 69.

9. On "non-reformative reforms," see Gorz, *Strategy for Labor*. On intersections of non-reformative reforms, transformative justice, and prison abolitionism, see Gilmore, *Golden Gulag*.

Christian theologies that informed and shaped carcerality and racism, and then to reconstruct restorative, transformative, and anti-racist theologies.

Antebellum Penitentiaries

The invention of the prison as a means of punishment in the United States came about in the early republic as a reaction against corporal and shame-based punishments of the colonial period.[10] Fines, whippings, stocks, banishment, and gallows were deemed monarchical and undemocratic in the new nation, ill-suited to a free people. Their severity was perceived as overly harsh, contributing to reluctance to impose these sanctions, and thus reducing their deterrent effect because of the uncertainty that they would actually be carried out. Critics found these punishments inhumane and ineffective, leading to experiments in incarceration as a criminal sanction at the Walnut Street Jail in Philadelphia (converted to a penitentiary in 1790) and Newgate Prison in New York (opened in 1796).

At the inception of the penitentiary, Quakers in the Philadelphia Society for Alleviating the Miseries of the Public Prisons led the reforms of Walnut Street Jail. The Society of Friends drew on their theology of the Inner Light to inform their recommendations.[11] "Society members' proposals for the prison were grounded in their belief that proper environment allowed lawbreakers to experience God's presence within."[12] In New York, Thomas Eddy took inspiration from his fellow Quakers in Pennsylvania. Challenging the punishment practices of the colonies (which he had personally experienced when mistakenly jailed as a spy), Eddy argued that prisons could prove more humane and effective. As director of Newgate, he implemented a regime of communal living and work based on Quaker practices of discipline (akin to their child-rearing practices). He "always heralded the institutions as a bastion against worldly distraction and a setting for wholesome living."[13] For Eddy, this environment was like an "enclosed garden" that shut out the corruptions of the world and allowed for the cultivation of virtues as citizens, laborers, and Christians.[14] He aimed not to inflict suffering, but to provide the conditions for the flourishing of people incarcerated in Newgate. With this idealism, Eddy and the Philadelphia Society

---

10. Rothman, "Perfecting the Prison," 112–16.
11. Graber, *Furnace of Affliction*, 21–24. See also Skotnicki, *Religion and the Development*.
12. Graber, *Furnace of Affliction*, 22.
13. Graber, *Furnace of Affliction*, 29.
14. Graber, *Furnace of Affliction*, 28–33.

viewed prisons as humanitarian advances, unable to recognize the suffering involved in incarceration. Nevertheless, as historian Jennifer Graber notes, "The regular occurrence of riots and escapes reveals that a significant portion of inmates refused to accept the Protestant patterns of piety imposed on them at Newgate."[15]

The Quakers in New York and Pennsylvania were sidelined from prison administration at the turn of the nineteenth century as they lost their official roles due to the emergence of political parties and the spoils system for public offices. Soon, however, prison inspectors found that in the absence of Quaker input, chaos erupted. Reform was necessary. To reemphasize the possibilities of rehabilitation through incarceration, prison inspectors hired John Stanford as chaplain at Newgate in 1807. Graber argues that whereas Eddy viewed the prison as an enclosed garden, Stanford saw it as a "furnace of affliction" (drawing the image from the text of Isa 48:10) in which the souls of incarcerated people could be refined with the fires of suffering.[16] A Baptist, Stanford drew on Calvinist theology that maintains the total depravity of humanity and the necessity of Christ's crucifixion for substitutionary atonement. Historian Timothy Gorringe argues that theologies like Stanford's tend to uphold the metaphysical necessity of punishment and thus justify punitive approaches to criminal justice: "A story which was a unique protest against judicial cruelty came to be a validation of it."[17] Stanford believed that people in prison deserved to suffer—both in the hands of an angry God and in the hands of the state, a this-worldly instrument of God's punishment. He held that "God not only approved of the prison but also worked through it."[18] When people experienced the suffering of incarceration, they might turn toward God's grace, as any depraved person ought to do in response to any divine punishment. The penitentiary was a tool for redemption. Although Stanford did not advocate making prisons any more afflicting than they were inherently (and indeed praised US prisons for their mildness compared to those in Europe), his theological reasoning helped support harsher treatments. By 1819, whipping was reintroduced into Newgate and justified publicly as bearing "a severity [that] will harmonize with the spirit of christianity [sic]."[19] Although Stanford criticized these

---

15. Graber, *Furnace of Affliction*, 42.

16. Graber, *Furnace of Affliction*, 54. The KJV reads, "Behold, I have refined thee, but not with silver; I have chosen thee in the furnace of affliction."

17. Gorringe, *God's Just Revenge*, 81.

18. Graber, *Furnace of Affliction*, 59.

19. Graber, *Furnace of Affliction*, 63; quoting *Journal of the Assembly of the State of New York*, Forty-Seventh Session (Jan. 1824), 252.

developments, his "theology of redemptive suffering" nonetheless helped legitimate these abuses.

By the 1820s, a new spirit of reform took hold.[20] Reformers of this decade hoped that ordered, regular, and disciplined prisons would be a bulwark of the social order, which many perceived to be collapsing with failures of families, churches, schools, and communities. The consequence of reformers' hopes were Auburn State Prison in New York (opened 1818) and Eastern State Prison in Pennsylvania (opened 1829). These prisons became competing models of penitentiaries, though both were based on rehabilitative ideals and implemented similar regimes of isolation, silence, and labor. Their main difference was that daytime work was done alone in one's cell in Eastern and done as a group at Auburn, although in complete silence. Because of its relative cost effectiveness, the Auburn model became dominant, and similar penitentiaries opened in several states over the following decades.[21]

Iterations of a theology of redemptive suffering informed the institutions and practices of these penitentiaries. When Elam Lynds began administering Auburn in 1822, with its nighttime solitary cells and daytime congregate labor, his innovations—including lockstep (a regimented style of walking around prison grounds in close single file), striped uniforms, and strict silence—received endorsements from both Thomas Eddy and John Stanford.[22] Eddy was then horrified in 1826 to learn of Lynds's extreme use of corporal punishment, especially flogging, which among other travesties resulted in the death of a woman, Rachel Welch, who had recently given birth to a child conceived when she was in solitary confinement. Following public outcry, Gershom Powers replaced Lynds in 1826, while Lynds was tasked with building Sing Sing Prison on the Auburn model using prisoner labor. Powers began reforms of the prison to reduce the use of corporal punishment, but also to maintain order, which required legitimation of prison discipline so that the people receiving punishment would find it deserved and just. Powers looked to Protestant clergy to justify the institutions and practices of the penitentiary.

Rev. Louis Dwight, a Congregationalist, held that all people need God's grace and that everyone who accepts God's grace can be saved. As the head of the Prison Discipline Society of Boston (PDSB), he viewed the prison as a mission field with a literally captive audience. Through his reports on prisons in several states and his advocacy of the Auburn model,

---

20. Rothman, "Perfecting the Prison," 115–19.
21. Rothman, "Perfecting the Prison," 119.
22. Graber, *Furnace of Affliction*, 84.

Dwight provided the legitimation that Powers needed. He argued that the state rightfully disciplines people in prison, who may come to accept God's grace because of the chastisement offered through incarceration. Describing his priorities, he held that the PDSB ought, first, to allow for people in prison to receive their merited punishment; second, to lobby for humane prison conditions; and third, to preach the word of God to the prisoner.[23] Through his advocacy, Dwight furthered Stanford's theology of redemptive suffering, legitimated Powers's administration of Auburn, and advanced the spread of this model across the United States through monitoring and reports conducted by the PDSB.

Dwight would come to regret his advocacy when Elam Lynds returned to Auburn in 1838 as warden and resuscitated the use of severe corporal punishments, including whippings with cowhide strips and cat-o'-nine-tails.[24] While Dwight denounced these practices as defeating the goal of Christian conversion, the chaplain of Auburn—Rev. Benjamin C. Smith—endorsed them, drawing on a more extreme theology of redemptive suffering. For Smith, Lynds's tactics delivered the docility and attention of incarcerated people, which were necessary for them to receive the saving word.[25] A similar pattern occurred at Sing Sing Penitentiary in New York, where Rev. John Dickerson sanctioned the abuses of Warden Robert Wiltse (Lynds's successor) as entirely deserved by a population that was clearly not—and clearly could not be, in his view—among the elect.[26] For Smith and Dickerson, salvation was unlikely for incarcerated people; the only recourse to their wrongdoing was punishment itself.

With Dickerson and Smith, in contrast to Eddy, Dwight, and Stanford, a spectrum of theological assessments of prisons and their practices emerges. At one end, Dickerson and Smith at best ignored and at worst validated not only the silence, separation, and labor of penitentiaries, but also the heaping of violence on incarcerated people through corporal punishments. Eddy, Dwight, and Stanford, in contrast, criticized corporal punishments as degrading, but maintained that well-run penitentiaries could redeem individuals and restore social order. Although critical of Dickerson and Smith (as well as Lynds and Wiltse), Eddy, Dwight, and Stanford's theological worldviews nevertheless could be readily appropriated to justify abuse. But further along the spectrum, in critique of even Eddy, Stanford, and Dwight, lie a minority of Christian reformers who understood the inherent failures

23. Graber, *Furnace of Affliction*, 92.
24. Graber, *Furnace of Affliction*, 126.
25. Graber, *Furnace of Affliction*, 127.
26. Graber, *Furnace of Affliction*, 111–24.

of penitentiaries. In the 1840s, Rev. John Luckey, for example, served as chaplain at Sing Sing, where he espoused a prison theology much like Stanford's or Dwight's.[27] However, in 1853 he published his *Prison Sketches*, in which he described how conversion of people in prison could not be brought about *through* the hellish environment of Sing Sing or Auburn. If grace is to be found by incarcerated people, he concluded, it is *despite*, not *because of*, prison.[28] Similarly, Isaac Hopper, a Quaker who assisted men returning from sentences in Sing Sing, collected testimonials of their experiences, beginning in 1846.[29] They reported floggings, strangulation, use of the gag (an iron tongue depressor locked in place by a chain around the neck), shower baths (a contraption in which a person's head is flooded in a box of water, akin to waterboarding, now known as a form of torture), disease, and inadequate and unsafe food. Although Hopper believed in the necessity of discipline, he concluded that the prison was neither garden nor furnace, but hell on earth. Neither Luckey nor Hopper rejected a theology of redemptive suffering, but they doubted that penitentiaries—even well administered—could be humane or effective. They remained among the minority of Christian reformers.

Importantly, all of these men were white Protestants, and their theologies—wherever they fell on this spectrum—often reflected white supremacist worldviews and contributed to racialized oppression through prisons. They were the "noble protagonists" of prison development. The presence of free Black people after abolition of slavery in the North (and increasing numbers of immigrants, such as the Irish, who were predominantly Catholic and would not yet be considered white) was perceived as a threat to the social order. The culture upheld a racial hierarchy in which the presumed responsibility, rationality, and freedom of white "civilization" were thought to be threatened by racialized "others." Black people were particularly portrayed as base, evil, and dangerous, in contrast to white purity, virtue, and godliness.[30] This ideology can be seen to influence the reformative impulse behind penitentiaries, for example, in the proceedings of the PDSB, the organization headed by Dwight. Rima Vesely-Flad notes,

> The first annual meeting passed a motion presented by two clergymen, the Rev. William Jenks and the Rev. Francis Wayland,

---

27. Graber, *Furnace of Affliction*, 141.
28. Graber, *Furnace of Affliction*, 168.
29. Graber, *Furnace of Affliction*, 162–67.
30. Vesely-Flad, "Social Covenant and Mass Incarceration"; *Racial Purity and Dangerous Bodies*. See also Kelly Douglas, *Stand Your Ground*.

which recognized the "degraded character of the coloured population" as the first "cause of the increase and frequency of crime."[31]

The PDSB also held that free Black people ought to be deported because they could not be incorporated successfully into democratic society.[32] Racist ideology infused theologies of redemptive suffering as nonwhite people were often thought to "lack the inherent qualities, such as an inspired work ethic, that were essential for Christian redemption."[33] If Black people were seen as inherently criminal, as not redeemable and innately lacking the work ethic of whites, then a prison program that sought redemption of criminals through silence, separation, and labor was not really for them; other sanctions—corporal and capital—were required.

Views of nonwhites, and Black people especially, as morally deficient fueled harsh treatment. As Graber observes, "The Irishman counterfeiting and the free black stealing went against all that was sacred. They were different, poor, and guilty."[34] Lynds, for instance, successfully defended against interventions by Dwight in Sing Sing by arguing to legislators that "tougher routines were necessary because Sing Sing's prisoners—usually urban and immigrant—were more dangerous and less human."[35] Immigrants and Black people increasingly occupied antebellum penitentiaries of the North; prison conditions correspondingly worsened.[36]

This conclusion is strengthened by consideration of carceral institutions and practices outside of the northeastern United States. The history recounted thus far has had a regional bias, emphasizing the influence of the Auburn model, which was exported westward and to the south. The latter, of course, had its own "peculiar institution" that impacted criminal legal systems. Prior to the Civil War, Southern penitentiaries based on the Auburn model incarcerated white people, while Black people—whether free or enslaved—were subject to corporal and capital punishments within the regime of chattel slavery.[37] The justification for these distinctions lies in white supremacy rooted in white Christian theology. White people were seen as redeemable through the practices of carceral institutions. Black people were not; only lashing and lynching could adequately respond to their crimes.

31. Vesely-Flad, *Racial Purity and Dangerous Bodies*, 37.
32. Vesely-Flad, *Racial Purity and Dangerous Bodies*, 37.
33. Vesely-Flad, "Social Covenant and Mass Incarceration," 544.
34. Graber, *Furnace of Affliction*, 110.
35. Graber, *Furnace of Affliction*, 116.
36. Rothman, "Perfecting the Prison," 126.
37. For further discussion, see Hindus, *Prison and Plantation*; Ayers, *Vengeance and Justice*; Vesely-Flad, *Racial Purity and Dangerous Bodies*.

While distinctions in treatment of Black and white people in prisons in the North might have been less stark than in the South, the distinctions were still there, and the distinctions enabled tolerance—if not outright approval—of inhumane punishments doled out along racial lines.

Proponents of penitentiaries argued that they could produce law-abiding citizens, productive workers, and devout Christians, but these noble ends often helped justify severe treatment. Compliance was deemed necessary for rehabilitation; many prison administrators deemed harsh means necessary to achieve compliance.[38] Rothman observes, "The rhetoric of the reform program continued to cloak the prison with the mantle of legitimacy long after the reality of reform had disappeared."[39] This rhetoric often drew on theologies of redemptive suffering and theological accounts of racial difference, and so Christian reformers offered legitimacy—intentionally (Dickerson and Smith) or not (Eddy, Stanford, and Dwight)—to severe treatments inflicted in penitentiaries. While penitentiaries were intrinsically prone to abuse, the extrinsic realities of budget constraints, political vicissitudes, and overcrowding exacerbated their internal contradictions. Rothman notes, "By the 1860s, and even more obviously by the 1870s and 1880s, the unique arrangements of the Auburn and Pennsylvania [Eastern] plans had disappeared. . . . The opportunities for prisoner unrest increased, which prompted wardens and guards to become all the more harsh in their discipline of inmates."[40]

Postbellum Reformatories

Following the Civil War, reformative impulses again took hold. In an 1867 report about prison conditions in eighteen states commissioned by the New York Prison Association, Enoch Cobb Wines and Theodore Dwight concluded that prisons failed to meet their rehabilitative goals, especially with their excessive use of corporal punishments.[41] Moving away from the lockstep marching, isolation, and striped uniforms of penitentiaries, Wines and Dwight advocated a new system of rewards for good behavior with indeterminate sentencing, classification based on criminal history, industrial and academic education, and post-release supervision. These practices were implemented in new reformatories, exemplified in the Elmira Reformatory

---

38. Rothman, "Perfecting the Prison," 122.
39. Rothman, "Perfecting the Prison," 125.
40. Rothman, "Perfecting the Prison," 124–25.
41. Pisciotta, *Benevolent Repression*, 11. Note: *Theodore*, not *Louis*, Dwight. Louis Dwight died in 1854.

in New York, opened in 1876. All prisons built in the United States through the 1890s were based on Elmira.[42] These prisons, however, retained the internal contradictions of penitentiaries as physical punishments remained common, still justified by the rhetoric and ideology of reformation.[43] Overcrowding and security concerns exacerbated these tensions, and by the end of the nineteenth century, the new reformatories were commonly viewed as failures. During the Progressive Era, reformatories were themselves reformed as psychotherapeutic prisons based on the pathologization of crime. Still employing indeterminate sentencing and classification, prisons also began employing psychiatrists and psychologists, who expanded upon previous rehabilitation schemes to treat people in prisons. Rotman notes, "Despite the therapeutic pretense, prescriptions were in fact not very different from old reformatory methods."[44]

The impact of Christianity on carcerality in the postbellum period was less direct and explicit than previously. Prison administration became more secularized and professionalized; Christian reformers were sidelined. Graber summarizes, "Their particular offerings were not only unwelcome but also unworkable. Their relevance lay only in their willingness to preach a religiosity of citizenship that invoked God's blessing on moral living, hard work, and obedience to secular authority."[45] Prison administrators relied on professionals in education, behavioral sciences, social work, and law to devise carceral institutions and practices. Many states also shifted the power of prison administration away from wardens and toward state-level commissions that drew their expertise from new penological and criminological sciences.[46]

Despite these shifts, Christian theology still provided rhetoric and ideology that spurred reformative impulses and shaped prisons. After issuing his 1867 report with Theodore Dwight, Enoch Wines founded the National Prison Congress in 1870, the first national conference of its kind, leading to the formation of the National Prison Association. The congress adopted a Declaration of Principles that reflects secularization and professionalization of penology with its emphasis on making public punishment "scientific,

---

42. Skotnicki, *Religion and the Development*, 124.

43. See Rotman, "Failure of Reform." The famous warden of Elmira, Zebulon Brockway, extolled the use of physical force in prisons "not so much for safety as . . . for the sake of serviceable industrial efficiency, the increase of prison earnings" (Brockway, *Fifty Years of Prison Service*, 46). Brockway based this conclusion on reports of the effects of a warden's use of a cat-of-nine-tails (a gift from Sing Sing's Robert Wiltse) on the general population at the prison in Wethersfield, CT.

44. Rotman, "Failure of Reform," 159.

45. Graber, *Furnace of Affliction*, 176–77.

46. Rotman, "Failure of Reform."

uniform, and successful" in order to foster "moral regeneration" (in contrast to "vindictive suffering").[47] Doing so would require "special training" for prison officers, raising them "to the dignity of a profession."[48] But the declaration also indicates the importance of religion. Principle 9 declares, "Of all reformatory agencies, religion is first importance, because most potent in its action upon the human heart and life." The congress also rejected "the imposition of degradation as a part of punishment" on the grounds that it is "trampling where we ought to raise, and is therefore unchristian in principle as it is unwise in policy."[49]

The institutionalization of the principles came under the superintendent of Elmira, Zebulon Brockway, whose practices widely influenced penology in the United States. Brockway adopted a faith that aligned with scientific progressivism, with a belief in the immanence of the "Infinite-Creative-Formative-Force by which all things are, and move, and have their being."[50] He perceived this faith to support a universal and rationalist ethic accessible to all people, but the ethic was actually the "Protestant ethic" of his childhood: "honesty, integrity, hard work, frugality, piety, sobriety, discipline, self-control, respect for authority and law."[51] This moral and theological worldview infused his structuring of Elmira, which "would . . . instill inmates with 'Christian character' and transform them into 'Christian gentlemen.'"[52] To become so, they needed to "become responsible workers, husbands, fathers, and citizens."[53] Although penal professionalization and secularization supplanted Christian reformers, Christian worldviews remained significant in shaping prisons even after the decline of the penitentiary.

The theology that came to the fore, however, differed from previous theologies of redemptive suffering. Earlier reformers endorsed some degree of pain in punishment insofar as it could discipline people in prison to accept God's word. They tended to assume that *all* people are sinful and in need of conversion, *but* people who commit crime need official reprobation by the state to foster their transformation. Brockway and the National Prison Congress aimed at an outcome different than evangelical conversion.

---

47. The Declaration of Principles is reprinted in Pisciotta, *Benevolent Repression*, 157–61. See principles 2 and 7.

48. Pisciotta, *Benevolent Repression*, prin. 7.

49. Pisciotta, *Benevolent Repression*, prin. 14.

50. Skotnicki, *Religion and the Development*, 122–23; quoting Brockway, *Fifty Years of Prison Service*, 64.

51. Pisciotta, *Benevolent Repression*, 28.

52. Pisciotta, *Benevolent Repression*, 18.

53. Pisciotta, *Benevolent Repression*, 18.

Reformatories had moralistic ends, but their morality was secularized—a "religiosity of citizenship."[54] Pisciotta observes that in sermons at mandatory religious services,

> The chaplain reminded [the Elmira boys] that the Lord wanted them to abide by the rules of the Elmira system and work hard to become good citizens. The penalty for noncompliance was severe: inmates who fought their keepers and rejected the Elmira system were spurning God and risking eternal damnation and the flames of Hell.[55]

Conversion produced Christian men—defined less by faith in God's grace and more by compliance with the requirements of dutiful citizens and productive workers.

As in the antebellum period, white Protestant men dominated reformatories and later psychotherapeutic prisons. The end of slavery did not end white supremacy, of course. The pattern of preserving racialized oppression through transformation is replicated in the shift from penitentiaries to reformatories. White Christian theologies that informed penitentiaries held that all human beings bear guilt and need redemption, but only white people were thought to bear qualities essential for Christian redemption. In contrast, reformatories did not depend upon theological anthropologies that maintained the commonality of human sinfulness. Rather, based on "scientific" punishment, these institutions classified incarcerated people according to whether and how they might be reformed—only some people commit crime, and they do so not because of a shared human condition but due to specific personal traits and social contexts.[56] Classification reflected stereotypes, and reformatory practice responded to classification—reflecting a notion that the punishment ought to fit the person deemed criminal, not the crime.[57] Treatments aimed at creating responsible workers and citi-

---

54. Graber, *Furnace of Affliction*, 177.

55. Pisciotta, *Benevolent Repression*, 20.

56. Rotman summarizes one classification scheme at the Norfolk Prison Colony in Massachusetts: "Inmates were divided into five categories: situational cases, comprising occasional offenders; custodial cases, in which treatment was not possible because of age or mental insufficiency; asocial cases, composed of sociopaths; medical cases, in which crime was connected to physical illness; and personality cases, represented by the mentally ill" ("Failure of Reform," 162).

57. Pisciotta, *Benevolent Repression*, 49. Pisciotta attributes this idea in reformatory practice to Beccaria, *On Crimes and Punishments* (1764), trans. by Henry Paolucci, but I cannot find the wording Pisciotta attributes to Beccaria. See Pisciotta, *Benevolent Repression*, 18.

zens, but work and citizenship meant different things depending on racial and gender-based classification. Pisciotta observes,

> The handling of minority offenders at . . . reformatories exposes four approaches to building docile bodies: white males (except those labelled mentally defective) were trained as craftsmen and prepared to assume their place as honest, obedient, lower-class workers; white females were trained as domestic servants and prepared to assume positions as wives and mothers; black males were channeled into the most menial laboring positions; black females, the victims of race and gender discrimination had the lowest position in the hierarchy of "reform": menial servants and the mothers of the next generation of social outcasts.[58]

If Black people were still seen as inherently criminal, then a prison program that sought reformation through personalized treatment protocols was still not really for them. The classification and treatment practices of reformatories institutionalized and maintained racialized oppression and white supremacy.

Again, the differentiation of Black and white people in prisons was most stark in Southern states, which followed a different reform trajectory, bent by the legacies of slavery and white resistance to abolition. Following the Civil War, Southern states converted some plantations into prisons, such as the Louisiana State Penitentiary (better known as Angola, named for the plantation on which it was built). Convict leasing through the turn of the twentieth century continued practices of slavery on a rental, rather than ownership, regime.[59] Otherwise, people in Southern prisons were used as laborers on chain gangs that completed public works such as road building and repair; or in prison mines, such as those owned by the Tennessee Coal, Iron and Railroad Company; or on farms, such as the Mississippi State Penitentiary (better known as Parchman Farm).[60] Because of Black codes and Jim Crow, three-quarters of incarcerated people in Southern states after

---

58. Pisciotta, *Benevolent Repression*, 148.

59. On convict leasing, see Lichtenstein, *Twice the Work*; Oshinsky, "*Worse Than Slavery*"; Blackmon, *Slavery by Another Name*.

60. On prison mines, see Aberg-Riger, "'It Didn't Pump Itself.'" Aaron Griffith writes, "Convict leasing had prominent religious advocates, such as Joseph E. Brown, the chair of the board of trustees at Southern Baptist Theological Seminary in Louisville, Kentucky, and its most important donor. Brown's horrific coal mines and furnaces were filled with black convict laborers, whose backbreaking work under threat of corporal punishment enriched Brown and allowed him to donate $50,000 to the seminary and save it from financial ruin. The continued ministerial preparation of Baptist pastors was made possible by forced black labor" (*God's Law and Order*, 19).

the Civil War were Black. Systems that treated Black and white people differently—the former as irredeemable laborers and the latter as redeemable citizens—marked the carceral institutions of the southern United States long after the Civil War. These distinctions also shaped northern and western institutions and practices, though not as starkly and overtly.

Conflicts between treatment staff and custodial staff along with lack of reliable treatment methods and resources led to the failures of reformatories, which "did not fundamentally alter the punitive structure of the prison."[61] Rotman concludes that "custody prevailed over treatment.... Punishments remained unfair and even brutal."[62] Big House prisons, such as San Quentin in California and Stateville in Illinois, followed in the 1920s in order to warehouse large numbers of people, especially under the pressures of overcrowding that had inundated previous prison models. A series of prison insurrections in the 1950s, which were interpreted as the result largely of a lack of rehabilitative services in Big House prisons, led to renewed reform efforts. Beginning in 1954, "correctional institutions" revitalized emphasis on treatment, although "in practice, attempts at rehabilitation were only peripheral, [and] the prevailing indeterminate sentencing statutes led to disparities, arbitrariness, and disproportionately high penalties."[63] In many ways, correctional institutions were reformatories in a new guise, maintaining their legitimacy—despite their failures—through appeal to the professionalization of carceral practices and "scientific" attempts at rehabilitating people in prison.[64]

Into the Twenty-First Century: The Rise of Mass Incarceration

By the 1960s, the failures of prisons in achieving social order and individual change were well documented. The 1966 Presidential Commission on Law Enforcement and Administration of Justice concluded,

> Life in many institutions is at best barren and futile, at worst unspeakably brutal and degrading. To be sure, the offenders in such institutions are incapacitated from committing further

61. Rotman, "Failure of Reform," 162.
62. Rotman, "Failure of Reform," 164.
63. Rotman, "Failure of Reform," 171.
64. The continuity of these institutions can be seen, for example, in that the American Correctional Association is the same organization as Wines's National Prison Association, renamed in 1954 (American Correctional Association, "Our History and Mission," s.vv. "The History of the American Correctional Association," paras. 1, 3).

crimes while serving their sentences, but the conditions in which they live are the poorest possible preparation for their successful reentry into society, and often merely reinforce in them a pattern of manipulation and destruction.[65]

Despite these failures, efforts to make carceral institutions more humane did not surface. Rather, the age of mass incarceration commenced with increasing calls to be "tough on crime."[66] With this period of reform, the emphasis fell more on ensuring public safety and less on redeeming individuals. The priority was making prisons more effective, where the aim shifted from rehabilitation toward retribution, deterrence, and incapacitation.[67] Fueled by backlash against the civil rights movement, doubts about the effectiveness of rehabilitation, and dog-whistle politics about drug abuse, crime, and violence, the United States began incarcerating more people for more crimes and for longer periods than ever before.[68] As criminologist Michael Tonry argues, "Ham-fisted laws—three-strikes, mandatory minimums, truth-in-sentencing, life without parole—were enacted throughout the country. Some states enacted all of them. All enacted some."[69] The stage was set for the development of mass incarceration, however, much earlier with a growing cultural consensus that crime was a national problem requiring state intervention.[70]

The rate of incarceration climbed steadily beginning in the 1920s. Historian Aaron Griffith summarizes, "After a brief, sharp rise in the 1880s, imprisonment rates grew only slightly from 1890 to the early 1920s. . . . From 1923 to 1930, however, the rate jumped from 74 to 98 [people in prison] per 100,000, and the decade after that from 98 to 125, a 69 percent increase."[71] Rates decreased slightly during World War II, but then continued to rise.

65. As quoted in Rotman, "Failure of Reform," 173.

66. The exception is the Prisoners' Rights Movement. Uniquely in the history of US prisons, this movement of the 1960s and 1970s was driven by people who were incarcerated themselves. It contributed to court interventions in prison administration, importantly led by Black Muslim appeals to religious freedom that generated the basis for the judiciary to abandon its previous "hands-off" approach in monitoring prison administration (C. Smith, "Black Muslims").

67. Clear, *Harm in American Penology*.

68. See Alexander, *New Jim Crow*; Pfaff, *Locked In*. Proponents of tough-on-crime approaches could justify their rejection of rehabilitation, in part, through appeal to a landmark study: Martinson, "What Works." Despite weaknesses of the study, its "nothing works" thesis caught on among criminologists and criminal justice professionals and then spread to policymakers and the general public. On dog-whistle politics, López, *Dog-Whistle Politics*.

69. Tonry, *Sentencing Fragments*, viii.

70. A. Griffith, *God's Law and Order*.

71. A. Griffith, *God's Law and Order*, 26.

Starting in the late 1960s, the rate of incarceration began a steep and relentless ascent with tougher sentencing laws. As of early 2021, the United States had an incarceration rate of 537 people in jails or state and federal prisons per 100,000 residents. The peak rate was in 2008 with 708 incarcerated people per 100,000.[72] While the decrease over the last decade reflects widespread recognition of the problems of mass incarceration, the Sentencing Project observed in 2018, "The overall impact of reforms has been quite modest. . . . If states and the federal government maintain their recent pace of decarceration, it will take seventy-five years—until 2093—to cut the U.S. prison population by fifty percent."[73]

As in previous periods, Christian theology provided rhetoric and ideology that spurred reformative impulses—though now toward mass incarceration. The landscape of Christianity in US culture and society, however, shifted greatly after the end of the Civil War. The relative unity of white Protestantism in the nineteenth century broke apart into two main movements at the beginning of the twentieth century: liberal Protestantism, informed by the social gospel, emphasizing a Christian mission to advance social justice (especially economic equity) in modern society, and fundamentalist Protestantism, which rejected the modern accommodations of liberalism and stressed the necessity of individual conversion.[74] After World War II, "new evangelical" Protestants emerged, eschewing the disengagement of fundamentalists from wider society, while "conserving what they saw as biblical Christian doctrine" and "emphasizing the recurring importance of conversion," in contrast to liberalism.[75] During the same period, the presence of Catholicism in public life became more palatable in the dominant Protestant culture, which had been previously marked by suspicions of Catholics as generally anti-democratic and of Catholics from Southern and Eastern European immigrant groups as not fully white. Many Catholics in the early and mid-twentieth century sought and gained acceptance through assimilation into norms of whiteness and practices of US democracy, culminating in John F. Kennedy's inauguration.[76] Christian theological influence on the rise of mass incarceration must be understood within a context of a fractured Protestantism and increased acceptance of Catholic participation in American culture and society.

72. Kang-Brown et al., "People in Jail."
73. Ghandnoosh, "Can We Wait 75 Years."
74. Dorrien, *Making of American Liberal Theology*, vols. 2–3; Marsden, *Understanding Fundamentalism and Evangelicalism*.
75. A. Griffith, *God's Law and Order*, 7.
76. Tentler, *American Catholics*.

Despite the complexity of this context, white Christians from these varied backgrounds supported the expansion of incarceration as a response to crime. From the 1920s onward, they shared "common ground on two points: the beliefs that rising crime reflected growing secularity and that disciplinary state power was ultimately responsible for addressing the problem."[77] These two points undergirded a "shared rhetorical culture" that helped to legitimate the "law and order" responses to crime.[78] On one hand, religious conservatives believed that secularism caused moral decline and individual culpability, and thus higher crime rates. Griffith notes, "Sin as an explanatory category was a powerful way to universalize wrongdoing, and preachers who needed a convenient shorthand to illustrate total depravity began relying on crime as a generalizable example."[79] If individual sinfulness is the root of a perceived crime problem, then law, justice, and proper punishment through the state are the correct answers, along with individual conversion. On the other hand, religious liberals saw social factors with growing secularity to be the cause of crime. The decline of the family, poverty, licentious entertainments, urbanism, poor hygiene—all could potentially explain criminal behavior, and all were traced to a failure to embody the social requirements of the gospel. "Crime's true reference point was not found exclusively in an individual's moral consciousness, but also in the living conditions that made unsavory choices more likely."[80] This reasoning helped bolster liberal support for increased social welfare programs, but it also refined the role of the prison chaplain "to highlight the 'social matrix,' to bring the latest tools of psychological and social scientific investigation to bear in the ministry, and to exhibit sensitivity to religious diversity."[81] Griffith concludes, "At a time when acceptance of the religious 'other' by the Protestant establishment was by no means a guarantee, the crime issue allowed Protestants, Catholics, and Jews to all seek state protection of . . . the 'common religion' of 'the American way of life.'"[82] Carceral institutions remained largely secularized and professionalized with an imprimatur from religious liberals and conservatives alike that prisons were necessary for social order.

While Christians across the spectrum enabled the rise of mass incarceration, the public advocacy of Evangelicals was especially influential.

---

77. A. Griffith, *God's Law and Order*, 9.
78. A. Griffith, *God's Law and Order*, 15.
79. A. Griffith, *God's Law and Order*, 28.
80. A. Griffith, *God's Law and Order*, 36.
81. A. Griffith, *God's Law and Order*, 38.
82. A. Griffith, *God's Law and Order*, 40.

Griffith documents the coinciding rise of Evangelicalism and "America's carceral state," which facilitated widespread support for law-and-order politics by "providing them a sacred valence that helped broaden and deepen their appeal."[83] He describes three "conceptual contributions evangelicals made to the framing of crime" that fostered wider support for tougher sentencing reforms. First, evangelical preachers in the mid-twentieth century often used crime to talk about the universal problem of sin and their understanding of its universal solution: conversion. To demonstrate that *anyone* and *everyone* could be saved, preachers would draw upon narratives of the "worst of the worst" finding forgiveness to demonstrate the power of the gospel.[84] Second, the evangelical focus on conversion stressed that individual redemption and a just social order come about not through legislation but through "dramatic heart change."[85] Finally, Evangelicals constructed "icons of sinfulness" in contrast to the goodness of the gospel.[86] Preachers connected several images with criminality to heighten the sense of menacing, especially imagery of "inner cities" and "godless ghettoes."[87] The answer to crime (and to urban Black poverty) was then to expand white Evangelicals' ministry in Black communities: "The heart, not redlined neighborhoods or segregated school systems, was the fundamental site of both sin's diagnosis and its hopeful solution."[88]

Notably, these three conceptual contributions are not significantly punitive, and aspects of each humanize people deemed criminal, even while emphasizing their degradation. However, most Evangelicals adopted increasingly punitive perspectives through the 1960s and seventies in reaction to civil rights decisions by the Warren Court, urban uprisings, and disagreements in Protestant denominations about whether systemic problems or individuals' lawlessness were to blame for social disorder. In such a context, individual conversion was seen as necessary, but not sufficient. The preaching of the law as well as the gospel was required to preserve justice and restrain evil in a fallen world, and the law—whether God's or that of temporal authorities—delivers what is due: rightful punishment for wrongdoing. Conversion could follow just deserts. An exception to the evangelical conviction that heart change, not legislation, brings about individual redemption and a just social order pertained to criminal law. In this instance,

---

83. A. Griffith, *God's Law and Order*, 57.
84. A. Griffith, *God's Law and Order*, 82.
85. A. Griffith, *God's Law and Order*, 84–85.
86. A. Griffith, *God's Law and Order*, 87.
87. A. Griffith, *God's Law and Order*, 87–94.
88. A. Griffith, *God's Law and Order*, 90.

new legislation was seen as necessary. This mixture of law and gospel then shapes evangelical engagement with carceral institutions and practices: supporting tough-on-crime measures *and* expansive prison ministries, such as Kairos and Prison Fellowship.[89]

Crime and punishment seem not to have mattered as much to other Christians during this period. Griffith summarizes, "Evangelicals were on the cutting edge of engagement with American criminal justice, prisons, and reform, outpacing nearly all other American religious and social constituencies in their interest, intensity, and influence."[90] He continues,

> By contrast, in the following decades [after World War II], African American and liberal Protestants, Catholics, and Jews made arguments for state influence in securing civil rights and economic welfare, while white evangelicals championed the law enforcement function of the state to address what they deemed social disorder.[91]

Members of these groups remained present in carceral institutions as chaplains, though with a decidedly non-evangelical bent. Drawing on training in clinical pastoral education (CPE), state-sponsored chaplains shifted away from a "conversion-centered paradigm" and "developed a *maintenance* role, a 'ministry of presence' to help prisoners avail themselves of the 'free market of religion.'"[92] These roles might have increased access to carceral institutions, but they also reduced opportunities for critiquing prisons as access for chaplains depended upon approval and acceptance by prison administrators, for whom chaplains could be "key allies."[93] Outside of prisons, the National Council of Churches and the national leadership of many liberal Protestant denominations offered a counterpoint to evangelical law-and-order rhetoric, but "the mainline movement lost steam after their initial work lobbying for civil rights."[94] Where these groups addressed questions of crime and punishment, they often did so in ways that were out of step with laity and local leadership. White non-evangelical Christians might not have led the way to the law-and-order politics of mass incarceration, but they did not brook much opposition and were often complicit in the growing

---

89. Erzen, *God in Captivity*.
90. A. Griffith, *God's Law and Order*, 4.
91. A. Griffith, *God's Law and Order*, 52–53.
92. Winnifred Fallers-Sullivan, *Ministry of Presence*, as quoted in A. Griffith, *God's Law and Order*, 41; emphasis in original.
93. A. Griffith, *God's Law and Order*, 39.
94. A. Griffith, *God's Law and Order*, 126.

apparatus of carceral institutions.[95] Meanwhile, Black Christians often navigated difficult terrain regarding law-and-order politics. While concerned about high rates of crime victimization among Black people, they also worried that growing criminal legal systems were another source of harm directed against their community.[96] Griffith notes, "Engaging in the anticrime cause also risked the dilution of black struggle or even the endorsement of racist sentiment. Some believed it was worth the risk."[97]

In previous periods, white Christian assumptions about race and redemption informed carceral institutions and practices. An irony of this period is that explicit stereotypes and prejudices became less socially acceptable just as this latest form of social control of Black people arose. With the advances of the civil rights movement, ideology and rhetoric about race shifted, but in a way that permitted the preservation of racialized oppression through transformation. Mid-century evangelical conceptions seemingly pushed against previous notions about who could be saved. Evangelicals wanted to promote the gospel by showing that *everyone* and *anyone* could be saved, which could best be shown through conversion stories of people in prison. This argument, however, depended on icons of sinfulness that aligned criminality with racially coded imagery (inner cities and godless ghettoes), which then implicitly suggested that the most degraded souls are those of Black people—all while avoiding overt acknowledgment of race, especially its systemic realities.[98] Tough-on-crime politicians could then portray inner-city lawlessness and civil rights advances as the cause of social disorder, and they could gain support from evangelical Christians and a growing social consensus that could then believe that law-and-order policies were not racist.[99] Of course, law in the United States has never been racially neutral, so suddenly opting for purportedly colorblind support for law and order in a society marked by white supremacy ultimately upheld racialized oppression under mass incarceration.

Evangelical Christians were not alone in their "colorblindness." Even as other Christians increased their engagement with questions of crime and punishment, often with a more critical eye, they typically did so without accounting adequately for the racialized context of carcerality. In an early denominational statement addressing the growth of incarceration rates, the General Conference of the Mennonite Church encouraged exploration of

95. A. Griffith, *God's Law and Order*, 129.
96. Forman, *Locking Up Our Own*.
97. A. Griffith, *God's Law and Order*, 50.
98. A. Griffith, *God's Law and Order*, 90.
99. A. Griffith, *God's Law and Order*, 134.

alternatives to prisons in its 1977 "Offender Ministries." It however did not mention racial disparities in criminal legal systems. The Catholic Bishops of the United States considered some racial disparities in their 2000 *Responsibility, Rehabilitation, and Restoration*, but they provided little analysis about why disparities exist. The Evangelical Lutheran Church in America issued its own statement in 2013, "The Church and Criminal Justice: Hearing the Cries." Like many liberal Protestant denominational statements, it endeavored to navigate between a critique of the failures of US criminal legal systems and praise for the principles and professionals of these systems. Like the USCCB, the ELCA acknowledges racial disparities, but without more substantive analysis. An early exception to this rule is the American Friends Service Committee's 1971 *Struggle for Justice*, which called for more humane reforms decades before most liberal Christians even acknowledged significant problems. In addition, the AFSC included fuller recognition of the roles carceral institutions and practices play in racialized oppression. With awareness of how Quakers contributed to the creation of penitentiaries, Quakers now worked to correct their legacy. Despite this exception, white Catholics and liberal Protestants have usually stopped with naming disparities without addressing how white supremacy has created them or how churches have contributed rhetoric and ideology that help maintain racialized oppression.

Reformative Impulses Today

Despite the optimism of reformers from one period to the next, one group has consistently criticized prisons as brutal institutions—people who were incarcerated themselves. Their critiques perhaps culminated in the Prisoners' Rights Movement of the 1960s and seventies, but the complaints of that movement were not new and have not gone away. Prison insurrections throughout the history of US prisons offer one testimony to protests from incarcerated people. William Coffey wrote in 1823 about his experiences as a prisoner at Newgate that the prison guards "practice upon the convicts without scruple or reserve, everything abominable, disgusting, and inhumane."[100] Hopper's collected testimonies recounted floggings, strangulation, shower baths, disease, and inadequate and unsafe food.[101] In 1923 Kate Richards O'Hare, who had been incarcerated because of protest against World War I, wrote of hideous conditions in a Missouri penitentiary, in which "every crack and every crevice of the cellhouse was full of vermin of

---

100. William Coffey, *Inside Out*; as quoted in Graber, *Furnace of Affliction*, 70.
101. Graber, *Furnace of Affliction*, 164.

every known sort, which no amount of scrubbing on the part of the women could permanently dislodge."[102] Innumerable lawsuits filed by people in prison, after courts recognized that "a prison environment could entail the infliction of cruel and unusual punishment," give evidence of prisoner critiques into the twenty-first century.[103] Contemporary accounts, such as Albert Woodfox's and Ian Manual's, testify to the current brokenness of carceral institutions and practices.[104] While the reformative impulse has waxed and waned over the last two centuries, people in prison have consistently made the case regarding prison abuses, violence, and failures since their inception.

In light of the scale of mass incarceration, we are in a new reformative movement. Tonry writes,

> Nearly everyone agrees. The *New York Times* and the *Wall Street Journal* publish interchangeable editorials decrying the system, condemning its excesses, and regretting what it has done. The Soros Foundation and Koch Industries fund major criminal justice reform initiatives aiming to repeal severe laws and facilitate offenders' reintegration into mainstream society. Conservative organizations like the Manhattan Institute, Justice Fellowship, the American Enterprise Institute, and the Texas Public Policy Foundation more often than not find common cause with liberal organizations like the American Civil Liberties Union, the Open Society Institute, the Sentencing Project, and NYU's Brennan Center.[105]

Across the political spectrum, people are coming to agree that our use of prisons is arbitrary, unjust, severe, and unwise. Prisons are both inhumane and ineffective. Christians across the religious spectrum have also come to this conclusion. Numerous denominations have selected Alexander's *The New Jim Crow*, as well as Bryan Stephenson's *Just Mercy*, for national awareness campaigns; congregations across the country have used them for reading clubs, adult education programs, and listening groups.[106] The annual meeting of Christian Churches Together promulgated a statement against

---

102. Kate Richards O'Hare, *In Prison*; as quoted in Rotman, "Failure of Reform," 157.

103. Rotman, "Failure of Reform," 171.

104. See Woodfox, *Solitary*; Manual, *My Time Will Come*.

105. Tonry, *Sentencing Fragments*, vii.

106. Garcia, "New Jim Crow." See also Levad, "Repairing the Breach"; Stevenson, *Just Mercy*.

mass incarceration at its 2014 meeting.[107] In 2017, the evangelical Prison Fellowship issued "The Justice Declaration," which states, "The Church has both the unique ability and unparalleled capacity to confront the staggering crisis of crime and incarceration in America and to respond with restorative solutions for communities, victims, and individuals responsible for crime."[108] Christians have increasingly acknowledged the injustices of mass incarceration, often sharing Alexander's recognition that "this is not simply a legal problem, or a political problem, or a policy problem. [It] raises profound moral and spiritual questions about who we are, individually and collectively, who we aim to become, and what we are willing to do now."[109]

The history presented here raises several challenges, especially to Christians, in this moment. Following Rotman's observation about the cycle of prison reform, if we are in a moment of exposé and report, how do we ensure that our proposals do not inevitably recreate and expand the intrinsic and extrinsic problems of carceral institutions and practices? Idealism about reforms has a tendency to legitimate them, even when they fail or are not actually implemented. Ideology and rhetoric that extol their humaneness and effectiveness mask abuses. The realities of limited budgets, overcrowding, and politics overwhelm idealism. Christians have repeatedly contributed to the reformative impulse without critically assessing this cycle. Yet the failures of past reforms do not go away; they accumulate as new institutions and practices build on old ones (Auburn, Sing Sing, Parchman, and Angola are all still fully operational). To be responsible to this history, Christians must meet this moment with non-reformative reforms and transformative justice and consider the possibilities of abolition.[110] Otherwise, the reforms that come out of this moment will "widen the net" of carceral institutions and practices while repeating the cycle demonstrated here.[111] We must address theologies that have provided rhetorical and ideological cover for prisons.[112] Liberationist theologies beginning from the experiences of people who have

---

107. Christian Churches Together, "Principles on Mass Incarceration."

108. Colson Center et al., "Justice Declaration," preface.

109. Michelle Alexander, Facebook post, Sept. 14, 2016, since deleted. This conclusion led Alexander to join the faculty of Union Theological Seminary in New York in 2016.

110. Dubler and Lloyd, *Break Every Yoke*. For a Catholic argument on abolitionism, see Soltis and Grimes, "Order, Reform, and Abolition."

111. Gilmore, *Golden Gulag*.

112. For an abolitionist critique of theologies of redemptive suffering, see H. Bowman, "From Substitution to Solidarity."

experienced incarceration are necessary to counter theologies that have permitted and sometimes supported their abuse and degradation.[113]

In addition, if white supremacy is preserved through transformation, and if mass incarceration is the latest among many forms of racialized oppression, how do we ensure that our proposals to end mass incarceration do not recreate and expand white supremacy and racialized oppression in new forms? White supremacy has shaped every reform of prisons in the United States since their inception. Assumptions about the purposes of incarceration and the possibilities of achieving those ends with white versus nonwhite people have contributed to disparate treatment, whether in penitentiaries, reformatories, Big Houses, prison farms and mines, or correctional institutions. These differences have been legitimated by rhetoric and ideology that portray white people (such as Christian reformers) as noble protagonists and nonwhite people, especially Black people, as dangerous and degenerate. Christians have contributed theologically to this rhetoric and ideology, whether explicitly in the notions of the Prison Discipline Society of Boston or the classification notes of Zebulon Brockway, or implicitly in the "color-blind" defense of law-and-order politics. To be responsible to this history, liberationist theologies that decenter whiteness are necessary to counter theologies that have permitted and supported the abuse and degradation of people of color. White Christians must address the theologies that have created and maintained these sins. We must meet this moment with honesty about our historical and ongoing complicity in and culpability for white supremacy and racialized oppression.

---

113. See, for example, Jobe, "Carceral Hermeneutics."

Part Three

PRACTICING THE BUSINESS OF INCARCERATION TODAY

6

Mass Incarceration as the Policy Outcome of the Presumed Pathology of the Black Urban Class

A Short History

JERMAINE M. MCDONALD

Mass incarceration in the United States is a relatively recent phenomenon in the United States. It is a common misconception that the war on drugs was its beginning and epicenter, but drug prohibition is merely one rung in the seemingly never-ending ladder that is mass incarceration in the United States. The purpose of this chapter is to provide more detailed information about the increasingly punitive and racialized nature of national criminal justice policy and rhetoric over the course of the last seventy years that have helped make mass incarceration the issue it is today.

Johnson Years: Wars on Poverty and Crime

According to historian Elizabeth Hinton, the advent of mass incarceration had an inauspicious beginning as a relatively good-faith attempt to alleviate poverty in general, but with an extra engagement with Black poverty as a continuation of the social gains won from desegregation and as a key pillar of President Lyndon Johnson's vision for shaping the "Great Society." In his 1964 State of the Union address to the nation, President Johnson declared "unconditional war on poverty in America,"[1] proposing a laundry list of programs, policies, and actions that would be social investments into impacted communities, aiming to address the principal causes of poverty. President Johnson's fierce advocacy pushed the United States Congress to pass the Economic Opportunity Act of 1964 (creating programs like Job Corps and Head Start, and providing loans to rural impoverished families, small businesses, and the like),[2] the Elementary and Secondary Education Act of 1965 (infused local schools with federal aid for the first time),[3] the Higher Education Act of 1965 (provided funding for higher education and greatly expanded the number of high school and college graduates),[4] and the Social Security Amendments of 1965 (establishing Medicaid and Medicare as health insurance programs for the elderly and people with limited income, respectively).[5] These four explicit measures to combat general poverty, along with the landmark civil rights legislation of the 1960s, the Civil Rights Act of 1964, the Voting Rights Act of 1965, and the Fair Housing Act of 1968 mark this time period as one of the most politically progressive in US history.

President Johnson's vision for the Great Society still impacts the nation well into the twenty-first century. Yet, the full force and potential of that vision was muted by Johnson's commitment to another major domestic policy agenda: law and order as a means of social control. Johnson's agenda here was deeply influenced by Daniel Patrick Moynihan's report, "The Negro Family: The Case for National Action." Published in March of 1965, Moynihan's report institutionalized the notion that Black poverty, delinquency, and crime were primarily caused by a self-perpetuating "tangle of pathology"[6] rooted in the brokenness of Black families resulting from "three centuries of injustice."[7] For the Johnson Administration, this pathology required both a commitment to the Great Society vision focusing on job training to increase opportunities in urban Black communities and an enhanced law enforcement strategy to surveille and manage the same population. Contemporarily, there were voices of dissent regarding Moynihan's conclusions; voices

1. Johnson, "Annual Message," sec. 3, para. 2.
2. National Archives Catalog, "Act of August 20, 1964."
3. GovInfo, "Elementary and Secondary Education."
4. GovInfo, "Higher Education Act of 1965."
5. National Archives, "Medicare and Medicaid Act (1965)."
6. Moynihan, "Negro Family," ch. 4, "Tangle of Pathology."
7. Moynihan, "Negro Family," ch. 5, para. 6. The pathology, it argues, was shaped by the matrilineal nature of Black families in contrast to the patrilineal nature of white families.

that would have cemented Johnson's affinity for the Great Society programs and negated his turn toward punitive carceral measures to supplement that work. William Ryan, for example, wrote in the November 22, 1965, edition of *The Nation* criticizing the report for providing yet another "explanation [that] almost always focus on supposed defects of the Negro victim as if those—and not the racist structure of American society—were the cause of all woes that Negroes suffer."[8] The "unstable Negro family" was the result of discrimination, not the cause of Black disfunction. President Johnson ignored pleas like Ryan's in favor of Moynihan's conclusions, thus providing the foundation for the rise of the carceral state.[9]

The first rung added to the mass incarceration ladder was the Law Enforcement Assistance Act of 1965.[10] Passed in September of that year, the law was a direct refutation of social unrest and rioting in South Central Los Angeles (commonly referred to as the Watts Riots or Rebellion) of August 1965. That rebellion lasted over six days, caused $40 million of property damage, and killed thirty-four people. Fourteen thousand California National Guard troops were brought in to help restore order. Though the spark was an incident of alleged police brutality witnessed by over two hundred residents, the underlying tension was the community's growing discontent with the poor social and economic conditions of their neighborhood.[11] Policymakers, in turn, used this communally violent cry for increased social welfare to intensify punitive measures of law enforcement in the same communities crying out for help.[12] The Law Enforcement Assistance Act provided urban police departments with federal funds to bolster their ranks, equipment, weaponry, and training and authorized the creation of the Office of Law Enforcement Assistance (later the Law Enforcement Assistance Administration [LEAA]). Grants went to various organizations for crime research, law enforcement training, weapons development, and computerized systems analysis to anticipate crime and improve surveillance tactics.[13]

Urban uprisings in the cities of Newark and Detroit in the summer of 1967 caused further alarm to authorities and the public. Much like the Watts rebellion, the unrest in Newark and Detroit began with the spark of seemingly unjust police encounters with the Black population under

8. W. Ryan, "D. Savage Discovery."

9. Hinton, *From War on Poverty*, 61.

10. GovInfo, "Law Enforcement Assistance Act." This law set aside $10 million annually "for the purpose of improving the quality of State and local law enforcement and correctional personnel . . . for the prevention or control of crime."

11. Civil Rights Digital Library, "Watts Riots."

12. Hinton, *From War on Poverty*, 65.

13. Hinton, *From War on Poverty*, 91.

the backdrop of poor socioeconomic conditions and an antagonistic relationship between police and the Black populations of those cities. Rather than seeing the uprisings as a violent appeal for proactive relief from these conditions, the authorities saw the uprisings as threats to the social order. President Johnson and Congress determined that urban police departments needed fortifying and militarization. The Omnibus Crime Control and Safe Streets Act of 1968 did just that, creating the aforementioned LEAA, establishing wiretapping rules, and setting aside funds to expand and improve law enforcement with "special emphasis, where appropriate or feasible, to programs and projects dealing with the prevention, detection, and control of organized crime and riots and other violent civil disorders."[14] With the passing of this law, the Johnson Administration had effectively curtailed their commitment to social programs of uplift to advance major crime control intervention, setting the stage for mass incarceration.

Nixon Years: Establishing Law and Order

President Johnson's efforts fortified law enforcement as the front line of the war on crime. With efforts well underway to modernize and militarize urban police forces across the nation, President Richard Nixon would fortify those interventions, then turn his attention toward the courts, the prison systems, and drugs as the next fronts in the war on crime. First, Nixon focused on innovations in the District of Columbia, hoping to demonstrate their effectiveness before expanding them elsewhere. The majority-Black nation's capital had been a testing ground for federal law enforcement innovations since the Kennedy Administration, and Nixon took full advantage of this precedent. The District of Columbia Court Reform and Criminal Procedure Act of 1970 required a mandatory minimum sentence of five years for a repeat armed offense and allowed a life sentence for a third. This rudimentary "three strikes" law informed the creation of the three strikes laws of New York and California.[15] It also required youth over sixteen who were charged with rape, murder, or armed robbery to be tried as adults, permitted preventative detention at a judge's discretion, and permitted "no-knock" raids on the homes of suspects without notice or announcement.[16] Thus, Nixon legitimized mandatory minimums, pretrial detaining of criminal

---

14. GovInfo, "Omnibus Crime Control," 202.

15. Hinton, *From War on Poverty*, 156. The actual law can be seen at GovInfo, "District of Columbia."

16. Hinton, *From War on Poverty*, 157–58.

subjects, and trying youth offenders of violent crime as adults, and reduced constraints on police searches, seizures, and raids.

Second, the Nixon Administration anticipated an increase in the prison population via its punitive law enforcement measures and planned for the construction of prisons. They created a ten-year "Long Range Master Plan" to expand and modernize the US prisons, setting the foundation for the prison-industrial complex.[17] Finding that the existing prison system was antiquated and inadequate, the administration sought to build better federal prisons, more suitable to holding prisoners long term, that would also serve as models and inspiration for states to do the same. The administration used the block grants and discretionary funding from the Organized Crime Control Act of 1970 to encourage and help states pay for new prison construction.[18] The administration also summarily abandoned the notion of rehabilitation for the "new class of inmates" (the majority of whom were Black or Latino), reasoning that incarceration and behavior modification in maximum security settings was the best punishment for these offenders and would serve as a crime deterrent for others.

Finally, the Nixon Administration pursued and encouraged police crime-fighting strategies that turned the war on crime into a literal battlefield of violent conflicts, real gun battles, and real victims.[19] Reasoning that social programs to uplift and prevent crime would not work, the administration sought to empower police with tactics to control and maintain order by forcefully confronting potential crime in urban localities. One means of establishing control was to institute plain clothes officers as highly armed foot patrols authorized for surveillance, harassment, decoy operations, and warrant-free no-knock raids to increase the number of arrests in "high-crime" areas as an anti-crime deterrent.[20]

One final innovation occurred during the Nixon years that would have a lasting impact on mass incarceration to this day: the establishment of the Rockefeller drug laws in New York in 1973. Governor Nelson Rockefeller birthed the idea and led the effort to toughen New York's drug laws,

17. Hinton, *From War on Poverty*, 164–79.
18. Hinton, *From War on Poverty*, 172.
19. Hinton, *From War on Poverty*, 184.
20. Hinton, *From War on Poverty*, 189. Two short-lived pilot programs, "Stop the Robberies, Enjoy Safe Streets (STRESS)" in Detroit and a nationalized campaign by the Office of Drug Abuse Law Enforcement (ODALE) deployed undercover military-style tactical units in "high-crime" urban communities. ODALE conducted 1439 raids in little over a year's time, many conducted without warrants, terrorizing these communities in the name of law enforcement and getting many innocent people caught in the crosshairs. For more about STRESS, see Lassiter and the Policing and Social Justice HistoryLab, "Creation of STRESS."

reasoning that convicted drug dealers should receive a mandatory "life sentence, no parole, no probation."[21] Through deterrence and the threat of imposing punishment for dealers and addicts, drug use was supposed to go down. Rockefeller's tough on crime stance earned him the vice presidency when Gerald Ford unexpectedly became president. His drug laws had no impact on drug use, but swelled New York's prison population. Nevertheless, mandatory minimums would spread across the country and become a key facet of President Ronald Reagan's reinvigoration of the war on drugs.

Ford and Carter Years: Career Criminals and Electronic Surveillance

President Gerald Ford's innovation in the war on crime and the acceleration of mass incarceration was to focus on streamlining courts, overburdened by the significant rise of cases due to the tactics, policies, and laws addressed above, by accelerating the prosecution of defendants deemed "career criminals."[22] Federal grant funds allowed state and local prosecutor offices to set up specialized units that would focus on career criminals. These units tended to have more resources and a much lighter case load and could prosecute cases much more efficiently. The Ford Administration would also expand the notion of criminal career to youth, getting Congress to authorize adult prosecutions for youth aged sixteen or older who were deemed "dangerous to the community." This would be yet another tool to combat crime in urban communities, particularly (Black and Latino) youth gang violence.

Contrary to the Ford Administration's view that crime and the lack of individual responsibility were the causes of urban decay, President Jimmy Carter believed that improving the economic conditions of these urban communities would reduce crime. In some ways, it was a return to Johnson's policy agenda. First, President Carter sought a better commitment to social programs. With the Public Housing Security Demonstration Act of 1978, the Carter Administration incorporated the Department of Housing and Urban Development into anti-crime measures to focus on addressing the quality of life of housing project communities, viewing those areas as hotbeds for urban crime. Rather than improving things like plumbing and deteriorating living conditions, HUD added electronic surveillance, gates, fences, and other security measures, as well as more uniformed patrols and (limited) community involvement. Second, President Carter sought to end the war on crime by dismantling federal control and funding for local law

21. Mann, "Drug Laws That Changed," para. 10.
22. Hinton, *From War on Poverty*, 257–58.

enforcement. The latter plan met so much resistance that Carter pivoted to an indirect plan of splitting the LEAA into three separate agencies, focusing on improving crime statistics collection, and reducing federal funding for police hardware.[23]

Reagan and Bush I Years: War on Drugs and Soft on Crime

In the 1980s President Ronald Reagan ratcheted up the battle against urban crime, promoting the notion that social programs and a lazy culture were the primary causes of the crime and social stagnation of those communities. By framing the crime problem in this way, Reagan convinced Congress to authorize the transformation of policing in the United States and wage the war on drugs in full force. Congress passed the Military Cooperation with Civilian Law Enforcement Agencies Act of 1981, which allowed the military to assist local law enforcement, particularly with drug interdiction.[24] In 1984, Reagan led Congress to pass, with an overwhelming majority, the Comprehensive Crime Control Act of 1984, essentially renewing and doubling down on the war on drugs. The legislation permitted judges to detain defendants pretrial without bail if the accused posed a danger to the community. It also imposed mandatory minimum sentences on felony with a firearm convictions, allowed police departments to keep some of the proceeds of civil asset forfeitures, and provided more federal funds for the construction of state prisons.[25]

Reagan's Anti-Drug Abuse Act of 1986 dramatically increased funding for crime and drug control programs and established mandatory minimum sentences for possession of one hundred grams of heroin, five hundred grams of cocaine, and five grams of crack cocaine.[26] The hundred-to-one sentence discrepancy between crack cocaine and powder cocaine was especially pernicious because crack cocaine was disproportionately available in the urban centers that had traditionally been the focus of crime war. Additionally, Reagan led Congress to pass the Anti-Drug Abuse Act of 1988, months before leaving office, mandating the eviction of drug abusers from public housing, denial of federal benefits for anyone convicted of drug offenses, and drug testing of all

---

23. Hinton, *From War on Poverty*, 283. See also Congress, "H.R. 2061."

24. Ronald F. Lauve testified to the impact of the legislation at a hearing before the House of Representatives Subcommittee on Crime in 1983 (Lauve, "Statement").

25. Hinton, *From War on Poverty*, 312. See also the full text of the resolution in GovInfo, "Department of the Interior."

26. Hinton, *From War on Poverty*, 317. For the full text, see Congress, "H.R. 5484."

federal employees and grant recipients. It should also be noted here that the work of Rockefeller, Nixon, and Reagan was not entirely opposed by the Black community. Black urban neighborhoods were most impacted by high crime and drug abuse. Black community and political leaders were on the forefront of raising the alarm about drug crime in their neighborhoods. According to historian Michael Javen Fortner, there was an active intracommunal debate about the solutions, but ultimately, many determined that "the risk of persecution were outweighed by the urgent need for protection."[27] To that end, there was virtually no Black political support for the initial Rockefeller laws in New York, but over two-thirds of Black elected officials in Congress subsequently voted for the Anti-Drug Abuse Act of 1986, the nationalization of the Rockefeller mandatory minimum invention. Poorly funded rehabilitative efforts had failed to rescue the addicted and transform the dealers; many Black leaders in high-crime, high-drug-abuse communities reasoned that perhaps punitive laws could protect everyone else.

President George H. W. Bush's innovation in mass incarceration was not policy related, but rhetorical. He successfully weaponized the notion that any politician who supported reforms that reduced the punitive nature of the carceral state was "soft on crime." The most prominent example of this was the "Willie Horton" ad, used in his successful 1988 presidential campaign, which used the example of Horton to declare that prison furlough and early release programs would put (Black) convicts back on the street, putting the rest of the population at risk for increased murders, rapes, and violent crime. It was a clear racist dog whistle[28] that neatly reinforced the idea of the presumed criminality of the Black urban class that had defined federal policy toward poverty and crime since the Johnson Administration. This duality of tough on crime vs. soft on crime still carries strong rhetorical weight in public political discourse in the United States today. Bush also led the passing of Section 1208 in the National Defense Authorization Act in late 1989, which authorized the transfer of excess military equipment to federal and state agencies for anti-drug operations at no cost to those agencies.[29] The legacy and legitimacy of this program, which effectively helped militarize police departments around the country, finally came into sharp focus in the aftermath of the 2014 Ferguson uprising, where a militarized police force engaged protesters angry about the police killing of Michael Brown.

27. Sanneh, "Body Count." See also Fortner, *Black Silent Majority*.
28. Withers, "George H. W. Bush's 'Wille Horton.'"
29. Wofford, "How America's Police Became an Army." The 1208 program was a precursor for and would be replaced by sec. 1033 in the "Clinton Crime Bill" of 1994. See also sec. 1208 of the National Defense Authorization Act for Fiscal Years 1990 and 1991 (GovTrack, "H.R. 2461"). The 1033 revision removed the requirement that equipment transfers were to support counter drug operations.

Clinton Years: Community Policing and the End of Welfare as an Entitlement

George H. W. Bush's rhetoric on crime was powerful enough to force the Democratic candidate in the 1992 US presidential election, William Clinton, to adopt similar rhetoric to neutralize his opponent's political advantages on the issue. Candidate Clinton pledged to be "tough on crime and good for civil rights."[30] President Clinton made good on the tough-on-crime aspect of his pledge with his executive advocacy for the Violent Crime Control and Law Enforcement Act of 1994, the single largest federal criminal justice legislation in the history of the United States. The bill authorized more than $30 billion of federal funds over six years toward law enforcement, spread across state and local agencies, federal agencies, prison construction, and crime prevention.[31] With the explicit goal of adding at least one hundred thousand more police officers, the bill created the office of the Police Corps and law enforcement education and scholarships to train new officers.[32] Improving the quantity and quality of policing was a key aspect of Clinton's innovation of community policing as a crime reduction remedy.[33] Punitive measures of punishment continued to be part of the federal law enforcement agenda. The 1994 crime bill allowed juveniles as young as thirteen to be charged as adults for violent crimes. Thrice-convicted offenders of violent crime or drug trafficking were mandated to receive life sentences. It encouraged states to increase their capacity to hold violent offenders and keep them imprisoned longer (at least 85 percent of their sentences) via the Violent Offender Incarceration and Truth-In-Sentencing grant programs.[34] Additionally, the bill created a national sex offender registry and authorized grants and other provisions to combat violence against women. According to a Gallup survey at the time, 58 percent of African Americans supported the crime bill. The crack epidemic was raging in urban Black communities, and those most impacted wanted something, anything done to curtail its devastating effects.[35]

As part of his effort to "end welfare as we know it,"[36] President Clinton also transformed welfare from a cash assistance entitlement program for

30. Ifill, "1992 Campaign," para. 4.

31. Rosenfeld, "Overview and Reflections." See the "Overview" section for the summary of federal spending authorized by the bill.

32. One Hundred Third Congress, "H.R. 3355." See specifically sec. 200104 of the bill.

33. See U.S. Department of Justice, *Clinton Administration's Law Enforcement Strategy*.

34. See Sabol and Johnson, "Impacts on Prison Populations."

35. Ray and Galston, "1994 Crime Bill."

36. Carcasson, "Ending Welfare."

families with children in poverty to a program of block grants to enable states to set up their own assistance and support services programs under four general guidelines: (1) provide assistance to needy families; (2) end the dependence of needy parents on government benefits by promoting job preparation, work, and marriage; (3) prevent and reduce out of-wedlock pregnancies; and (4) encourage the formation of two-parent families.[37] Under the Temporary Assistance to Needy Families (TANF) grants established by the 1996 law, states were empowered to develop their own metrics as to what qualified a family for assistance, were forced to include work provisions in order to continue receiving the grants, and could divert funds from cash assistance to support programs that addressed the wedlock provisions for any family regardless of need.[38] If we can cast the increasingly punitive nature of law enforcement policy as the attempt to control, manage, and contain the bad pathology of Black urban communities, the Clinton Administration's welfare reform can be viewed in a similar light. According to the theory, poverty, drug abuse, and crime are the direct result of the inferior cultural pathology of the people in these urban centers and only punitive measures can control this population. The 1996 law also continued the tradition of harshly punishing (poor) drug abusers by including a provision that denied benefits in TANF or food stamps for individuals with a felony conviction for drug use, possession, or distribution.[39]

The Twenty-First Century: Drawing Down on Mass Incarceration

The twenty-first century has seen a slight drawdown on mass incarceration. First, President George W. Bush signed the Second Chance Act of 2007, formalizing his prisoner reentry initiative.[40] That initiative, announced in his 2004 State of the Union address, sought to help nonviolent ex-offenders successfully reintegrate back into society via enhanced drug treatment, mentoring, and transitional services, partnering with local corrections, faith-based, and community organizations. The legislation authorized $165 million in federal grants to state and local governments as well as nonprofit organizations to fund programs that provided assistance to formerly incarcerated individuals to reduce the chance that those individuals would

37. See Congress, "H.R. 3734," sec. 401.
38. Center on Budget and Policy Priorities, "Policy Basics."
39. Congress, "H.R. 3734," sec. 115.
40. White House, "Fact Sheet: President Bush."

reoffend.[41] It was a signature program in President Bush's "faith-based and community initiative" designed to allow faith-based organizations to better compete for federal funds to aid the poor and needy.[42] Reducing recidivism, the chance that a formerly incarcerated person commits another criminal act that results in rearrest, reconviction, or return to prison within three years of being released from incarceration,[43] is a core criminal justice concern and a noteworthy public policy goal. The recidivism rate in the United States has fluctuated across states and time due to changes in what counts as criminal activity, the demographics of incarcerated persons, time after first incarceration, and other factors. One can find national recidivism rates between 43 percent and 66 percent after three years, and as high as 82 percent after ten years.[44] Some states have had better luck than others at tackling the issue, however. For instance, a study conducted by Jonny Amasa-Annang and Gina Scutelnicu on the impact of the 2007 Second Chance Act among male ex-offenders in Alabama, Georgia, and Mississippi revealed a wide discrepancy of success rates in the three-year period following the implementation of the Second Chance Act. Georgia, which received more money and funded more grant programs, had a 12.4-percent decrease of new sentences to prison releases; Mississippi, funding only two grant programs, had a 10-percent decrease; and Alabama, also funding only two grant programs, had a 2.5-percent increase.[45] The researchers concluded that recidivism rates could potentially be reduced with comprehensive and compulsory rehabilitative reentry services for ex-offenders.[46] According to the Bureau of Justice Assistance, a division of the US Department of Justice, released ex-offenders often need support in the following five categories: mental health, substance abuse, housing, education and employment, and familial support.[47] Despite the monetary intervention of the Second Chance Act and its reauthorization in 2018, the overall recidivism rate has not budged.

President Barack Obama's key contribution to the drawing down on mass incarceration was the Fair Sentencing Act of 2010. That legislation reduced the drug quantity ratio disparity between crack cocaine and powder cocaine from 100 to 1 to 18 to 1, meaning it now takes possession of

41. National Reentry Resource Center, "Second Chance Act," s.vv. "The Second Chance Act."

42. White House, "White House Faith-Based and Community Initiative."

43. National Institute of Justice, "Recidivism."

44. Pew Center on the States, *State of Recidivism*; Antenangeli and Durose, *Recidivism of Prisoners*.

45. Amasa-Annang and Scutelnicu, "How Promising," 33.

46. Amasa-Annang and Scutelnicu, "How Promising," 33.

47. National Reentry Resource Center, "Second Chance Act," s.v. "Background."

28 grams of crack cocaine (up from 5 grams) versus 500 grams of powder cocaine to trigger a mandatory 5-year sentence, and 280 grams of crack (up from 50 grams) versus 5000 grams of powder to trigger a mandatory 10-year sentence.[48] A report from the US Sentencing Commission estimates that the discrepancy reduction resulted in 29,653 prison bed–years saved for the Bureau of Prisons in year three of the enactment of the FSA (2013).[49] Further, the trend of declining crack cocaine use, starting in 2008, was not interrupted by the enactment of the FSA.[50] In other words, more people did not start using crack cocaine when the sentencing of possession was lightened, calling into question the idea that strict sentencing is a deterrent for drug use and possession. While certainly a step in the right direction, the reduction, rather than the elimination, of the sentencing discrepancy still places a discriminatory burden on Black and Brown communities, as crack use and possession are more prevalent in those communities while cocaine is more prevalent in white communities. It is, perhaps, an admission by the US government that the punitive measures that marked the rise of mass incarceration need some correction.

Conclusion

The rise of mass incarceration in the United States was a mid- to late-twentieth-century phenomenon directly resulting from the punitive crime prevention measures imagined by presidential policies, cemented by congressional legislation, and affirmed by the judiciary of that era. It set the stage for states and municipalities to follow suit. Reversing it will require federal, state, and local governments to listen to and enact the imaginative solutions of grassroots justice organizations committed to restorative justice ideals, some of which are profiled in this book. If the same vigor, energy, and resolve that were used to create the shackles of mass incarceration are deployed to tear it down, then perhaps the twenty-first century will be known as the century of decarceration in the United States.

---

48. See Congress, "S. 1789." Specific reference for the mandatory minimum change can be found in sec. 2, "Cocaine Sentencing Disparity Reduction."

49. U.S. Sentencing Commission, *Report to the Congress*, 26.

50. U.S. Sentencing Commission, *Report to the Congress*, 27.

7

Immigration and the Business of Incarceration

BRITTA MEIERS CARLSON

An Encounter with the Immigrant Detention Apparatus

It was the same story any time I left my neighborhood. Traffic, confusing directions, and scarce parking options made it feel impossible to arrive on time to any unfamiliar neighborhood of Boston. The sinking stomach feeling that often plagued me in the bottlenecks under the Inner Harbor, while I watched the estimated arrival time get later and later on the screen of my phone, was especially awful this day. Being late to the jail was not an option.

It was my first day as a spiritual caregiver with Refugee Immigration Ministry. Since 1986, this interfaith group had been training and organizing volunteer chaplains to provide spiritual care to migrants in detention. I was one of a group of volunteers scheduled to meet in the lobby before proceeding to the immigration unit for our session with men detained for immigration proceedings or awaiting deportation. Volunteers were not permitted to bring cell phones into the jail, and there would be no way to contact the group if I arrived late. So, when I saw a parking spot open on the street just one block from the facility, I raised a quick thanksgiving and pulled in. I was still out of breath as I joined the small circle of volunteers and our escort, who walked us through the double-locked door entrance for security screening.

I had been inside the facility only once before, on a tour with other individuals from a neighborhood coalition working to prevent recidivism. In my capacity as a pastor in a community with many undocumented immigrants and people living outside, the South Bay House of Correction was well known to many I encountered daily. It seemed important to have some sense of the place. On this visit, the lighting was just as severe, the hallways remained bleak, and the whole place still smelled a bit too much like cleaning products. On the day of my tour, however, our guide had motioned dismissively toward the ICE detention unit as we had passed. Today we walked through the security doors and onto the unit.

Almost immediately after we arrived at our assigned meeting room, the men began shuffling in to join us. We formed an oval around the edges of the room with our chairs. Some of the men quietly greeted volunteers whom they remembered from previous visits. Then one of the more experienced caregivers opened the space for conversation, asking the prisoners to share how they were doing and update us on their cases.

One individual who had emigrated from Egypt had recently been transported to Boston from Texas, where he had been living with his wife and children. Having lost easy access to his lawyer, he wondered how he might continue to pursue his asylum case. A young man from Guatemala kept a slight smile on his face as he proclaimed his trust that God would be with him, no matter the outcome of his claim. Another man from Trinidad suppressed tears as he shared his disappointment that a date had been set for his removal later that week. As he finished his check-in, his voice was almost a whisper. "If only we'd gotten DAPA [deferred action for parents of Americans]."

His reference to President Obama's blocked executive action to prevent deportation for undocumented parents of US citizens and permanent residents brought me back to the day, several years prior, when we had celebrated the announcement of that order as well as the also-defeated expansion of DACA (deferred action for childhood arrivals). Immigration advocates and migrants from Algeria, Morocco, Guatemala, El Salvador, and Colombia had crowded into the basement of our church. The mood was both festive and anxious. This might mean work permits and freedom from fear of deportation for some in our community, but already Republican opposition to the president's announcement was provoking promises of legal challenges. A community organizer had led the crowd in an upbeat chant. "¡Cuando luchamos: ganamos! When we fight, we win!" A frazzled attorney from a local immigrant rights organization had stood at the podium and shared what little information he had, promising to return with more details once the government provided procedures and timelines. One by one, community members had come to the microphone to share excitement and questions. Then the crowd was brought to a reflective hush at the words of a middle-aged widow from El Salvador. "I am happy for our young people and for all the parents," she had said. "I really am. But I worry for the rest of us."

Five years later, on the immigration detention unit, we volunteers could do little more than listen. These men had few protections under the law. We shared the phone number for a legal support network with them. The last such number had been shut down by the jail for unexplained reasons two months prior. Because we could not bring anything in with us, the only way to share the number was to memorize it. Several of the men jotted the number down and promised to disseminate it. One asylum seeker explained that he had not heard from his lawyer and had been unable to get through to the organization that referred him. He was running low on money in his phone account. The volunteers collaborated to commit the details of his case to memory and relay a message to his lawyer. The jail did not permit volunteers to advocate publicly for those who had been detained, but we could pass the word along.

I did not expect we would move mountains that day, but I was unprepared for the helplessness and gloom that remained with me as I exited through layers of secure doors and into the daylight of the lobby. After a debrief with the other volunteers, I plodded slowly back to my car. Even as the jail grew smaller in my rearview mirror, I could not shake the dread I had encountered inside those iron-clad walls. How could it be that in my city, just a few miles from that church basement, people were being so violently discarded, and with such little resistance?

The Context

Immigration enforcement is a contentious issue in the United States that is often used as a political football. Donald Trump's 2016 campaign and subsequent election to the presidency brought a renewed focus on the US-Mexico border as a symbol of the campaign to keep undocumented migrants out of the country. The president's words and actions also inspired criticism from his political opponents, and from immigrant advocates, who called for humane discourse and softer policies.[1] However, history has not exonerated Trump's political opponents from their own punitive posture toward immigrants. At the completion of his second term, President Barack Obama was credited with creating "the harshest and largest immigration enforcement

---

1. Collinson and Fox, "Outrage Grows."

regime in American history."² Despite the adversarial discourse, neither political party has garnered the political will to enact comprehensive immigration reform, which has been in discussion since 2001 and debated three times in the US Senate. Furthermore, both parties have made significant contributions to the criminalization of immigrants and the creation of a system designed to remove them from society. As the following discussion illustrates, blueprints for the US detention and deportation regime were drafted under President Reagan. Regardless of who is in the White House or which party controls Congress, the system has continued to grow since the 1980s. The US now oversees the largest immigrant detention system in the world.[3]

One result of this bipartisan consensus is broad acceptance of the notion that immigrants who do not enter the United States "the right way" should not be allowed to remain. Broad acceptance of this narrative can be a stumbling block for churches and faith-based organizations who wish to be in solidarity with migrants.[4] Those with compassion for the plight of undocumented immigrants fleeing violence, poverty, or persecution may operate out of a personal piety telling them it is wrong to break the law. Shouldn't undocumented immigrants be held accountable for their crimes? Faith leaders and activists have found that their members' discomfort with criminality can be a source of division and that strategies to mitigate this discomfort are necessary to mobilize their communities in support of migrants.[5]

In what follows, I hope to demonstrate that "criminal" is a slippery category and that the various immigration "crisis" moments in the last forty years are crises of the government's own making. I begin by describing the expansion of immigrant detention practices since the 1980s. I illustrate enforcement trends by surveying some of the relevant laws and policies as well as their effects on the detention system. This section will include a brief overview of the phenomenon some legal scholars are calling "crimmigration." As the lines blur between immigration law and criminal law, both corresponding detention systems expand with new pathways by which immigrants are forced in. Next, I describe how unprecedented growth in immigrant detention has contributed to the development of the prison-industrial complex (PIC). I indicate how the system implicates corporations, government entities, and everyday workers and citizens. I also include some details about a prison

2. Nowrasteh, "Obama's Mixed Legacy," subheading.

3. Young, *Forever Prisoners*, 17.

4. Throughout the chapter I address the role of "churches and faith-based organizations." I frame it in this way to confess my perspective as a Christian theologian and to acknowledge the interfaith nature of much immigrant advocacy work.

5. Freeland, "Negotiating Place, Space and Borders," 493, 497.

work program that exposes the degree to which private prison companies rely on criminalized detainees to make their line of business profitable. In the final section, I describe how churches and advocacy organizations can inadvertently uphold the logic behind the immigrant detention apparatus by failing to critically challenge the criminalization narrative, even as they advocate for individuals and families they see as victims of an unjust system. I conclude by suggesting strategies to examine immigrant advocacy practices in faith-based activism. A new framework may allow us to accompany immigrant communities more holistically, not by obscuring the criminality of migrants, but by problematizing the laws that made them criminal.

Changes in Immigration Law and Enforcement Since the 1980s

Legal scholars began recognizing a phenomenon they call "crimmigration" in the early 2000s. They noted a shift from civil proceedings to criminal ones in prosecuting immigrants.[6] Civil immigration law and criminal law, which had been separated in US judicial tradition, remained separate in name only while in practice they became deeply intertwined and mutually constitutive.[7] I have employed this lens, drawing on legal and sociological scholarship of immigration policy and enforcement since the 1980s. Elliott Young cautions that these trends should not be too closely associated with the war on drugs or 9/11, which are featured in the discussion that follows, as there are precedents for detention practices that criminalize and racialize immigrants.[8] I choose to begin with the 1980s because of this volume's focus on the PIC. As that system has developed meaningfully since the 1980s, exponential growth in immigrant detention has come alongside it.

The War on Drugs

The mass immigrant detention trends that are so pervasive today emerged from the US war on drugs.[9] The Anti-Drug Abuse Act of 1986 made drug offenses grounds for inadmissibility to the United States for the first time.[10]

    6. Stumpf, "Crimmigration Crisis," 371.

    7. Stumpf, "Crimmigration Crisis," 376.

    8. Young, *Forever Prisoners*, 7. Historical examples of immigrant detention include the incarceration of Chinese immigrants in the late nineteenth century and high rates of immigrants confined to insane asylums in the early twentieth century.

    9. Stumpf, "Civil Detention," 58–59.

    10. Kurzban, "Democracy and Immigration," 64.

Noncitizens who had previously been fined for drug offenses, either in the US or in their countries of origin, suddenly faced the possibility of deportation, even if the offense occurred before the act was passed. In like manner, the Alien Criminal Apprehension Program of 1986 established cooperation between the Federal Bureau of Prisons (BOP) and the Immigration and Naturalization Service (INS) to identify migrants with criminal records, including those who had already completed their sentences.[11]

Perhaps the more impactful legislation from this period is the Omnibus Anti-Drug Abuse Act of 1988, which established a new category of offense, the "aggravated felony." Regardless of an individual's immigration status, a noncitizen charged with an aggravated felony may face particularly harsh immigration enforcement consequences, such as deportation without a removal hearing, ineligibility for cancellation of removal, and permanent inadmissibility to the United States.[12] It may also render someone ineligible for voluntary departure. The alternative to voluntary departure, removal, often makes legal reentry impossible for at least ten years.[13]

After an aggravated felony conviction, authorized immigrants, including permanent residents, may serve a sentence for the criminal conviction, only to be transferred to Immigration and Customs Enforcement (ICE) custody for removal proceedings. Although the aggravated felony category originally referred to a narrow set of violations (drug and weapon trafficking, murder), Congress has gradually added new offenses to the list. The category includes criminalized acts that in other situations may be considered low-level felonies or misdemeanors. By the 2010s, a mother of three who had been brought to the US as a child could be deported for a ten-year-old $1500 check fraud conviction for which she had long since completed her criminal sentence.[14]

Although immigrant detention and deportation grew out of drug enforcement policies, they now operate on their own accord. In fact, recent federal enforcement priorities have shifted away from the war on drugs, allocating more resources to concentrate intensely on immigration enforcement.[15] In 2004, immigration-related offenses surpassed, for the first time, all other types of federal prosecutions, including drug prosecutions.[16]

    11. Karen Douglas and Sáenz, "Criminalization of Immigrants," 211; U.S. Immigration and Customs Enforcement, "Fact Sheet," 3.
    12. American Immigration Council, "Aggravated Felonies."
    13. Ashfaq, "Invisible Removal, Endless Detention," 186.
    14. Young, *Forever Prisoners*, 162.
    15. Kretsedemas and Brotherton, "Open Markets and Militarized Borders?," 4.
    16. Nopper, "Why Black Immigrants Matter," 211.

Tough on Crime

Building on the precedent set by the war on drugs as well as fear of terrorism resulting from such events as the World Trade Center bombing of 1993, the 1990s brought a wave of tough-on-crime policies. The Violent Crime Control and Law Enforcement Act of 1994 made it possible for the first time for immigration officers to order the summary removal of noncitizens. The government no longer had to prove deportability in court if an individual had an aggravated felony conviction on their record. As a result of this change, ICE, which replaced INS in 2003, can incarcerate a noncitizen without due process or bond until removal proceedings are completed. Removal can take anywhere from days or weeks to months or years.[17] Likewise, the Antiterrorism and Effective Death Penalty Act of 1996 placed new limits on the application of habeas corpus for federal prisoners, making it easier for the government to imprison immigration and other federal detainees without recourse for the incarcerated.

The Illegal Immigration Reform and Immigrant Responsibility Act (IIRAIRA) of 1996 further limited legal options for noncitizens. It promoted deportation for unauthorized migrants and made reentry more evasive.[18] IIRAIRA expanded the list of aggravated felonies. It built on the Personal Responsibility and Work Opportunity Reconciliation Act of 1996, which barred immigrants from many social programs, by expanding the basis for the removal of legal migrants who are judged to be a potential public charge.[19] The act also "mandated detention for most people convicted of crimes thus limiting the discretion individual judges can exercise in considering humane and mitigating factors in a case that would justify the release of even the most sympathetic individuals."[20] IIRAIRA set a precedent for cooperation between federal and local law enforcement on matters of immigration control, a trend discussed below. The tough-on-crime policies of the 1990s generated demand for a larger immigration enforcement apparatus. Between 1993 and 1999, the budget for INS tripled, from $1.5 billion to $4.2 billion a year.[21]

Although the narrative shifted after 9/11, tough-on-crime remains an influential framework in political discourse. In a 2014 address to the nation, President Obama famously noted that his administration was concerned

---

17. Kurzban, "Democracy and Immigration," 65.
18. Brotherton and Kretsedemas, "Annotated List of Immigration Laws," 377.
19. Brotherton and Kretsedemas, "Annotated List of Immigration Laws," 376–77.
20. Ashfaq, "Invisible Removal, Endless Detention," 183.
21. Karen Douglas and Sáenz, "Criminalization of Immigrants," 204.

about "felons, not families. Criminals, not children. Gang members, not a mom who's working hard to provide for her kids."[22] This was to highlight the way his administration prioritized the deportation of migrants with criminal records. The problem with this characterization, as many analysts have noted, is that putting "families" and "felons" into such contrast creates a false dichotomy.[23] "Moms" can commit crimes, and the list of deportable offenses has grown dramatically since the 1980s. Moreover, the distinction becomes meaningless in a world where the act of entering the country without authorization is made a crime.

9/11 and Creation of the Department of Homeland Security

Although the US established several harsh immigration laws during the Clinton Administration, these were better resourced and more fully deployed by the Bush Administration with the political will developed in response to the September 11, 2001, terror attacks.[24] The Enhanced Border Security and Visa Entry Reform Act of 2002 formalized connections between antiterrorism work and immigration enforcement, including investment in technologies meant to enhance border control.[25] The Uniting and Strengthening America by Providing Appropriate Tools Required to Intercept and Obstruct Terrorism (USA PATRIOT) Act of 2001 tripled the number of border patrol agents at the northern border of the United States, established a special registry for Arab and Muslim immigrants, and indicated deportation as a penalty for failure to comply.[26] These trends were further realized with the creation of the cabinet-level Department of Homeland Security (DHS) in 2002. Better coordination between federal law enforcement agencies and with state and local governments was a key objective in creating DHS.[27] All immigration and border security functions were moved into the department, and two new agencies, ICE and US Customs and Border Protection (CBP), were created. Under DHS, the number of border agents increased from 10,000 in 2003 to 17,000 in 2008, while ICE agents increased from 2,700 to 5,000.[28]

22. Obama, "Remarks by the President," para. 14.
23. Young, *Forever Prisoners*, 183.
24. Chishti et al., "Obama Record on Deportations."
25. Brotherton and Kretsedemas, "Annotated List of Immigration Laws," 378.
26. Karen Douglas and Sáenz, "Criminalization of Immigrants," 206.
27. Bush, *Department of Homeland Security*, 2.
28. Chishti et al., "Obama Record on Deportations."

The post-9/11 era also mobilized immigration law to eliminate some of the protections that had previously provided noncitizens with legal channels that could shorten detention stays and prevent deportation. The REAL ID Act of 2005 allowed judges to deny asylum claims and other measures to prevent removal based on an individual's demeanor in the courtroom, paving the way for a judge's individual biases or cultural insensitivities to determine the outcome of an immigration proceeding.[29] It also introduced more rigorous criteria for asylum claims and eliminated habeas corpus for Convention Against Torture claims that could otherwise protect a noncitizen from deportation to a hostile receiving country.[30]

In the post-9/11 era, the federal government discovered that immigration law provided more efficient strategies to control noncitizens than the criminal justice system ever had.[31] The Military Commissions Act of 2006 allowed the government to use immigration laws to detain noncitizens indefinitely without a criminal trial.[32] Thus, immigrants who never had had due process were rounded up and deported, carrying the stigma of criminal terrorists with them to their countries of citizenship.[33] Immigration law allowed the government to use racial profiling as grounds to initiate an investigation against an individual, a precondition that would render evidence inadmissible in a criminal court.[34] Although much of this "anti-terrorism" legislation was initially aimed at migrants from certain Muslim and Arab countries, it transformed the whole immigration enforcement and detention apparatus for noncitizens of many racial and national identities. In 2004 only 4 percent of people apprehended on immigration violations were from the government's list of countries representing "terrorist threats," and only a small number of these were apprehended for national security–related concerns. That same year, 71 percent of immigration apprehensions were of Mexican nationals.[35] Although fear of terrorism might have been used to justify increased spending on immigration enforcement, immigrants did not need to be suspected terrorists to feel the effects of the enhanced system.

---

29. Ashfaq, "Invisible Removal, Endless Detention," 192.

30. Brotherton and Kretsedemas, "Annotated List of Immigration Laws," 378; Ashfaq, "Invisible Removal, Endless Detention," 192.

31. Sheikh, "Racializing, Criminalizing, and Silencing," 89; Arriaga, "Understanding Crimmigration," 806. See also T. Miller, "Blurring the Boundaries," 96.

32. Kurzban, "Democracy and Immigration," 67.

33. Sheikh, "Racializing, Criminalizing, and Silencing," 95.

34. Karen Douglas and Sáenz, "Criminalization of Immigrants," 206.

35. Nopper, "Why Black Immigrants Matter," 206-7.

Increased Cooperation Between Government Entities

One of the first times in recent history that the federal government relied on local governments to hold immigrants was upon the arrival of Haitians and Mariel Cubans during the Reagan Administration.[36] The 1996 IIRAIRA included provision 287(g), which allowed officers of state and local policing agencies to enforce immigration law on behalf of the federal government. The program grew through the years so that, by 2011, sixty-eight separate law enforcement agencies were participating.[37]

Another program, the Criminal Alien Program, was created in 2007. This program allows ICE to request local jails to hold undocumented immigrants on detainers. Under this program, local governments keep noncitizens behind bars after they have completed their sentences. This is to make time for ICE agents to come and arrest them on their immigration violations. These types of arrests now account for most ICE apprehensions.[38]

The Secure Communities program was created in 2008. This program gives ICE access to an FBI database to view biometric data for people in local jails and compare it to their own records. Under President Bush, the program was optional for states. The Obama Administration made it mandatory.[39] In 2015, the Priority Enforcement Program replaced Secure Communities. This change was short lived, however, as President Trump reinstated Secure Communities and the 287(g) program in 2017.

Zero Tolerance

President Trump is well known for his zero-tolerance policy on unauthorized entry, but this policy was not without precedent. Operation Streamline, established in 2005 by DHS and DOJ, mandates that all migrants who enter the US without documentation be "detained while awaiting trial, prosecuted with a misdemeanor or felony charge, and eventually deported."[40] The previous practice had been for immigrants to be released after an initial encounter with CBP to await immigration proceedings, with the exception of Mexican immigrants, who were often kept in detention.[41] "Operation

36. Nopper, "Why Black Immigrants Matter," 228.
37. Young, *Forever Prisoners*, 167.
38. Amuedo-Dorantes and Lopez, "Immigration Policy, Immigrant Detention," 438.
39. Nowrasteh, "Obama's Mixed Legacy."
40. Doty and Wheatley, "Private Detention," 431.
41. Karen Douglas and Sáenz, "Criminalization of Immigrants," 206.

Streamline led to a quadrupling of criminal prosecutions for first-time illegal entry or reentry from 4,000 in 2003 to 16,500 in 2005. As Operation Streamline expanded from Texas to all border states except California, criminal prosecutions grew to 44,000 in 2010 and peaked at 97,000 in 2013."[42] The act dramatically increased the demand for detention beds by criminalizing violations that would previously have been handled through civil immigration proceedings.[43]

In May of 2017, CBP began enforcing the Criminal Consequence Initiative, a new iteration of Operation Streamline. Under this policy, children could be separated from their families while parents faced prosecution. This led to 234 separations between July and December of 2017.[44] Then, in November of that year, CBP mandated that all families be slated for expedited removal. This required that families be held for the duration of removal proceedings unless family detention facilities were full.[45] Finally, in April 2018 DOJ instructed its prosecutors to prioritize immigration crimes. Thus, migrants who were apprehended at the US-Mexico border were handed over to DOJ rather than remaining under the jurisdiction of DHS. DHS began separating families in higher volumes as DOJ was not authorized to detain children. From July 2017 to June 2018, when the president ended family separation by executive order amid public outcry, 3,900 to 4,100 migrant children had been placed in government custody.[46]

President Trump also gave an executive order in January 2017 that imposed priority arrest status on all unauthorized immigrants. Because so many resources were going to the border and political shifts were causing some local communities to stop cooperating with ICE, arrests and removals decreased under Trump compared to his predecessor.[47] There was, however, a significant shift in the numbers of migrants whose only crime was illegal entry arrested under Trump's leadership. Thirty-two percent of people arrested by ICE in 2020 had no criminal record, compared to 14 percent in 2016.[48]

While Trump sought to dramatize the arrival of migrant caravans and portray the situation on the border as an urgent scenario in need of a strong response, it was a government-produced crisis. Border apprehensions during

---

42. Young, *Forever Prisoners*, 164.
43. Doty and Wheatley, "Private Detention," 431.
44. Bolter et al., *Four Years of Profound Change*, 31.
45. Bolter et al., *Four Years of Profound Change*, 32.
46. Bolter et al., *Four Years of Profound Change*, 33.
47. Bolter et al., *Four Years of Profound Change*, 3.
48. Bolter et al., *Four Years of Profound Change*, 4.

the Trump Administration were at their lowest since the early 1970s.[49] The backlog of asylum cases, and the resulting shortages of immigration judges and detention facilities, were direct results of the administration's aggressive immigration enforcement priorities.[50]

An Excursus on the Biden Administration

Two years into his presidency, Joe Biden's record on immigration was still uncertain, and the impacts of the COVID-19 pandemic make it difficult to interpret the statistics. Initial analysis indicates that, much like President Obama, Biden's success in reforming the system was mixed. On the one hand, Biden de-prioritized interior enforcement; interior removals decreased to 28,200 in 2022 compared to an average of 81,000 per year under President Trump and 155,000 per year under President Obama.[51] On the other hand, ICE nearly doubled its administrative arrests from 2021 to 2022, a figure that can be attributed to ICE's support of CBP in responding to a surge in apprehensions at the southwest border.[52] The administration developed a "parole" program that allows Venezuelan, Haitian, Cuban, and Nicaraguan migrants to enter the country legally and apply for a two-year work permit, while simultaneously vowing to expand the use of expedited removal for those who enter without authorization.[53] The Biden Administration expanded the use of alternatives to detention, which use technologies like cell phone apps and ankle monitors to track noncitizens while they await their immigration hearing, and vowed to decrease ICE's daily detention capacity, but even a Democratic Congress refused the proposed decrease.[54] With Republicans in control of the House, it is difficult to imagine that Biden might have had any more success moving forward. Biden's mixed record reveals the inertia of a system that was built over many decades through bipartisan appeals to law and order.

---

49. United States Border Patrol, "Southwest Border Sectors."
50. Young, *Forever Prisoners*, 170.
51. Chishti and Bush-Joseph, "Biden at Two-Year Mark."
52. U.S. Immigration and Customs Enforcement, "ICE Releases FY2022 Annual Report."
53. White House, "Fact Sheet: Biden-Harris Administration."
54. Chishti and Bush-Joseph, "Biden at Two-Year Mark."

Impacts on the Prison-Industrial Complex

The strain on the immigrant detention system that became apparent during the latter years of the Trump Administration is revelatory of a trend that has been growing since the 1980s. Both the criminalization of undocumented immigrants and the use of immigration procedures to prosecute crimes for authorized migrants led to dramatic increases in the numbers of noncitizens in detention. It is difficult to capture these trends through detention numbers alone as reporting on noncitizens in detention is not consistent from one state to the next and federal reporting can change from year to year based on the whims of an administration. Additionally, even the so-called raw data can be misleading. Elliot Young notes that, for 2016, DOJ counted 83,000 noncitizens in federal or state custody, while the Cato Institute estimated the number at 160,000.[55] Therefore, while noting that the historical developments surveyed above have contributed significantly to the numbers of noncitizens in DOJ custody, I will explore the growth of immigrant detention through ICE contracts.

The demand for immigrant detention beds is up. ICE detained about 20,000 people per day when it was created.[56] Even then, the system could not keep up with the demand. The ICE strategic plan from 2003 notes that an increased detention population, higher numbers of "criminal" detainees, and an aging system was straining the agency's ability to imprison immigrants in its service processing centers.[57] In the years that followed, ICE began to rely heavily on service agreements with private prisons and with state and local jails to meet the growing demand. By 2009, 16 percent of ICE detainees were held in private prisons.[58]

ICE initiated reforms during the early years of the Obama Administration, including the cancellation of some private prison contracts, but President Trump reversed this trend decisively.[59] Under Trump, the immigration detention system expanded by over 50 percent; the administration signed contracts for more than forty new detention facilities.[60] By 2018, 65

---

55. Young, *Forever Prisoners*, 164–65.
56. Siskin, *Immigration-Related Detention*, 13.
57. Immigration and Customs Enforcement, *Endgame*, 2–6.
58. Schriro, *Immigration Detention Overview*, 15. This percentage does not include the many federal, state, and local facilities that are owned by government entities but operated by private corporations. I discuss the complexities of such arrangements below.
59. Luan, "Profiting from Enforcement."
60. Cho, "More of the Same."

percent of immigration detainees were held in private prisons.[61] By January 2020, that percentage had climbed to 81 and did not decrease significantly under the Biden Administration, despite decreases in migrants crossing the border as a result of the COVID-19 pandemic and related policies.[62]

In the words of one prison company, "immigrants are not just a problem, they are an opportunity."[63] Although the industry claims it does not "lobby for or against policies or legislation that would determine the basis for or duration of an individual's incarceration or detention,"[64] it has also acknowledged that legislative and administrative changes that relax immigration enforcement could negatively impact its ability to make a profit.[65] For example, Corrections Corporation of America (CCA—now CoreCivic) was seriously considering closing in 2004 as it struggled to fill detention beds. Instead, the company invested $3 million in lobbying that year to leverage increasing demands for places to incarcerate immigrants.[66] GEO Group is notorious for its political entanglements. Its founder, George Zoley, was a major contributor to President George W. Bush's reelection campaign in 2004. By 2007 GEO Group had earned more than $100 million from its immigrant detention business alone.[67] These political efforts continue into the present. A 2021 study of prison political action committees found that such PACs were more likely to donate to legislators after they had cosponsored punitive immigration legislation and that, while Republican lawmakers were more likely to receive funding from the industry, Democrats who cosponsored punitive bills related to immigration were disproportionately rewarded compared to their colleagues across the aisle.[68] The study authors conclude that Democrats are being rewarded for taking political risks when they support harsh legislation on immigration.[69]

The political strategies of private prison corporations are paying off. ICE detention now accounts for about one quarter of the revenue for both GEO Group and CoreCivic, the nation's two largest private prison

61. Eisen, "Trump's First Year."
62. Cho, "More of the Same," paras. 5–6.
63. Advertisement for ComDef Tucson Conference, 2006; as cited in Doty and Wheatley, "Private Detention," 432.
64. CoreCivic, "Political and Lobbying Activity," para. 1.
65. CCA, *2014 Annual Report*, 24.
66. Trujillo-Pagán, "Emphasizing the 'Complex,'" 42.
67. Trujillo-Pagán, "Emphasizing the 'Complex,'" 42.
68. Morín et al., "Cosponsoring and Cashing In," 501.
69. Morín et al., "Cosponsoring and Cashing In," 502.

companies.⁷⁰ In 2019, CoreCivic's ICE detention contracts contributed $574 million in revenue, while GEO's revenue from ICE contracts totaled $708 million.⁷¹ Furthermore, ICE contracts have helped prison corporations to make up for revenues lost under the Biden Administration due to criminal justice reforms and cancelled contracts with the BOP, even when those cancellations resulted from poor conditions in the prisons.⁷² President Biden came under scrutiny from immigrant advocates, who claimed that his administration's sanctioning of private immigration detention contracts violated campaign promises.⁷³

Lucrative contracts are made even more profitable by an immigrant work program that allows ICE contractors to exploit the labor of immigration detainees. According to ICE's Performance-Based National Detention Standards, detainees are permitted to "volunteer" for work assignments that are meant to enhance "essential operations and services . . . through detainee productivity" with the additional benefit of improving morale and discipline among detainees.⁷⁴ In exchange for their labor, detainees are to be compensated with a minimum of $1 per day, which ICE reimburses to prison contractors.⁷⁵ Thus, although it is illegal to employ immigrants who do not have work authorization, the immigrant detention system is effectively the largest employer of undocumented immigrants in the United States.⁷⁶ A 2015 *New York Times* report estimated that this program saved the government and private companies at least $40 million per year because they do not have to pay the federal minimum wage of $7.25 for basic, required functions like cooking and cleaning in their facilities.⁷⁷ This is a conservative estimate. It does not account for higher minimum wages in some states, like Washington, where GEO Group is being sued by the state and some detainees over its labor practices at the Northwest ICE Processing Center.

70. Cho, "More of the Same," para. 7. Other companies that are major players in the immigration detention business include Akal Security, Inc.; Ahtna Technical Services, LLC; Asset Protection and Security Services LP; and Akima.

71. Cho, "More of the Same," para. 8. Two thousand nineteen was a record year for private detention profits. The COVID-19 pandemic disrupted the detention industry as well as immigration enforcement strategies. It is yet to be seen if and how these industries will fare moving forward.

72. Cho, "More of the Same," para. 10.

73. Orozco, "Major Immigrant Detention Center," para. 14.

74. U.S. Immigration and Customs Enforcement, "5.8 Voluntary Work Program," 405.

75. U.S. Immigration and Customs Enforcement, "5.8 Voluntary Work Program," 407.

76. Hollister, "Litigating ICE's 'Voluntary Work Program,'" para. 1.

77. Urbina, "Using Jailed Migrants," para. 5.

Washington has a minimum wage of $15.74 per hour. GEO Group's annual profits from that facility between 2010 and 2018 ranged from $18.6 to $23.5 million per year.[78]

Some analysts believe that, if ICE contractors were required to pay legally sanctioned wages, it would make immigration detention so expensive that Congress would no longer be willing to authorize spending for the current scale of the system.[79] While the legality of the work program has been questioned from many angles, it has been difficult to cancel the program or increase wages for detainees because of a 1990 federal case that found that immigration detainees are not defined as employees and are exempt from the Fair Labor Standards Act.[80] Increased scrutiny of the private detention industry has brought with it a rise in lawsuits and immigrant labor strikes that highlight new potential legal pathways to reform or end the program. Some campaigns have highlighted situations wherein detainees experience intense pressure to participate in the "voluntary" labor programs, such as threats of solitary confinement if they do not sign up.[81] Litigating based on these instances has limited impact, however, because it applies only to workers who have faced such pressures. Many detainees do not claim these particular abuses and are willing to sign up for the program because it may be their only source of income to purchase essentials such as toothpaste, toilet paper, and phone calls.[82] More effective strategies may seek protections for detainee workers under state labor laws. This was the case in California, where a federal judge recently ruled that detainees are considered employees under state law at one GEO-run facility.[83] Another promising strategy claims that detainee labor is a source of unjust enrichment for ICE contractors. This strategy is being used in the Washington case with some success.[84]

It is yet to be seen what will come of these cases as they move their way through the courts. The outcomes are worthy of attention from immigrant rights advocates; the ICE Voluntary Work Program is one piece of a complex puzzle that makes immigration detention such a profitable business for private prison corporations. These companies are paying detainees $1 a day, less than thirteen cents an hour, to carry out necessary functions for their

78. Nwauzor v. The GEO Group, Inc., D.C. No. 3:17-cv-05769-RJB (9th Cir. Court of Appeals 2023).
79. Starr, "At Low Pay," para. 14.
80. Guevara v. INS, 902 F.2d 394 (5th Cir. 1990).
81. Urbina, "Using Jailed Migrants," para. 23.
82. Hollister, "Litigating ICE's 'Voluntary Work Program,'" para. 2.
83. Romero, "Immigrant Detainees Strike," para. 25.
84. Nwauzor v. The GEO Group.

prisons. Would CoreCivic and GEO be able to keep their businesses afloat if they were not propped up by a system that is essentially legalized slavery? Perhaps a more fundamental question for US citizens and for faith communities is why we allow a private corporation to enslave someone simply because the government has labeled them a criminal.

For-profit corporations are not the only entities that benefit from the unprecedented demand brought about by changes in immigration enforcement. In 2015, 43 percent of ICE facilities were part of an intergovernmental service contract.[85] Local jails, and the communities that surround them, directly benefit from financial compensation in exchange for detaining migrants. According to one 2019 NPR report, ICE may pay a sheriff in Louisiana five times what the state would pay the county for someone convicted of a state-level crime.[86] In their 2013 study of two "prison towns" in Arizona, sociologists Roxanne Lynne Doty and Elizabeth Shannon Wheatley highlighted the ample compensation that often comes with ICE detention arrangements. The city of Eloy, Arizona, received $95 million from ICE, which it passed on to CCA, to receive a kickback of twenty-five cents per day per inmate at the Eloy Detention Center.[87] At the time, CCA was the largest employer in Eloy, which was home to four prisons.[88] In a more recent example, a five-year deal between ICE, GEO Group, and Clearfield County, Pennsylvania, was estimated to bring $263 million in revenue for the county for converting the 1,878-bed Moshannon Valley Correctional Facility into an ICE processing center.[89] GEO Group is the biggest taxpayer in the school district where the facility is located.[90]

The lucrative nature of these contracts leads some small towns to view the prisons as "salvation" when they see no other option to promote survival for their communities.[91] In Doty and Wheatley's study, even those who regretted the presence of the prisons could not imagine an alternative future.[92] The situation in Eloy highlights the "complex" in the prison-industrial complex. While private prison corporations are making enormous profits from immigrant detention and detainee labor, local governments and everyday workers depend on the same system for their livelihood.

85. Ryo and Peacock, "National Study of Immigration Detention," 29.
86. Noguchi, "Unequal Outcomes," para. 21.
87. Doty and Wheatley, "Private Detention," 427.
88. Doty and Wheatley, "Private Detention," 426.
89. Orozco, "Major Immigrant Detention Center," paras. 6, 9.
90. Orozco, "Major Immigrant Detention Center," para. 12.
91. Doty and Wheatley, "Private Detention," 434.
92. Doty and Wheatley, "Private Detention," 438.

Doty and Wheatley also note that, in spite of the government's performance of sovereignty over the lives of immigrants through its incarceration strategy, the tactic has not meaningfully reduced the numbers of undocumented immigrants in the United States.[93] If the immigrant detention system is so ineffective at achieving the stated goals on which it was founded, we should question the ends it actually serves. Punitive immigration enforcement measures allow the government to project the illusion of control over the situation.[94] Meanwhile, private prison corporations and local government entities have a vested interest in the expansion of immigrant detention and, therefore, a financial incentive to destabilize the social order by advocating policies that malign and criminalize immigrants.[95]

While the commodification of immigrant bodies is a boon for some, it results in grievous injuries to immigrants and their communities. Whether or not a migrant crossed the border, and whether that person did so without authorization, the border "surrounds, separates, and follows migrants wherever they go." Immigrants live in fear, pushing them to inhabit shadows and accept substandard wages for their work, within the prisons and beyond them. They may be less likely to seek help for illness, injury, or victimization. Criminalization also produces a state of "perpetual foreignness" that applies even to permanent residents and naturalized citizens who, because of their race, ethnicity, or language, are associated with "criminal aliens."[96]

Faithful Resistance

As pro-detention policies have gradually but decisively intensified in the past several decades, faith communities have noticed and responded. For example, the New Sanctuary Movement (NSM) was established in 2007 as a response to anti-immigrant legislation and high-profile immigrant workplace raids. The movement promotes traditional sanctuary, following the sanctuary movement of the 1980s. Congregations provide housing for immigrants facing deportation, which may allow for more time and resources to formulate a case and prevent removal. NSM also facilitates other types of solidarity such as courtroom accompaniment, detention center visitation, and legal funds. Similarly, in response to the vicious anti-immigrant posture of the Trump Administration, many congregations, which may or may not

---

93. Doty and Wheatley, "Private Detention," 428.
94. Doty and Wheatley, "Private Detention," 428.
95. Karen Douglas and Sáenz, "Criminalization of Immigrants," 221. See also Sjoberg, "Corporate Control of Industry," 98.
96. Chase, "Carceral Networks," 9.

be affiliated with NSM, began hosting know-your-rights trainings and participating in rapid response networks for undocumented migrants in their communities. These activities have undoubtedly benefited the immigrant rights movement by mobilizing human and financial resources and putting pressure on local governments to enact sanctuary city and other noncooperation policies with federal immigration agencies.

Despite this contribution, there is one feature of such faith-based involvement in immigrant advocacy that requires examination if churches and faith-based organizations wish to avoid supporting the expansion of the PIC through immigrant detention. The scandal of family separation has dominated the movement. A desire to make known the "deep suffering caused by family separations" has motivated many people of faith to get involved in immigrant rights advocacy since at least 2007.[97] Gregory Freeland notes that centering this issue has proven to be highly effective because it builds solidarity across political and cultural barriers.[98] As a result, immigrant rights groups have highlighted stories of parents who have been deported, leaving their traumatized children behind in the care of relatives. They have disseminated photos of children sleeping alone in detention cells under mylar blankets.

It is right that Christians should protest such vicious treatment of children and their families. These images and narratives are also meant to challenge unflattering stereotypes.[99] By casting some migrants as victims of an unjust system rather than as criminals, faith-based movements can more easily engage supporters who may otherwise be uncomfortable challenging the government's prosecution of someone who has broken the law.[100] While this strategy may be helpful for recruitment, it also has a negative consequence for immigrants. In centering the experience of immigrants *whose only crime was crossing the border*, activists unwittingly malign those migrants who have committed other crimes and condemn them to detention, exploitation, and deportation under the power of the carceral state.[101] In fact, a criminal record has been among the criteria that exclude immigrants from public support. Some NSM coalitions have required that the immigrants they take into sanctuary have US citizen children, a viable case under current law, a "good work record," and no other criminal convictions.[102]

97. Caminero-Santangelo, "Responding to Human Costs," 120.
98. Freeland, "Negotiating Place, Space and Borders," 492.
99. Yukich, "Constructing the Model Immigrant," 310.
100. Freeland, "Negotiating Place, Space and Borders," 496–97.
101. Yukich, "Constructing the Model Immigrant," 311.
102. Paik, "Abolitionist Futures," 14. See also Freeland, "Negotiating Place, Space and Borders," 494.

In the exploration of immigration law above, I illustrated how changes in both criminal and immigration law have contributed to an expansion of the various types of crimes, such as "aggravated felonies," that are considered deportable offenses. Thus, "criminal" is an unstable category. It is entirely within the government's power to determine who is a criminal and to decide which migrants must be deported for their crimes. When changes to immigration law result in migrants being deported because of decades-old violations for which they have already served their time, it demonstrates that "criminals" are made not only by individual choices to violate the law. They are also produced by the law.[103]

By participating in the "felons, not families" narrative, churches gloss over decades of decisions resulting in the expanding criminalization of immigrants. This approach unwittingly supports the government's detention and deportation regime and allows private prison corporations to continue profiting from the imprisonment and labor of racialized immigrants. As A. Naomi Paik so aptly puts it, "Though many immigrants and advocates respond to federal deportation regimes by asserting that they are not criminals, this defence does not destabilise, but affirms, the legitimacy of criminalisation overall, even while demanding exception to it."[104] In other words, immigrant rights advocates frame individual cases as government overreach but do not question the fundamental logic of a system that casts some immigrants as "so bad" they must be removed. Thus, the family-centered strategy reproduces the very exclusions it was intended to dismantle in its efforts to combat stereotypes.[105] Meanwhile, the government continues to add more categories to its list of "bad" immigrants. Private prison companies, who lobby for this expansion, continue to acquire new contracts.

Focusing efforts on "noncriminal" immigrants facing deportation will become even less impactful as the criminalization of immigrants grows more pervasive and immigration detention becomes more profitable. While continuing to advocate for family togetherness and for comprehensive immigration reform, advocacy groups can contribute to the destabilization of the immigrant detention system by examining the way criminality is leveraged in the immigration policy conversation and in their activism. Therefore, to conclude the chapter, I suggest some strategies and practices for Christian and other faith-based organizations to consider as they incorporate critique of the PIC into their advocacy for a more just immigration system.

---

103. Paik, "Abolitionist Futures" 9.
104. Paik, "Abolitionist Futures," 16.
105. Paik, "Abolitionist Futures," 3.

Learn the History

As the survey above demonstrates, the growth of the immigrant detention system is not an accident. It is the result of decades-long trends that made criminals of immigrants and immigration a crime. Churches and faith-based organizations advocating for immigrants have a responsibility to learn about this history so that they are better equipped to decode the rhetoric used by politicians, including those who seize on the fear of "criminal aliens" to advance their own agenda and those who avert responsibility for a broken immigration system by appealing to law and order.

Follow the Money

Immigrant advocates will be more effective in their solidarity work if they have a basic understanding of who profits from the detention of immigrants. Knowing which public and private entities have ICE contracts in one's region, and how much revenue they bring in, may encourage faith communities to view the immigration debate more critically. Rather than understanding immigration enforcement as a cat-and-mouse game between ICE agents and individual immigrants, members of congregations and organizations could start asking about the laws those ICE agents are enforcing and who lobbied for their passage.

Tend to Moral Injury

Dismantling the immigrant detention apparatus requires accountability for those who benefit from the system. The PIC is an intricate web, touching many aspects of life in the US and around the globe, so assigning responsibility is not as simple as identifying perpetrators and victims. While corporate executives and politicians may stand to gain the most in terms of wealth and power, we all bear responsibility for creating and maintaining the system. Individual workers who are directly employed by the PIC and residents of communities that are sustained by it may feel the responsibility more personally. However, all who have accepted the criminalization narrative, and who have benefited from suppressed migrant wages and valuable stock portfolios, are responsible for the harms done to immigrant communities. It is also important to consider how taxpayer dollars are subsidizing the private prison industry through contracts and worker programs. Attention to these varying levels of responsibility can meaningfully shape the prophetic actions and pastoral resources that communities bring to bear in advocating for better treatment of migrants.

Tell a Different Story

Finally, faith communities can resist the narrative that incarceration is a natural response to immigration as well as the broadly accepted notion that noncitizens do not deserve the same legal protections that citizens expect. Our faith traditions give us different frameworks for criminality and identity that can provide alternatives to the rationale that undergirds the PIC. Churches and Christian organizations facing discomfort with criminality might consider exploring the following themes:

- Jesus was executed by the government. What were his crimes, and why did the Roman Empire deem it necessary to kill him? If we consider that Jesus was a criminal, what difference does it make in how we respond to the law, people who make and enforce laws, and people who break them?

- The apostle Paul wrote of the church that "our citizenship is in heaven" (Phil 3:20). One of Saint Augustine's most well-known books, *The City of God*, explores what it means to have our citizenship in God's kingdom, even as we dwell in earthly nations. What difference does it make to think about US immigration laws if we imagine ourselves to be citizens of heaven instead of, or in addition to, citizens of a particular country?

- Many Christians and other people of faith who were active in the civil rights movement of the 1960s participated in nonviolent civil disobedience. They did this because they believed the law discriminated against Black Americans. Some of those activists were arrested and jailed for their crimes. How might we compare our current immigration system to the unjust laws that led to the civil rights movement? How do Christians know whether we may be called to participate in civil disobedience?

Different congregations and denominations may have similar resources to explore, and interfaith partners can illuminate other sources of wisdom on the matter of criminality. The goal in accessing these traditions is to inspire our communities to see alternatives to the narratives that have acquired such broad consensus in our society and on which the PIC is built. Learning to assess the situation in which immigration detainees so often find themselves through new lenses may help faith-based activists move beyond discomfort with criminality to advocate for immigrants more holistically as friends and neighbors.

In Remembrance

It was a cold night in early November. We were gathered in the church basement once again. This time, the atmosphere was a bit more somber. The last few years had been heart wrenching for the immigrant rights movement. The rhetoric was difficult to stomach, and the politics seemed hopeless.

We had been approached by a local immigrant rights group to partner with them on an art festival to celebrate the Día de los Muertos. Young adults from all over the city were strewn about the floor, painting, making posters, and arranging flowers. Members of our congregation spoke in hushed tones from the kitchen while they prepared a simple meal. In one corner, a Mexican woman who was connected to our congregation had gathered a group of children from the neighborhood to tell them about the festival as she remembered it from her youth.

After the artists had finished their work, one of the community organizers instructed us to put on our coats and gather our art pieces. We carried them out of the church to the metro station that sat a mere two blocks away. There, we constructed our altar. The colorful arrangement of flowers, candles, and sweets was interspersed with photos and names. We said prayers for family members who had died across borders, whose graves we could not visit. We said prayers for immigrants who had died in detention and for immigrants who, because they were deported, had gone silent and were presumed dead. We said prayers for the countless migrants who had disappeared in the treacherous borderlands, whose names were known only to their loved ones.

We remembered them, not as criminals, but as family, as friends, as saints. As we made our way back to the church to share the meal, we left our altar behind for a time in the bustling square. Our candles glowed in the cold, dark night as a stubborn reminder that the US immigration system was killing people who were loved and missed.

Part Four

RESISTING THE BUSINESS OF INCARCERATION

8

"Develop a Love for Freedom"
Education and Power in Prison Systems

ELIZABETH M. BOUNDS

Getting In/Introduction

We start at six a.m. in a parking lot in complete darkness. Then there is the ride, weaving through the crazed traffic on the perimeter and on the interstate, followed by the easier drive on the smaller state highway. Just past the schoolbus graveyard and the Chik-fil-A billboard, we turn off, hugging concrete walls and chain fences topped with loops of barbed wire until we reach the prison parking lot. We make our way through the entrance sally port[1]—that is, through signing in, checking IDs, scanning of book bags and persons for illegal items, and jostling with staff and officers in the small entrance area. All of us are subject to standard operating procedures (SOPs)—the correctional rule book with prison-specific variation that bans countless items, from cell phones (which enable unauthorized contacts) to wire-bound notebooks (wire can be used as a weapon) to gum (which can be used to jam automatic gates). We volunteers in particular are subject to whatever is the current authoritative interpretation of the SOPs, often determined by the mood and stress level of a particular officer.

---

1. A sally port is a secure, controlled entry way, usually with two sets of doors and a guard. It is a military term, originally referring to the protected entry of a castle.

It is always a relief when we are actually inside. We navigate two more locked doors and a set of gates, walking through the entrance and administrative buildings. When we finally reach the main part of the yard and turn downhill on the roofed walkway, we see clusters of women[2] in khaki yelling out to those farther away, while officers in blue in turn yell at the women to keep moving. We make it to the B building and go to the open right-hand corridor door, where Officer Y, on duty, is located. A short, compact woman in the standard blue uniform, she is trying to mark down names and collect IDs as a few women cluster at the door, shouting out their names and waving paper strips of their weekly schedules, which they must have at all times. In theory, the prison must know at every minute the location of every single one of the more than one thousand women incarcerated here. Prison-wide counts happen at least four times a day, and if the numbers of who is where do not add up, everything shuts down until it does. Not surprisingly, I have experienced innumerable shutdowns over the years, waiting for the count to clear.

Waving a greeting at the officer, we squeeze through the crowded door and start down a long dull green hall, with a row of doors on each side. We have made it to the education "hall," two parallel hallways of classrooms on either side of a gym where everything called "education"—from GED classes to behavioral classes to college classes—occurs. As does our theological certificate program.[3]

~

From the moment plans were made for the first US prison,[4] key contested questions have shaped US prison education. One foundational question has always been: *Why education at all?* The degree of support for education depends upon what has been considered the prevailing purpose of punishment. The purposes generally cited are retribution, rehabilitation, incapacitation (separating criminal from community), deterrence (discouraging criminal behavior), and restitution. Prisons were founded as alternatives to

---

2. My use of "women" here is a shorthand that I will generally employ throughout this work. While this institution is classified as a women's institution, there are, in fact, a number of persons inside who do not identity as female. Although this shorthand is exclusionary, I choose it over different possible collective nouns such as "students" because over the years "the women" has become an important positive reference among those who teach there.

3. Prison descriptions and quotations come from an unpublished, IRB-approved research study of the certificate program, Bounds et al., "Incarcerated Women's Understanding," which I carried out with three other co-investigators.

4. In 1790, a block of solitary cells was added to Walnut Street Jail in Philadelphia to provide a new type of incarceration, a "penitentiary house."

the harsh physical retributive punishments of the premodern world, where public physical punishment was used to demonstrate the power of the rulers. Putting people in closed and disciplined environments was considered a modern, rehabilitative improvement. However, while the US prison system has generally claimed a rehabilitative mission, it has far more often functioned to incapacitate and punish retributively. For those who believe that punishment is simply for the purposes of retribution, there is no reason for education, which would be superfluous to punishment. For those who believe punishment is for the purposes of rehabilitation, some kind of formative and educative process is essential in order to enable the person to return to the community as an "acceptable" citizen.[5]

However, even if education is accepted as part of prison programming, there are three further questions. The first is: *For what purposes do we educate?* To create better Christians? More obedient citizens? More productive workers? Then: *Who should be educated?* For reasons generally linked to race and gender, not all those confined may be deemed deserving of education. Finally, there is the question: *What kind(s) of education should be offered?*

These questions are, of course, always asked about education. Until modernity, education was only for elites, the citizen leaders in ancient Greece or the aristocratic lords in later Western Europe. However, with modern industrial nation-states came a requirement for workers to have certain skills and for citizens to have participatory capacities. As the idea of citizenship slowly became more inclusive and the need for more skilled labor more evident, the question of education became more urgent. The sociologist Émile Durkheim, considering the challenge of legitimacy in the newly formed modern states, believed education, particularly moral education, was key to teaching the discipline for what he termed the "wholesome self-control" required for social order.[6] In the development of compulsory public education in the US, concern for authority was woven together with commitments to "equality" expressed in a "comprehensive" approach, which rejected the forms of class tracking used in Europe. The same kind of education was, in principle, to be offered to all.

Of course, the principle has often not been the practice, particularly for African Americans and other persons of color, especially when incarcerated. The answers prison education gave to the key questions above have been shaped both by the dominant understandings of the purposes of

---

5. The five purposes of punishment generally cited are retribution, rehabilitation, incapacitation, deterrence, and restitution. Deterrence (making the punishment a deterring example to others) and incapacitation (removing the person from society) align with retribution in terms of education, while restitution can be linked to rehabilitation.

6. Durkheim, *Moral Education*, 49.

punishment, ranging between retribution and rehabilitation, along with the dominant educational currents. The two main purposes of prison education—disciplinary and therapeutic—track the retributive and rehabilitative purposes. These purposes can operate in multiple ways and can co-exist in different combinations at different times in any one form of education. One type of education may have therapeutic goals such as moral formation and/or moral/psychological improvement. Another may simply provide cheap labor for profit or for institutional maintenance. These opportunities may be distributed differently, with certain types of incarcerated persons receiving more disciplinary forms of education and others receiving more therapeutic forms. Or access to a therapeutic educational program can depend upon disciplinary records, so that therapeutic forms are being used for disciplinary purposes.

Christian theologies have been formative to both the disciplinary and therapeutic visions. A disciplinary emphasis draws upon a certain strand of Calvinism, emphasizing the depravity of humans redeemed through a powerful God. This God requires suffering and obedience as the price of redemption. The therapeutic vision has roots in the more optimistic Evangelicalism shaped by the Second Great Awakening, which touted the redemption of defective human nature by the act of turning to a "loving but offended Father."[7]

Also present in this contested educational space, however, have been fragile threads of transformative education. Such education aims to enable incarcerated persons to develop their own "practices of freedom," as Paolo Freire puts it, whether in a prison classroom or alone in their cell.[8] In theological terms, this thread connects to the idea of a God who frees and a faith that forms a transforming and loving community. This thread also has been found in secular liberal arts models aiming to form persons who, as Amy Gutmann puts it, "creatively and constructively understand their world . . . with a more comprehensive understanding."[9]

Where do I stand after over two decades of teaching inside women's prisons, including founding/administering a theological certificate program to provide higher educational opportunities in a women's prison? Central to my work has been the effort to support moments of transformative education, use forms of therapeutic education positively, and resist disciplinary frameworks. As I thought about how to write about the "business" of prison

7. Wines, *True Penitent*, 30. See also Bounds, "What Must I Do."

8. My understanding of the ongoing reality, historical and current, of those inside educating themselves in their own practices of freedom connects to what Vincent Lloyd and Josh Dubler call "a religious spirit of abolition" (*Break Every Yoke*, 193–227).

9. Gutmann, "What Makes a University Education," paras. 31–32.

education, I realized that the journey to our classrooms, with which I began this essay, where we pass by classrooms offering different forms of education, tracks the historical development of prison education. Therefore, I frame the first part of this chapter, where I give an overview of the history of prison education, with accounts of this journey, ending with the current critical moment where the slow return of Pell monies has opened up new possibilities for access to higher education. There I will pause between two corridors to sketch current forms of education.

While I will occasionally draw upon the voices of our students throughout this essay, in the final section, I will give a portrait of our classrooms. There I use our classroom work as small moments of education as resistance and transformation, pointing to creativity, hope, and possibility. These fragments of flourishing[10] are always in tension with the surrounding realities of structured power where education is a means of control. I suggest how the Christian theological framing of our program understands punishment, redemption, and worth quite differently than the Christian theologies that shaped the early nineteenth-century education and that continue to shape many forms of prison education today. Finally, I will suggest what it means for prison education to enable practices of freedom, or as Illianna, an incarcerated student put it, to "develop a love for freedom."

Top of Corridor/Beginnings of Education

Passing down the hall, we look into different classrooms. The first rooms, on both sides of the hall, are rooms for GED test preparation and for the charter schools. When I first started working in this system, there were few GED prep classes available, and I was told by my inside students that a person had to be within five years of release to be permitted to do the GED classes. However, in recent years, the state Department of Corrections has worked hard to provide broader access to high school diplomas and GEDs. In several states, inmates under a certain age are required to enroll in the GED, but here participation is voluntary, except for juveniles under eighteen with an adult sentence. There are "fast-track" GED classes for those who have tested well in math and reading, which take ten to twelve weeks to prepare for the test offered every month. There are regular GED programs that take twelve months. Women inside who are under twenty-one may attend a charter school program, which offers the more prestigious high school diploma. Several lifers I know have teachers' aides as their work detail (which is a very desirable placement, in contrast to something like kitchen duty or bathroom cleaning). I generally hear about

10. Curtis, "Fragmented Flourishing."

passing the GED test and little about the classes themselves. Looking at the room packed with small desks, with a large teacher desk, I suspect that most material is taught to the test—which of course is what happens in "regular" high schools! Usually a couple of these women emerge to say hello as we move down the hall. Because of the never-ending challenges of getting people cleared to leave their "dormitories,"[11] none of our various students seem to have arrived, so we have time to talk.

～

When Thomas Eddy built the first New York prison in 1796, he insisted upon educational programs because "it is generally from ignorance and corrupt manners that crimes proceed."[12] Unlike the previous forms of public physical punishment, the secluded and controlled prison environment, considered a progressive innovation, allowed for programs of reformation. However, the predominant opinion was (and often still is) that such reforming required prisons to be places of fear and suffering. As such, they could serve both as a warning to potential criminals and as transformative environments where, as the first paid chaplain in the US put it, experiencing the "furnace of affliction" would lead to redemption.[13] Protestant Calvinist notions of redemption at the hands of an angry God framed this vision. In its service, all aspects of prison life were to shape the sinner, from the architecture to the schedule to forms of discipline. The concrete program for redemption would come through enforced labor to counter idleness and through spiritual teaching to overcome sinfulness.

For much of the nineteenth century, education meant Christian formation under the purview of the chaplain. The warden at Auburn prison in New York in the 1820s, Gershom Powers, "wanted ministers not only to teach basic reading and writing to inmates in Sunday school but also to instruct inmates in the humility and degradation proper to their position."[14] By the mid-nineteenth century, penology began to turn from explicitly theological language to more therapeutic language, seeing the criminal as someone to be cured rather than as someone to be redeemed. The reformed

---

11. Dormitory is the official language for prison housing units, signifying some kind of collective living, which can range from two-bed to multiple-bed units. It is used in contrast to "cell," which is a one-person locked unit. For me, dormitories are the housing I had in college and resonate with friendship and connection. While there are indeed friendships and connections in these dormitories, the word in this context feels false to me.

12. Graber, *Furnace of Affliction*, 33.

13. Graber, *Furnace of Affliction*, 54–55.

14. Graber, *Furnace of Affliction*, 87.

Evangelicalism of the Second Great Awakening was part of this reframing, as severe Calvinism was softened through a more liberal theology that "downgraded the role of suffering in moral growth."[15] Chaplains were part of the curative process but maintained a focus on moral formation rather than on broader education.

More comprehensive educational programming began with the reformatory movements in the 1870s. In its 1870 Declaration of Principles, the new National Prison Association (NPA) stated:

> Education is a vital force in the reformation of fallen men and women. Its tendency is to quicken the intellect, inspire self-respect, excite to higher aims, and afford a healthful substitute for low and vicious amusements. Education is, therefore, a matter of primary importance in prisons, and should be carried to the utmost extent consistent with the other purposes of such institutions.[16]

A founder of the NPA, Zebulon Brockway, introduced both higher and vocational education carried out by professional teachers at his new reformatory for young men in Elmira, New York.[17] For Brockway, education was a critical part of the overall reform that should occur inside. However, his educational vision was linked to disciplinary incentives. Rather than being sentenced to serve a particular amount of time, a person's sentence was determined by their overall performance inside—grades, work habits, obedience, etc., as reported by the warden to the relevant managing board. As a result, Brockway wrote, "each day . . . each prisoner felt the pressure of some of duty the observance of which gained a credit, or neglect of which involved a loss; the effect being a help or hindrance toward release."[18]

Although education beyond religious formation began to be seen as a regular part of prison life, relatively few prisons had either the interest or the resources to implement the kinds of programs that reformers like Brockway envisioned. As legal scholar Edgardo Rotman puts it, by the end of the nineteenth century, "rudimentary education programs, prison libraries, and the intercessions of official chaplains affected only an insignificant portion of the prison population."[19] However, by 1918, all US children were required to attend primary school, and compulsory education through

15. Clark, "'Sacred Rights of the Weak,'" 472.
16. American Correctional Association Congress of Correction, *Resolutions*, 5.
17. At first the reformatory programs had the incarcerated engage in crafts and industrial production, but these programs were attacked by emerging labor unions.
18. Brockway, *Fifty Years of Prison Service*, 317.
19. Rotman, "Failure of Reform," 156.

secondary school became more common.[20] The growing assumption that primary and secondary education were a right and a requirement led to more self-conscious development of prison education programs. In 1928, Austin MacCormick, a Northern reformer, conducted an overall survey of prison education, which revealed virtually no regular educational programs. A standing committee of the American Prison Association (formerly NPA) on education was formed and, finally, in 1945 the Correctional Education Association was founded, which developed standards for accrediting prison educational programs.

Lack of educational programming was partly due to the ongoing reluctance to support the expense of prisons. However, there were also other reasons. If the purpose of rehabilitation was to prepare those convicted to be better citizens, then, it was assumed, there was little need for education for those who would never be full citizens. Reformatory prisons for women in the North and Midwest offered education in only the domestic arts as preparation for service employment. As MacCormick put it in his report, since many female prisoners were of "low" and "limited" intelligence, penal officials should carefully calculate "the exact knowledge of reading, writing, and arithmetic necessary" for women "as a supplement to specific vocational skills," since "how much English or arithmetic does the waitress need?"[21] In both Northern and Southern states, Black persons were generally not considered deserving of education, or at least not the same types of education as whites. In the North, young Black men and women were generally sent to custodial prisons (with little educational programming), not reformatories. In the South, Blacks were essential convict labor in fields, quarries, and steel mills.[22] Usually housed in camps, they were not offered basic or vocational education or, often, even Christian teaching. As sociologist Heather Schoenfeld puts it, "In the Jim Crow South, the belief that black people were intellectually and morally inferior to whites and therefore good for manual labor and prone to criminal activity was an orienting idea that shaped everyday life for black and white residents."[23] Indeed MacCormick's survey included few Southern prisons, since work camps and prison farms housed many of the incarcerated.

20. Education is compulsory for all children, but the age at which one can discontinue schooling varies from fourteen to eighteen years in different states.
21. MacCormick, *Education of Adult Prisoners*, 47.
22. Blackmon, *Slavery by Another Name*.
23. Schoenfeld, "Delayed Emergence of Penal Modernism," 263.

Nevertheless, as US society began to enforce secondary education, state prison systems slowly followed.[24] Depending on state law concerning mandatory attendance age, this education may be compulsory for inmates under eighteen; otherwise, it is voluntary. These programs are critical starting places for education, since perhaps 40 percent of those incarcerated have not completed high school.[25] For many women I know, the GED experience has been a turning point, simply because they experienced what it meant to try and to succeed. As Spicy, one of our students, put it, her school experience had given her a fear of failing, but when she got her GED, she said she had such a sense of accomplishment that she thought she "could do anything."

End of Corridor/College

At the end of the hall, we go into the college AA and BA classrooms to say hello. We have known most of these students for several years, since they graduated from our program before applying for the AA degree. From Mondays to Thursdays, two cohorts of students study and learn all day, with study halls during the morning and a mix of study hall and classes in the afternoon and evening. In these rooms, between twenty and twenty-five Formica desks are in a loose loop, with little "breakout" clusters where students are working together on a project or problem (one student is tutoring the others in math, which has been the subject of many groans). Laptops are out and in use, since they cannot be taken back to their living quarters. Usually the college supervisor is sitting with them, possibly working on his own laptop or answering questions, reading over a piece of writing, etc. We always stop to talk, either as we come in or go out, discussing their different research plans and projects. This is one place in the prison where you feel energy and joy.

~

While private higher education had been present from before the founding of the United States, public higher education began to grow through agricultural schools in the nineteenth century and community colleges in the twentieth century. The post–World War II growth of public colleges and college education eventually came to affect prison systems. In the mid-1960s, Lyndon Johnson's Great Society program included legislation that increased access to education, particularly through the funding eventually known as

---

24. Such programs are more likely to be GEDs rather than high school diplomas. Some states, however, are partnering with charter schools to offer full high school diploma programs.

25. Harlow, *Education and Correctional Populations*, para. 1.

Pell Grants instituted in the early seventies. Persons with low income could receive federal funding to support AA and BA degrees. Incarcerated persons had generally been included in federal education funding programs, such as the GI Bill, although before the 1964 Civil Rights Act, Black persons often were blocked from accessing these funds.[26] Pell grants made possible an extraordinary growth in prison higher education programs, from perhaps 46 programs in 1967, to 218 by 1973, to 350 by 1982.[27]

However, conservative politicians immediately began to campaign against the inclusion of incarcerated persons in Pell funding, part of the growing white conservative response to the passage of the civil rights bill. Every year from 1982 to 1994, conservative congressional members introduced legislation banning Pell Grants for incarcerated persons as part of the overall "tough on crime" approach fueling retributive mass incarceration.[28] Similarly, conservative state legislators campaigned for reductions in funding for education, among other inmate programs. Finally, as part of the 1993 Violent Crime Control and Law Enforcement Act and the Higher Education Act Reauthorization of 1994, Pell Grant eligibility was eliminated, resulting in a 44-percent drop in prison college enrollments the following year.[29]

By the next decade, however, the climate began to shift toward greater concern for those who were reentering society. The most visible signal was the Second Chance Act, approved by Congress in 2007, which prioritized programming for the increasing number of individuals released from prisons, jails, and juvenile residential facilities who were returning to communities upon release. By 2019, the Department of Justice survey noted that nearly 50 percent of state and federal prisons offered college courses, although there was no data about the kinds of programs or whether these courses offered credit.[30] In 2015, the Obama Administration began the Second Chance experimental program as part of overall criminal justice reforms that allowed a pilot group of in-prison higher education programs to apply for Pell aid. By 2016, sixty-seven higher education institutions were awarded Pell Grants for

---

26. Blakemore, "How the GI Bill's Promise." For example, Southern legislators forced the GI Bill to be administered by states, not by the federal government.

27. Ubah, "Abolition of Pell Grants," 75.

28. Ubah, "Abolition of Pell Grants," 76.

29. Ubah, "Abolition of Pell Grants," 79. Wright argues that there was already a slow decline in enrollments because of the overall shifts in higher education to increasing reliance on tuition-based funding, rather than government support (K. Wright, "Pell Grants, Politics"). See late nineties stats in Crayton and Neusteter, "Current State of Correctional Education."

30. Maruschak and Buehler, *Census*.

twelve thousand students.[31] In 2019, the program was expanded, and in 2020 the FAFSA [Free Application for Federal Student Aid] Simplification Act was ratified and signed, which removed the ban on Pell Grants for incarcerated persons no later than the 2023–24 academic year.

The dominant arguments for reinstating Pell have generally been pragmatic rather than moral. In 2014 the RAND Corporation published an evaluation of research on correctional education, concluding that while overall recidivism rates (within three years) are 40 percent, incarcerated people who participate in postsecondary education programs were 43 percent less likely to return to prison. Returning citizens, on average, are less educated than the general population (4.4 percent of state prison inmates had at least some postsecondary education, compared with 51 percent of the general US adult population). Thus, the report said it was particularly crucial that education and training be available while persons were still incarcerated.[32] More recent work by the Vera Institute continues to support the positive impact of education, stating that "greater educational attainment in prison will enable formerly incarcerated people to enter the labor market better positioned for good-paying jobs."[33]

Another reason for support of higher education programs in prisons may be even more pragmatic. Increased Pell access coincides with significant declines in college enrollment, particularly in public colleges and community colleges.[34] Public schools were about two-thirds of the seventy-three new schools awarded Pell Grant access for prison education for 2023. For-profit schools have also been seeking Pell funds. Ashland University, a for-profit Christian school favored by former Education Secretary Betsy DeVos, was able to enroll several thousand students in tablet-based classes in over one hundred prisons and jails. Pell funding for these students allowed the school to leave behind its large debt and junk rating. In 2018, a college accrediting commission found that Ashland had not enabled many of its students in prison to complete the program before running out of Pell funding.[35]

While the policy arguments may be pragmatic, greater access to higher education significantly affects the lives of those inside. Christopher Blackwell, serving a forty-five-year sentence in a Washington state prison, writes,

> College changed the way I thought about myself and others. I worked with men from all backgrounds to complete

31. Custer, "Denying Federal Financial Aid," 6.
32. Lois Davis et al., *How Effective Is Correctional Education*.
33. Oakford et al., *Investing in Futures*, 19.
34. Moody, "5th Straight Semester."
35. See Hager, "How Trump Made."

assignments, and even taught other students. Before I knew it, I was getting A's on my essays and solving quadratic equations in math class. My confidence spread to other parts of my life. I started to feel like I was destined to be more than a drug dealer from a community no one cared about. I could be anything I pushed myself to be.[36]

Space in Between/the Multiple Forms of Prison Education

At the end of the college/HS corridor, we turn left into the front hall of the building and pause. To the right is a locked gate to the counseling and chaplaincy areas. We move past bathrooms for inmates (staff have separate bathrooms in another corridor) and educational staff offices. We pause in the central reception space, which on one side has doors to the outside (always locked) and on the other side double doors to a run-down gym which is used not only for sports but for programs, graduations, large-scale package distributions, and random containment of groups of women. In this area is a large glass-fronted case where displays are rotated—or not, depending on how chaotic the prison is at a given moment. These displays track high school display cases—colorful and cheerful pictures and decorations noting graduations or other educational accomplishments. This space is an intersection where students from different classes connect. Depending on the prison atmosphere that day, the far gate that leads to "our" hall may or may not be locked. At different times in the morning, we stand there waiting for the gate to be unlocked by staff so that we can enter our classroom corridor, go out to the staff restroom, or leave the building. Our students begin to cluster around, having navigated their own more challenging sets of gates and check-ins. We answer an increasing volley of hellos, along with an occasional "Do you have my paper?" "Did you get my note last week?" "Carol sent you a note—she has medical today."

~

In this pause, I want to return to where this essay started, naming education in prison as a contested area, and highlight how the current trends in prison education answer my key questions: (1) *For what purposes do we educate?* (2) *Who should be educated?* (3) *What kind(s) of education should we offer?*

To respond to the first question of the purposes of education, the slow increase in access to education inside prison has demonstrated a limited consensus about the general importance of education, at least until Pell

---

36. Blackwell, "I Grew Up Believing," para. 9.

Grant funding was revoked in 1994. However, funding has always been contentious as education can easily be seen as a programmatic "extra" that can be cut when budgets are tight. The history of prison reform in general is marked by experiments ended by reductions in state funds.[37]

To respond to the second question about who should be educated, educational programming over time has become more inclusive from the nineteenth-century focus on white male students. Some of the current arguments for increased educational programming stress inclusivity within the reality of the over incarceration of persons of color.[38] However, the pragmatic approach to education in partnership with the disciplinary structure of prisons creates its own forms of exclusion. For example, those who are serving life or very long sentences may experience limitation of access. Years ago, it was announced at graduation that our certificate program would be counted as performance incentive credit points, which could be used as evidence of the "good behavior" required for parole consideration. When the ceremony ended, I was surrounded by our many lifer students asking if this meant they would be excluded from our classes. Just as GED classes used to be available only to those within five years of release, many opportunities for education inside are not open to those with life sentences, especially without possibility of parole. There is no pragmatic argument about the impact on recidivism to be made for those who will never return. This is also an equity issue since two-thirds of those receiving life sentences in the US are persons of color.[39] Disciplinary practices are another area of exclusion. Participation in educational programs is usually dependent on a record devoid of any "write-ups" or certainly any time in lockdown. There is a logic of incentive here, as I have heard many stories from women for whom the desire to be in classes and groups was part of a change in how they saw themselves and their futures. However, in practice, it may be hard to avoid a write-up if an officer is having a bad day or if another inmate wants to make trouble for you.

Perhaps the most challenging question for prison education, however, may be the third question, of what kind of education should be offered. The typical range of educational offerings in a prison includes:

- Special Education: Addressing different physical, cognitive, and social disabilities

- Adult Basic Education: Literacy, basic skills instruction in arithmetic, reading, writing, and, if needed, English as a second language

37. Hirschberger, "'Imprisonment Is Expensive.'"
38. diZerega and Chochos, "Postsecondary Education in Prison."
39. Sentencing Project, "Report to the United Nations," s.v. "C. Sentencing."

- Adult Secondary Education: Instruction to complete the high school diploma or prepare for a certificate of high school equivalency, such as the General Education Development

- Vocational Education: Training in general employment skills and in skills for specific jobs or industries

- Postsecondary Education: College-level instruction that enables an individual to earn college credit that may be applied toward a two- or four-year postsecondary degree[40]

While adult basic and secondary education are usually available (or even, in some state and federal prisons, mandated), other forms of education may not be. As public policy, higher education in prison tends to focus on supporting the development of skills that will enable incarcerated persons to become productive workers on reentry—or at least workers who do not return to prison.

In US education broadly, also, there have been struggles over education as technical preparation in contrast to education as formation.[41] Liberal arts education came from the heritage of elite education that stressed understanding of the humanistic traditions. Underlying the liberal arts model is the idea of education as formative or as *paideia*. The purpose of this education is to form the well-rounded human (until recently, assumed to be male, of European heritage, and elite) who was both a good person and a person of culture. Such a person, as the nineteenth-century English reformer Matthew Arnold put it, would have a command of "the best that has been thought and said in the world."[42] By contrast, as I have noted, the drive to extend education to poor and marginalized groups has often been the need to form appropriate skilled and compliant workers and citizens. However, as access to college increased in the postwar US, the liberal arts model still predominated. When prison college education was developed in the 1960s and seventies, this model of education was still assumed. Since that time, however, the place of liberal arts curricula has weakened considerably in relation to what are considered market-driven student interests in "career readiness competencies."[43] Yet in the Pell-less period of higher

---

40. Summarized from Levy, "Prison Education Across the U.S."

41. "The struggle between the liberal arts and vocationalism has been an ongoing one, spanning much of the history of American higher education" (Horowitz, "Balancing Hopes and Limits," 17).

42. Arnold, *Culture and Anarchy*, 5.

43. National Association of Colleges and Employers, "What Is Career Readiness?," subheading. See also K. Wright, "Pell Grants, Politics."

education, from 1994 until recently, more liberal arts institutions have come to be involved in providing higher education in prisons.

Currently, over 110 four-year nonprofit colleges or universities offer programs inside prisons.[44] Over the last decade, there have been national- and state-level efforts for networking among these programs, strengthened by the increasing availability of Pell Grants. Within these networks, there can still be separation between schools focused on liberal arts and technical/vocational schools.[45]

Much of the "formative" programming is now, in fact, offered by therapeutic and/or religious prison staff. The most prevalent formative therapeutic programs are Thinking for a Change and Moral Reconation Therapy, which are structured prepackaged programs used (often mandated) in the majority of prison systems in the US. Both are cognitive behavioral programs directed at developing better "reasoning, better decision making, and more *appropriate behavior*."[46] Since "security" is now the priority of the US prison system, it is not surprising that "appropriate behavior" can often mean simply obeying the rules.

By law, persons inside must be able to practice the religion of their choice, and the vast majority of religious programming is Christian, generally evangelical Protestant Christian. Prison Fellowship, the largest in-prison Christian program provider, runs the Prison Fellowship Academy in over one hundred prisons: "Located in select prisons across the country, the Prison Fellowship Academy takes men and women through a holistic life transformation spanning weeks or months. They are guided by Prison Fellowship staff and volunteers to lead lives of purpose and productivity inside and outside of prison."[47] The Prison Seminaries Foundation lists twenty-three seminary programs run by different Baptist schools, which train inmates for peer-to-peer ministry with an "ethos of service"[48] and "geared toward moral orientation."[49] In 1826, Gershom Powers, the prison warden, wrote that prisoners must be made to "realize the necessity and duty of repentance, of amendment, and of

---

44. Alliance for Higher Education in Prison, *National Directory*.

45. However, the state-wide coalition with which I work, the Georgia Coalition for Higher Education in Prison, is trying to keep these different schools in conversation, committed to a full range of possibilities for reentering citizens. See https://www.gachep.org/.

46. See https://www.moral-reconation-therapy.com/, s.vv. "What Is MRT—Moral Reconation Therapy*?*"; emphasis added.

47. Prison Fellowship, "Celebrating 101," para. 2.

48. Prison Seminaries Foundation, "Prison Seminary Model," para. 1.

49. Prison Seminaries Foundation, "Prison Seminary Model," s.vv. "A Four-Year Accredited Degree Program," para. 2.

humble and strict obedience ... to make them better convicts; and whenever restored to their liberty, better citizens."[50] Close to two hundred years later, the Prison Fellowship Academy continues this role, providing "the Good Citizenship Model," which promotes Christian principles of "good citizenship," such as productivity, responsibility, and integrity.[51]

Reaching Our Destination/Education as Transformation

Officer Y shows up again to unlock the gate. The women appreciate her, for she treats them fairly and often is quite kind (although both the SOPs and the officer culture strongly discourages more humane interactions). We joke with her as we turn into our class corridor, the teachers fanning out as she unlocks the different classrooms. Ms. X, the director, and I run interference, fielding requests for paper, pens, access to a pencil sharpener, a moment of our time. It is chaotic, but it is joyful. There have been so many times over the years at which this chaos did not happen, times when we were told not to come as there was no security officer available for our building, but the women had already been released from their dormitories and were waiting for us. There have likewise been times when we sat waiting for them, but their building officers would not release them, falsely telling them we were not there. And times when we were delayed getting in because of something "illegal," whether in a bag (paints) or on a body (blue jeans).

The classrooms are painted a puke green. Each is furnished with a battered metal or wooden teacher's desk, along with assorted metal and plastic desks, some with chairs attached to tablet arms, and some with separate chairs, remnants of past school furniture. Because so many different types of classes occur in these rooms, the blackboards in each room are always coated with old chalk dust. Often, the walls are taped with poster paper with bullet points from required prison classes highlighting "rational" behavior and recognition of "negative" emotions. Women shift desks with scraping screeches, teachers unpack bags and hand out paper and pens, women joke with each other and with the teacher. All students are in khaki, with their last name printed on the chest pocket in black letters. If it's cold, everyone will be wearing standard-issue blue jackets and white knit caps. The foray through several locked gates to track down the cart with the DVD player has been successful, so a couple of the women are busy plugging it in, as only they know how to press the pen into the broken power button in exactly the right way to get it to work.

---

50. Graber, *Furnace of Affliction*, 87.
51. Prison Fellowship, "Good Citizenship Model."

The transition noises diminish, and I can begin to hear the voices of the teachers more centrally as they get started. The rhythms shift. I sit at the end of the hall perched on a little wooden desk pushed up under the internal wall phone (for officers, no one else). This is one of my favorite spots, as I can sit but still see down the front hall whether anyone is late in arriving and down the classroom hall to hear whether anyone needs anything.

Soon what I call "ordinary" class voices can be heard . . . students saying things to teachers ("Why does God take it out on Miriam and not on anyone else?"), to each other ("Toni, are you fooling me? What kind of an answer is that?"), and always lots of laughter. I walk down the hall, looking through the small window in each wooden door, partly to be certain all is well and partly out of the pleasure of seeing them learning, from the teacher and from each other. Once classes have some momentum, Ms. X and I slip in to listen . . . or participate, as we are always seen as part of the class. I watch B bending over the Xerox pages, scrunching up her forehead to concentrate. Something from those pages is being read aloud by Z who, fresh from a GED she acquired after she was incarcerated, stumbles over some of the words. No one laughs, no one ever laughs, unless we can laugh with *her at some particularly wild pronunciation.*

∼

We have been running this theological certificate program, offering a basic and an advanced certificate, since 2009.[52] Since our program is not accredited, there is considerable freedom about what we offer. Our teachers are mostly master's students in theology and doctoral students in religion. We decide what course to offer on the bases both of what we know our inside students want and of what our outside teachers are able to teach. We have been able to offer an extraordinary range of courses, from Greek and Hebrew to art and creative writing, from studies of Christian biblical texts to overviews of Islam and Hinduism, from Christian history to political philosophy. We also have offered various forms of research, writing, and reading support, both built into classes and as stand-alone classes.

Our classrooms are places of creativity *and* knowledge.[53] The women name what *they* see, often linking it back to something they have experienced in their lives, both as it is lived now behind bars and as it was lived

---

52. The certificate is offered by a consortium of southern seminaries. I should note that as I write this, the program has been on hiatus, at first because of COVID but more recently as the prison will no longer be housing persons in the main prison population.

53. My thoughts here are deeply influenced by the work of three former directors of our program, Sarah Farmer, Rachelle Green, and Shari Madkins.

before outside. We have laughed, applauded, and cried many times: having conversations about which caring practices are present inside, listening to spoken-word poetry on whether belief in God does anything at all, experiencing a shared dance performance about endurance and hope (drawing upon the experiences of a brother's murder outside and an attack inside). And there is always the annual assignment in our core-required biblical class in writing a psalm of lamentation: "I fall alone / I take your hand," "The world is filled with your absence/your silence . . . . You are silent / So am I," "I quiet my spirit and block out the noise / I want to hear thee."[54]

Every text, film, picture our students engage, they enjoy as the encounter itself, the possibility of stepping outside of prison walls. As one student said, "I'm not in prison when I'm in theology." However, they are also assessing it as a resource for living now. Even when we have classes in ancient Hebrew and Greek, women love not only the languages themselves but the power felt in the acquired knowledge. Students in a prison classroom can enter into a literary text with focus and depth that I have rarely experienced in a college or seminary classroom. Our incarcerated students engage readings as resources for life in ways that can make texts come alive. As Meghan Sweeney says in her studies of women's reading practices inside, "Women in prison often exhibit a greater sense of intensity and exigency as they use reading to foster self-discovery, create a sense of community, and develop a language for reckoning with their experiences."[55] For them, education is always formative. Classified as a chaplaincy program, we are indeed supposed to be a formative program. However, we are not providing therapeutic or faith-based programming focused on fixing individual selves in isolation from wider social forces. Our formation occurs through engaging new knowledges in ways that help students encounter themselves, one another, *and* the world outside.

Our classrooms are also places for building relations. We are learning together in this fragile, humming, inventive space in ways that depend upon the quality of relationships among students and between teacher and students. The world of prisons is filled with distorted relationships. Officers and incarcerated persons live out an oddly intimate institutionalized power relationship. "Fraternizing" is strictly forbidden, and the ongoing external and internalized policing of boundaries means that humanity is also forbidden. Educational and therapeutic staff have a little more space, but the demands of security procedures (along with low salaries) wears on them. Relationships among the women inside can be complicated. Some are built on the

---

54. Class materials, gathered as part of IRB-approved research.
55. Sweeney, "Reading and Reckoning," 305.

exchange of "I'll do this for you if you do this for me." Some are non-relationships of fear, especially on the part of older women lifers/long-termers who struggle to live amid young, new, sometimes violent women. There are also (forbidden) romantic relationships. However, there are also enduring deep friendships, which we are told are nurtured by our classes, as places to be with "good people" around whom "you can let your guard down" and find "closeness," even if they are "people you would not normally relate to."

We try to enable education to be an open space, where our students can view themselves as free even in prison, where they can develop capacities, explore identities. Comments about our program must be read against this background: our students say our classrooms are a place inside where they can have "free expression," "be yourself," "find your voice," "be heard without being overlooked," and "don't have to be put in a box." Our time and our relationships are also filled with the annoyances, irritations, and disappointments that are part of human interaction. There are plenty of moments where I know I have let down our students and moments where they have let us (and themselves) down. But when you are immersed in an institutional space that can be described as "a human warehouse or even a kind of social waste management facility,"[56] those moments when you are treated as human rather than an inmate, when you feel you are not in prison, those are moments of immense value, the fragments of flourishing.[57]

I return to my three starting questions and give the answers I have found inside prison. *For what purposes do we educate?* To enable the greatest possible flourishing—which requires not only job-related education but education of the whole person. *Who should be educated?* Everyone. *What kind(s) of education should be offered?* Different kinds, of course, but taught in ways that enhance confidence in one's self and one's possibilities, along with some space to dream and hope.

In *The Courage to Teach*, Parker Palmer writes about knowing and the sacred, pointing to the experience of mystery, the transcendent subject or truth possible in a classroom. Palmer links this vision to the disciplines of knowledge, but I link it to the conviction of full personhood in a connected world. It is paideia, radically reformed from its elite heritage in both Western culture and Christian traditions, rooted in love.[58] This is a theological

---

56. Simon, *Governing Through Crime*, 142.

57. These moments could also be described as creating a space where "human dignity was important . . . increasing the likelihood that participants would feel morally and ethically 'seen'" (Little, "Moral Sight and Ethical Praxis," s.vv. "Discussion of Findings," para. 6).

58. As Paulo Freire puts it, "Love cannot be sentimental . . . it must generate other acts of freedom. . . . If I do not love the world—if I do not love life—if I do not love

vision very different than the Calvinist forms of Protestantism that have underwritten so much of the history of prisons in the US, including education programs in prisons. This vision has been appealed to countless times when people are searching for new ways of living. In our classroom, we dream of a world where we can live "all things new" (Rev 21:5 NRSVUE) and justice is real.

---

people—I cannot enter into dialogue" (*Pedagogy of the Oppressed*, 89–90).

9

Whole People and Communities Through Restorative Justice

JUSTIN BRONSON BARRINGER and JIM BUFFINGTON

In 1976 a twelve-year-old boy's mother was found dead in the back seat of her car. She had been raped and murdered. As if this were not horrific enough, the boy's father was accused of hiring two hitmen to kill her. It seems fitting that this boy, now grown, should tell some of his own story to set the stage for a reflection on the ideas and practices of restorative justice, particularly its moral and fiscal appeal.

Jim's Story

I never thought I would be helping run a restorative justice ministry like Bridges to Life (BTL). I am sixty-one years old and have been married for thirty-eight years to Marilyn, a retired elementary special education schoolteacher. We have one son, Bryce, who is thirty-four and works as a financial analyst. Bryce is married to Caitlyn, and they had our first grandchild in 2022 and our second grandchild in 2024. I grew up in the church with my two younger brothers, Oscar and Louis. My dad, James, was minister of music at a Baptist church in San Antonio, Texas. My mom, Chere, was the church pianist. Dad also owned a construction company.

When I was eleven, my parents got divorced. About a year later Dad went out of town for the weekend. On that Saturday night, Mom was found murdered. She had been shot three times at close range in the face. Her clothes had been ripped off of her, and she was found naked on the backseat floorboard of her car, which had been left in a school parking lot. The police said it looked like a rape and robbery gone bad.

My brothers and I clung to Dad because we were scared and had a lot of fear. For Mom to be killed and to be found naked had a devastating impact on me as a kid. But about a year later things were slowly trying to get back to normal. Then, when I was thirteen, Dad and two of his employees at the construction business were arrested for the murder of Mom. Dad was charged with capital murder and criminal solicitation in having hired two of his employees to murder Mom. Dad said he didn't do it and that he was innocent. The only evidence against Dad was circumstantial. Both of the men said that the other had committed the crime, and one of the men said he had overheard Dad hiring the other.

Now, instead of just being a victim's kid, I was also an inmate's kid. People treated us differently than they did when the only story they had known was my mother was murdered. As a victim's kid, people want to help you. As an inmate's kid, people treat you as damaged and like you will not amount to anything good. But we believed in Dad. We visited him every weekend in the county jail in San Antonio until he finally went to trial two and a half years later when I was sixteen. Dad was found guilty of capital murder and criminal solicitation for the murder of Mom. The jury sentenced him to the death penalty, and he was sent to death row in Huntsville, Texas, at the Ellis Unit to live in solitary confinement until he was to be executed by lethal injection.

About five years later, the district attorney's secretary came forward and made a confession. She confessed that the DA had altered evidence to gain a conviction in Dad's case. The court of appeals awarded Dad a new trial when I was twenty-one, and he was sent back to the San Antonio county jail for a new trial. This further reinforced my belief that Dad was really innocent.

Dad's new trial was again in San Antonio a few years later in 1988 when I was twenty-five, and my brothers and I went to testify in Dad's defense. I had so many questions about Mom's murder. Most murder victims' family members obsess over the details of the crime, and I was no exception. I carried that baggage of hurt, fear, shame, and obsession with me at most times. I wanted to know every detail about Mom and Dad and any details about her murder. I wanted to know what had happened to her, and why, and who actually killed her. I testified for Dad for hours and was very much treated by the police and district attorney's office as an offender's kid and not a victim's kid since I was testifying in Dad's defense.[1]

The trial ended, and it went to the jury. At the first vote, eleven jurors voted not guilty, and only one man voted guilty, and he was not going to change his mind. The jury deliberated for about three days and finally came back with the verdict. They decided to find him guilty of a lesser charge so he would be immediately eligible for parole. He was found guilty of murder instead of capital murder and was given life in prison. However, since he had been on death row so long previously, he was immediately eligible for parole and was to be released within a week. That night Marilyn and I went to go see Dad at the San Antonio Bexar County Jail.

We went to visit Dad because I hoped he could help answer my many questions. The questions were not all about him but were about some details that had come out in the trial about Mom's death. After we got through the first few questions, he said, "I did it and she deserved it!" We were shocked, and I could not believe it. Not only had he lied to me all these years and had now confessed, but he was also not sorry that he had had her killed. In addition, he actually blamed it on her! Dad felt like he was the victim, and I was furious. I guess he thought that I would support him regardless of his guilt and since he was getting out of jail within the week, he finally told me the truth. I told him right then that I would do everything I could to keep him in jail and not let him get granted release on parole.

Dad's murder trial had a lot of media attention, and my brothers and I were exposed to much of the media. We told reporters that Dad had confessed and that he was neither sorry nor remorseful. We asked the people of San Antonio to protest Dad's parole. We wrote letters of protest, and the parole board revoted and denied his parole.

At this second trial, the jury had sentenced him to life in prison. So now Dad had to go back to Huntsville, Ellis Unit. This time, however, he was not sent to death row but to general population in a maximum security prison. On death row, he had been very protected and isolated from other criminals, but now he was going to serve a life sentence in general

---

1. This evidences a real problem in the American justice system in that it tends to treat every accused person like a criminal, even though we supposedly subscribe to innocent until proven guilty; and worse still, it treats friends and family members of accused folks as guilty parties as well. In Jim's case, the DA/police would not answer any of my questions as they thought I might share with the defense. The defense would not answer any questions as they feared I would turn against Dad and then share with the DA. A restorative justice approach like the one described in this chapter might mitigate some of these issues by decreasing the antagonism between prosecution and defense, which would ultimately help the families and communities of those who have committed a serious crime.

population. We told Dad before he left that he would never see us again. I remember going to Mom's grave, and for the first time I sobbed uncontrollably. I was so angry that I had believed in Dad. We had found out at the trial that not only had he hired two men to kill Mom; he had also hired them to kill my brothers and me too—*all for life insurance money*. I picked up more baggage of anger, bitterness, hurt, and betrayal. I wanted Dad to rot in prison. I was not ever going to forgive him.

About a year later when I was twenty-six, thirteen years after this saga began, my son Bryce was born in 1990. I noticed after he was born that I was just like Dad in many ways. I would react in the same ways he did, and it was not a good thing. It really bothered me. I could not understand how Dad had gone from being a minister, a happily married man with a loving and kind wife and three good boys, to hiring two men to kill that wife and those three kids. I was also concerned, now that I was a father myself, that my own son might turn out to be just like me.

After not having seen or had any contact with Dad for four years, I decided to go see him one more time. I wanted him to know that I now had a son and he would never be able to see him. I had more unanswered questions that I had let fester in my life for years. I went to Ellis Unit in Huntsville, and I was scared to death. I now knew this was the man who had had Mom killed and had hired men to kill me too. However, I knew something was different as soon as I saw him. I was there with my list of questions, and I wanted answers. The very first thing he said after not seeing me for four years was that he was sorry. He said he was sorry for what he had done to Mom, and he was sorry for what he had put my brothers and me through. I did not believe him. This was a man who never said he was sorry. In his own mind, he was always right. It was always his way. In fact, he was very abusive to me and my brothers, something that at the time I had thought was normal. I had never realized the extent of the abuse until I got married and saw how a real family treated each other within my wife's family.

Dad then explained that since his last trial he had hit rock bottom in prison. All of his friends and family had turned on him and continued to protest his release on parole. Finally, he said that he had truly given his life over to God. I have to admit, I did not believe him. I thought this was probably just a "jail-house" conversion, one brought on by the stresses of prison but without real substantive change in the incarcerated person. But he then answered all of my questions about Mom's murder. He seemed different, and I kept going back to see him once a month for the next year. I spent a lot of our visits trying to understand how he had gone from being a happily married man to a killer. I did forgive him during this process but still protested his parole because I believed there were still consequences he had to face for the choices he had made.

About a year later in 1994, I got a call from the prison chaplain, Richard Lopez, who later became a BTL staff member after he retired from prison chaplaincy. He said I had to get to Huntsville immediately because something had happened to Dad. When I got to Huntsville, the chaplain said that Dad had had a brain aneurysm, a blood vessel that had burst in his brain, and he died later that evening. The chaplain said the warden had approved a memorial service for Dad in the prison chapel at Ellis Unit in Huntsville about a week later. There had never been a service for an inmate in the history of the Texas prison system and has not been another since. The warden also said that we were invited. Also, there had never been any family allowed inside the prison except for the visitation area. My brothers and our wives decided to attend.

The first thing that happened during the memorial service was a men's chorus came up front and sang some Christian songs. Apparently, everyone had had a job in prison, and Dad had become the chaplain's assistant. Dad had started the first men's chorus on the unit. We then listened as, one by one, three hundred men came forward to the microphone for about three hours, and each of them said, "I became a Christian because your Dad shared Christ with me." It was shocking to hear the first man say it, but it was overwhelming to hear three hundred men say the same thing. I learned that it is one thing to say something when everyone is looking, but it is entirely different to say something when no one was looking. *For the last three years* after Dad had become a Christian, he had spent his time winning others to Christ by just telling his story. Dad would meet a man in prison and tell him that he had committed a horrible crime but had asked God for forgiveness and accepted responsibility and accountability for his actions and was now going in a new direction and living a new way. We realized that Dad had truly changed. At the end of the service the chaplain asked if I wanted to say something to the men. When I walked up front and turned around, I saw three hundred men in white prison jumpsuits. I realized immediately they were no different than I was. The only difference between us was they had been caught making bad choices that nearly any of us could make, and the consequence was that they had landed in prison. The only thing I could think to tell them was that it was now their opportunity to go back to their dorms and tell other men who were not in the room that God could change their lives. We left prison that night, and my family finally forgave our dad and felt a real release and burden lifted. We let go of the hurt, betrayal, and anger we had held on to for years.

We are now able to explain to our kids about our parents. We tell them that our dad (their grandfather) made a horrible mistake and bad choices that culminated in our mom having been raped and murdered. But, even through such enormous tragedy, God can take a bad situation and still redeem it for God's good purposes. We learned to forgive and let go. God tells us to forgive not so we can let the person who offended us off the hook, but so we can let ourselves off the hook. Many people I know who have been hurt and do not forgive end up bitter, angry, and depressed. I did not want to be that guy. I had to let the luggage go.

During that last year of Dad's life, I learned how he had gone from minister to murderer, a series of bad choices he had made over time that included drinking too much, having an affair, not coming home until very late, and hitting Mom in the face. She had then filed for divorce, a bitter custody battle had ensued, and then Dad had taken out life insurance on all of us and hired two men to commit murder. In 2005, I also had the opportunity to meet with the man who actually shot Mom with the gun. He is still in prison serving a life sentence. I went to visit Charles through the Texas Victim Offender Mediation Dialogue program and was also able to finally forgive him too.[2]

Restorative Justice Primer

Jim met Connie Hilton as a fellow Victim Impact Panel speaker during his volunteer work with Texas Victim Services. Connie, who was a BTL staff member, invited him to volunteer with BTL in 2004 at the Hutchins Unit in Dallas. Bridges to Life is a Texas-based nonprofit founded in 1998 that provides a high-impact restorative justice program to incarcerated offenders. Along with exploring concepts from confession to restitution in our fourteen-week curriculum, offenders also hear firsthand from crime victims and face the true impact of crime on others. Through our unique faith-based process, offenders experience a change of heart that allows them to make positive changes in their lives. Since its inception, more than 87,000 men and women have graduated from the BTL program with the help of over 4,000 volunteers in eighteen states and seven countries.

Ever since my first experience of restorative justice practices, I have been a very active volunteer and participate each week in sharing my story and helping to restore peace to both victims of crime and offenders. Bridges to Life utilizes group discussions among victims and offenders, along with

---

2. You can hear more of Jim's story: Buffington, *Seventy Times Seven*. You can also read Jim's book: Buffington, *Betrayed by Choices*.

other volunteers, to help each person in the group find healing by sharing their story and hearing the stories of others, an activity that often takes a while for participants to embrace as a restorative practice. When I first started sharing my victim story as a speaker to inmates in prison, my motive was to make them feel bad and hope that would help them change. It did appear to cause them to get victim empathy. I also wanted the inmate to understand what it is like to be an offender's kid. But then I started sitting in the group circle each week and participated as a volunteer facilitator. My healing did happen each time I told my story, but I then got to hear the inmates' perspective when they shared their stories, and I experienced offender empathy. Both sides, victim and offender, experience hope and healing in these group circle discussions. Over the past twenty years, I have now completed about forty fourteen-week projects at the Hutchins Unit and shared my story countless times. As I have seen the effectiveness of this approach, I have recruited numerous active volunteers, including my son, who is also a BTL volunteer at the Hutchins Unit.

There has been so much healing that I have witnessed and been a part of that has happened with both victims and offenders, and I am so thankful to be a part of this awesome restorative justice program. My unique experience from both the victim's side of crime and the offender's side has helped me to impact positive life change with offenders and help victims heal. This is where restorative justice shines; it helps both victims and offenders move to accepting God's love and forgiveness and restoring peace in their lives.

After thirty years of business and sales management experience combined with other community involvement, along with my BTL volunteerism, I really felt God called me into full-time prison ministry. In 2016, I became the chief operating officer with BTL and my life story has come full circle. This has allowed all I have been through and learned to help others on a much broader scale. Restorative justice is a way to help inmates change and transform their lives for the better, helps heal crime victims, and also reduces the number of victims through our efforts, which will save some further lives from tragedy by improving safety in our communities. In short, restorative justice is a moral good for many stakeholders.

In the case of BTL, volunteers from all walks of life, including many victims and former offenders, join inmates in the BTL program for twelve to fourteen weeks. The volunteers, including those who have graduated from the program and who now serve as encouragers, accompany offenders as they share their stories of hurt and how they have harmed others, while they also listen to and read stories of victims. At the start of each new BTL cohort, a multi-weeklong class and discussion time among both criminal offenders and survivors as well as other volunteers, participants do an activity that works much like Jesus's instruction that those without sin could throw a rock at the woman. The group is divided into theoretical perpetrators of crime and victims of crime. The perpetrators are asked to come up with words that would describe how they would feel if they were being arrested for a crime. Likewise, they ask the victims how they would feel if they had just been victimized. When the two lists are compared, they are nearly identical. They both have words on them like "afraid," "angry," "confused," and "worried." This is the start of creating common ground, ground initially made up of hurt and fear, so that everyone involved can find healing and comfort.

Howard Zehr, often regarded as the "founding father" of restorative justice in the modern West, notes that restorative justice is difficult to define because the work is ever in flux and new discoveries about restorative practices are being made regularly. Nonetheless, he offers a working definition: "Restorative justice is an approach to achieving justice that involves to the extent possible those who have a stake in a specific offense or harm to collectively identify and address harms, needs, and obligations in order to heal and put things as right as possible."[3] Restorative justice scholar and practitioner Marian Liebmann points to a definition of restorative justice that was created by the Restorative Justice Consortium. They write, "Restorative Justice works to resolve conflict and repair harm. It encourages those who have caused harm to acknowledge the impact of what they have done and gives them an opportunity to make reparation. It offers those who have suffered harm the opportunity to have their harm or loss acknowledged and amends made."[4] In both definitions, reparation of harm is central to the approach, in contrast to more common approaches to criminal justice that are focused either on punishment or ostensible reform of an individual. Restorative justice aims to reform individuals as well, but it aims at doing so in the context of communal healing. It is not dissimilar from steps 4 and 8 in the Big Book used by Alcoholics Anonymous, which are respectively about recognizing the harm one has caused and why, and then seeking to make amends for that harm. In fact, BTL created a revised version of their program, which is focused on people fighting addiction, because the basic principles apply to both recovery and restorative justice, namely, seeking to understand the reasons one has harmed others and then seeking to repair that harm to the extent possible. Restorative justice, in short, at least for Christians, is an outworking or imitation of God's work to redeem and restore all of the cosmos.

3. Zehr, *Little Book of Restorative Justice*, 48.
4. Liebmann, *Restorative Justice*, 25.

Although working definitions like those offered above are helpful, it is pertinent to be mindful that restorative justice, whether as a field of practice, social movement, and/or scholarly discipline, is still trying to figure out its best philosophies and practices even as proponents tend to agree on many of its key pillars. For example, Zehr argues, "Restorative justice is not primarily designed to reduce recidivism or repeat offenses," although it often has that effect, as the reader will see shortly in BTL's assessment of its graduates' recidivism rates compared to state and national averages.[5] Yet, Liebmann writes, "Restorative justice aims to restore the well-being of victims, offenders and communities damaged by crime, and to prevent further offending."[6] This, however, is a relatively minor quibble. For Zehr, it seems reducing recidivism is a by-product of restorative justice, while for Liebmann, reducing recidivism is a direct goal of the restorative justice process. Whatever the case, the focus is on recognizing harm and attempting to make amends for that harm, not only for the sake of the one harmed or the one who caused harm, but for the wider community seeking to create a society that is ultimately more peaceable and just.

There are a number of criticisms of restorative justice, but perhaps the most common is some version of the charge that restorative justice is jejune and ultimately incapable of addressing serious criminal offenses or making a better society. Jim's story is a reminder that proponents of restorative justice are not ignorant, naïve, or pie in the sky. Many of them are victims of crime, are related to victims of crime, and are or are related to perpetrators of crime. They have spent time in jails and prisons witnessing the reality of the conditions there, and it is through their experiences, rather than in spite of them, that they come to believe that people can indeed find positive change and redemption. It is this belief, again formed out of experience and practice rather than mere theorizing, that sets the basic foundation for restorative justice. People can change, victims can heal, and society can be safe without equating punishment and justice.

In John 8, Jesus sets out a basic model for how we could approach those who have caused harm as well as those who have experienced harm. In this story a woman is brought to Jesus because she has been caught in adultery—notably only the woman and not the man presumed to be with her—and the prescribed punishment is being stoned to death. She has been caught committing a crime, and the crowd wants to punish her. This woman, viewed by the crowd as a criminal offender, quickly becomes a victim as she is used as a pawn in the game to catch Jesus in a trap. Jesus immediately

---

5. Zehr, *Little Book of Restorative Justice*, 16.
6. Liebmann, *Restorative Justice*, 25.

takes the focus of the crowd off the woman as he bends down and scribbles in the dirt. Eventually, he says to the crowd that anyone without sin could cast a stone at the woman. Upon realizing that no one in the mob met that criterion, they eventually vanish. Once it is only Jesus and the woman who are left, he asks her a question: "Where are all those who condemn you?" The woman responds that they have all left. Jesus, who by his very own criterion has the right to condemn the woman and stone her, instead says, "Neither do I condemn you." It is only after Jesus has refocused the crowd's ire on himself rather than the woman, after he has made himself a human shield, after he asks her about her situation, and finally after he expresses his own lack of condemnation that he then tells the woman to "go and sin no more."

Conventional wisdom in many cultures, including both Jesus's and contemporary America's, says punishment is the best response to a criminal offense, but Jesus says, "Neither do I condemn you," before exhorting, "Go and sin no more." Restorative justice allows us to be able to say, "Neither do I condemn you" to criminal perpetrators and victims alike. In a punishment culture, like the one in the US, society often attaches moral value not only to those who commit crimes but those who are victims as well. These values in practice (as illustrated in Jim's story) suggest that people, not merely the crimes they committed or the harms they have endured, are irredeemably evil or morally broken. Restorative justice, through this lens, is not merely about reforming or even replacing our present justice system. It's about much more than that.

Theological Reflections on Restorative Justice

One may ask themselves, especially if they are a Christian, if our current system is not meant to help people make amends, forgive and reconcile, reduce recidivism, or replace our present system, then what's the point? For the folks at BTL, the point is peace—peace of mind, peace in relationships, and peace in communities. John Sage, the founder and CEO of BTL as well a victim who lost his sister Marilyn to murder during a carjacking, writes, "A significant part of my journey after Marilyn was murdered was toward becoming strong where I had been broken. For a number of years, that seemed impossible. I continued to feel broken by Marilyn's murder and other difficulties and hardships that life presented me. I continued to seek the path toward restoring my inner peace and, eventually, it led me to establish BTL. I believe that all who continue to seek will find their way to peace."[7] If the purpose or goal of restorative justice is anything, it seems to be God's shalom.

Restorative justice scholar Chris Marshall puts it this way, "Shalom is when everything is as it ought to be . . . shalom encapsulates God's basic intention for humanity—that people live in a condition of 'all rightness' in every department of life. Shalom thus combines in one concept the meaning of justice and peace. To know shalom requires the achievement of both justice and peace. They are inseparable ingredients of the same reality."[8] If that is the case, then can a Christian seeking to live God's shalom rightly believe and practice attempts at justice that are not founded in a peaceable pursuit of "all rightness"? Marshall responds, "Human justice-making should be patterned after divine justice-making. And since the justice of God disclosed in the life, death, and resurrection of Christ is a redeeming or restoring justice, so the pursuit in general society should also be qualified by a commitment to restorative methods and outcomes."[9] For Christians, ministers of reconciliation (2 Cor 5:16–21), it is difficult to imagine how justice could be anything other than a step toward shalom, and restorative justice is a practice of doing just that.

In the biblical story, *shalom*, usually translated as "peace," is a result of *hesed*, typically translated as "loving-kindness" but also as "mercy" and "goodness," which is to say that peace, wholeness, and right relationships are preceded by love, kindness, mercy, and goodness. We are even told that God wins us to repentance with kindness (Rom 2:4). Unfortunately, the current justice system discourages, and often even actively prevents, the love, mercy, compassion, and even justice that *hesed* demands. If the ravages of mass incarceration, and the massive industry surrounding the caging of people, are to be meaningfully transformed in the direction of shalom, the attitude of restoration must become the primary aim rather than punishment; those running the interlocking systems of oppression need a change of mind and heart that places *hesed* at the forefront rather than ostracization.

Hospitality and Accompaniment as the Modality of Restorative Justice

Restorative justice, read through the lens of *hesed*, is a practice of hospitality. While it is not common to talk about restorative justice in these terms, in the definitions above from Zehr and Liebmann, hospitality, that is mutual

---

7. Sage, "Foreword," 3.
8. Marshall, *Little Book of Biblical Justice*, 13.
9. Marshall, *Compassionate Justice*, 3.

welcome, is fundamental to the process. Christine Pohl explains why hospitality is important for working with anyone on the margins. She writes, "Because the practice of hospitality is so significant in establishing and reinforcing social relationships and moral bonds, we notice its more subversive character only when socially undervalued persons are welcomed," and this causes the wider society to "reassess its standards and methods of valuing."[10] Approaching restorative justice as hospitality has the potential to reshape society because it compels us to see people as nothing less than human, demanding that both victims and offenders are valued differently than the culture of punishment and incarceration currently allows.

As hospitality develops, it often demands many kinds of accompaniment. Sometimes, and perhaps ideally, those who have caused harm and who have been harmed accompany one another. However, this is not always possible or desirable depending on context. One inmate participant in BTL offered thoughts on how being accompanied by victims and other volunteers has changed their outlook. They wrote, "The interest of free people giving of their time, people who have been victimized by people like me, put to rest a lot of cynicism towards society."[11] Likewise, a BTL victim volunteer stated, "I have learned to forgive, because I have come face to face with people who have committed similar crimes, and have seen that change of heart is possible."[12] So, we see that hospitality and accompaniment can both change the way society, even members who have been victims of crime, values people, particularly those on the margins, and how those very people then interact with that society in healthier and more peaceable ways.

This way of understanding restorative justice as part of the Christian tradition of radical hospitality should change our approach to crime. Restorative justice is about accompaniment, about journeying with one another toward more whole selves and communities. Jesus's own mission statement in Luke 4:18–19 includes release to the captives, and ideally those released would be repentant if guilty and forgiving if not. Further, when Jesus separates out the faithful sheep from the disobedient goats (Matt 25:31–46), one of his central criteria has to do with visiting those in prison, with no mention about doing so based on innocence or guilt. And, in 1 Peter, we have an account that shows Jesus himself visiting prisoners in hell with the message of freedom and restoration. In short, if justice is to be restorative, it requires visitors to carceral facilities who are working to improve people's lives and

---

10. Pohl, *Making Room*, 62.
11. Blackard, *Restoring Peace*, 187.
12. Blackard, *Restoring Peace*, 185.

work toward the personal and systemic changes needed for the healing of inmates and victims.

Whatever the specific goals in restorative justice, the consensus is that it should attempt to help both victims and offenders to heal and find peace, and that healing and peace require walking with folks through some incredibly painful remembering and sharing of victimhood as well as sometimes equally painful recognition of the harm one's crime has done to others. For victims, particularly Christian ones, it may be helpful to recognize Jesus in offenders, and thus be able to realize that when we walk with them, it is akin to being in the garden alone with Jesus, as the 1912 C. Austin Miles hymn "In the Garden" says:

> And He walks with me, and He talks with me,
> And He tells me I am his own,
> And the joy we share as we tarry there,
> None other has ever known.[13]

One might not expect that joy could be an outcome of a process that begins with the committing of a crime, but this is evidence of the God who can redeem all things, even the ones guilty of hanging the innocent Jesus on a cross to die. Can we, too, learn to ask God to forgive those who have hurt us, with the recognition that they often do not know what they are doing because they are responding out of their own traumatic experiences? Perhaps then we can recognize the release of the captives not as a threat to society but as an opportunity to bear witness to the world of the transformative power of God's love.

Unfortunately, the logic of neoliberalism presents a formidable obstacle in this work because it shifts the focus from justice to efficiency (namely, getting potential criminals off the streets as quickly as possible) and profit. This logic also tells us that people get what they earn or deserve. The logic of restorative justice, particularly its hospitality element, could help subvert and even replace the neoliberal logic. Hospitality to the stranger, the outcast, and the prisoner declares a different logic, which says people are more than what they earn or deserve, because of grace. In one BTL meeting I (Justin) expressed that my own choice to pursue a PhD was because of similar trauma I had experienced in my life, and I was desperately trying to prove myself or find some kind of meaning in life. While my choices were certainly more societally acceptable, the motivation was much the same as many who commit crime. The men in our group recognized that, and they then offered me the hospitality of acknowledging the similarities in our otherwise vastly different experiences. Thus, the hospitality was mutual.

13. Miles, "In the Garden," refrain.

This way of viewing criminal justice, in fact, uses some of the logic of neoliberalism against itself when one considers the financial cost of mass incarceration versus restorative justice programs like BTL in light of the fact that their results that have made recidivism rates plummet. For example, "86% of BTL graduates do not return to prison within 3 years after release!"[14] That means, only 14 percent of their graduates return to prison compared to the national average (over a five-year period), which is somewhere between 41 and 68 percent.[15] Bridges to Life has a higher percentage of people who do not return to prison than the percentage of those who do return to prison nationally.

Further, the Federal Bureau of Prisons calculated in 2020 that it cost on average $39,158 annually, or $120.59 per day to house an inmate.[16] In contrast, the BTL program costs less than $200 per graduate. So, for less than the cost of two days in prison, an inmate can participate in BTL, which statistically will lead to a lower chance of inmates returning to prison. Ultimately, this would add up to countless millions of dollars saved by US taxpayers, making restorative justice programs like BTL not only morally compelling but more fiscally responsible than the dominant approach to addressing criminal offenses. Thus, restorative justice initiatives should speak to both social progressives and fiscal conservatives as a compelling alternative that will both shape a more just society and save taxpayers money.

So, perhaps a mix of Christian hospitality and a temporary commandeering of neoliberalism's perverted logic can convince others that it is more effective and efficient than being "tough on crime" as a strategic path forward. Further, BTL has significant evidence from surveys of volunteers that they find great joy and healing in the program as well, which is why so many of them return with each session.

Bridges to Life by the Numbers

We recognize that not everyone is persuaded by the theological and moral arguments that often surround restorative justice. So, we thought it would be prudent to discuss restorative justice from a fiscal standpoint. Since 1999, BTL has graduated over 87,000 people in carceral and transitional living

---

14. Bridges to Life, "Program Impact."

15. These numbers vary depending on the source. For the lower end of the recidivism rate, see North Carolina Sentencing and Policy Advisory Commission, *Correctional Program Evaluation*, iii. For the higher number, see Prison Policy Initiative, "Reentry and Recidivism," callout box, "Key Statistics."

16. Hyle, "Annual Determination of Average Cost."

facilities in eighteen states and seven foreign countries. Of those graduates, over 86 percent of them do not recidivate within three years of their release. This is remarkable when one considers the range of percentages offered for national recidivism rates. However one runs the numbers, BTL's program and resources reduce recidivism by well over half.

Although Zehr asserts that reducing recidivism is not a primary goal of restorative justice, he points out, "There are good reasons to believe that, in fact, such programs will reduce offending. Indeed, the research thus far is quite encouraging on this issue."[17] Bridges to Life has among its goals "to reduce recidivism rates of program graduates, enhancing public safety and saving taxpayer dollars." Fiscal, and even social, conservatives should rejoice at this reality—a safer community and lower taxes.

This is a place that turns neoliberalism's perverse logic—the logic that puts the number of beds filled in a private prison above the current and future well-being of inmates, staff, and the wider community—against itself by reducing the supply of humans as commodities through the minimization of reoffending. Restorative justice programs like BTL quite simply take people off the market. By reducing the supply of prisoners, the market for bodies to put in cages could be so impacted that it would necessitate a change of strategy for corporations like CoreCivic and GEO Group.[18] Perhaps if the attitudes that drive restorative justice could influence those changes, then those groups would find ways to make money by helping restore lives rather than commodify and enslave them.

Then again, this could be difficult because restorative justice practices and programs like BTL are exponentially cheaper, and thus not incentivized by potential profit. For example, the nearly $100 billion spent on corrections annually in the US could be reduced to a mere fraction of that cost.[19] Further, the lost wages incarcerated people incur during their time in prison, and the lower wages most inmates will earn after their release than they likely would have prior to being incarcerated, along with other social costs, including the likelihood that children of incarcerated parents are more likely to be incarcerated themselves, ultimately costs the US taxpayers for all of this upheaval around $500 billion annually.[20] By comparison, the recent student loan forgiveness plan will be a mere one-time cost of $400 billion. In other words, it

---

17. Zehr, *Little Book of Restorative Justice*, 16.
18. See this book's introduction.
19. Bridges to Life, "Fact Sheet."
20. The Institute for Advancing Justice Research and Innovation is a helpful resource, particularly their Oct. 2016 report: McLaughlin et al., "Economic Burden of Incarceration."

is currently costing society more to incarcerate people annually than it is to offer a one-time debt relief program for higher education.

Bridges to Life's program, by contrast, costs only about $226 per graduate, and merely a little over 13 percent of those graduates will return to prison, while many of them will use the broad network of resources that BTL offers to get quality jobs, housing, therapy, and whatever else they may need to flourish outside of prison walls. In Texas, where BTL was founded and currently serves the most inmates and victims, it costs over $30,000 to incarcerate someone for a year, meaning that it could cost hundreds of thousands of dollars to incarcerate someone over the course of their sentence, and they are still more likely to reoffend than inmates who graduate BTL.[21] In short, the financial savings to taxpayers could be massive if BTL and similar restorative justice programs were more widely utilized in the Texas prison system, and the same is true for other states as well.

And this does not directly account for the cost to victims, including the need for medical attention, the repair or replacement of property, and the ongoing expenses related to healing from trauma. If fewer people are being victimized, then the need to pay for these goods and services will also decrease, which frees up would-be victims to spend money on paying down debt, education, recreation, and sometimes even just meeting basic needs. Again, in short, this saves communities money by preventing crime.

Conclusion: Restoration to Self and Community

Much of this book is focused on the plight of incarcerated people, folks convicted of crimes, but restorative justice attempts to address all stakeholders related to a harm committed, including not only the perpetrator but also those who were harmed, as well as considerations about the wider community. Restorative justice tries to ensure the well-being of those harmed and create safer communities, while also offering opportunities for accountability and mercy to offenders. It is, perhaps, the human condition to be separated from ourselves, fragmented. As Martin Luther said, we are *simul iustus et peccator*, simultaneously sinners and saints, but the restorative justice process attempts to help all stakeholders embrace our saintly impulses as ministers of reconciliation who can become reconciled to ourselves first so that we can be whole to then help entire communities be reconciled. The tendency to be adrift from ourselves has been exacerbated in the age of neoliberalism when people's value is measured by what they can add to the ever-growing market rather than by their humanity. Individuals thus

---

21. See Henrichson and Delaney, *Price of Prisons*.

find themselves in a quandary about how to find wholeness in a world increasingly fractured by wealth inequality, political division, and social strife. While many folks are able to find their place as a cog in the machine, there are many others who do not fit, and they end up being forced into the system of neoliberalism through mass incarceration.

This provides good reason for some folks to argue against restorative justice because it does not appear to address those larger socioeconomic issues. However, whole and healthy people are better equipped to create a whole and healthy society, so transformation must begin within people and communities wherein they recognize the way they have been hurt and in turn hurt others as they try to hustle to make it in a world seemingly ruled by Mammon. However, through restorative justice programs like BTL, people begin to find the healing that leads to wholeness, making those folks excellent ambassadors for a healthier and more just society. Many of the social benefits of restorative justice have been touted in the narratives and analysis above, but it is necessary to emphasize the power this approach has to change individuals and their communities. A restorative justice approach also has the benefit of being able to appeal to both social liberals and fiscal conservatives. In fact, even we, the authors of this chapter, have many disagreements about how society ought to approach justice, prison, discipline, punishment, and societal safety. Restorative justice work can be done by folks who see it merely as a stopgap measure on the way to greater prison reforms or even prison abolition as well as those who take more common approaches regarding long-term incarceration. Restorative justice tells us the story, the truth, about a son being reconciled with the father who had his mother murdered. And, this society needs this story, these stories, if ever we are going to be a society of whole people working to restore one another rather than punish as we seek out God's restored shalom.

10

Prison-Industrial Complex Abolition and Transformative Justice

A Primer for Christians

JOHONNA MCCANTS-TURNER and JAMES W. MCCARTY

In Luke 4, Jesus announces the launch of his ministry by declaring good news for the poor, including "release to prisoners," setting "free those who are oppressed," and declaring "the year of the Lord's favor." In other words, he declares the liberation of prisoners and the forgiveness of debts that kept and continue to keep so many oppressed people on a direct path to imprisonment. In effect, Jesus declares his ministry to include the abolition of prisons.

In Luke 10, Jesus tells a story to help a lawyer understand what it means to love one's neighbor. The story depicts a person (denigrated in the eyes of Jesus's listening audience) intervening when someone has been hurt, creatively using resources such as a roadside inn for support and healing, and responding to harm in ways that are neither negligent nor punitive. This kind of direct aid and creative intervention are central to what is now called transformative justice.

Paired together, prison-industrial complex abolition (PIC abolition) and transformative justice (TJ) make up two of the most radical responses to enduring forms of interpersonal and state violence, including the crisis of mass incarceration in the United States. Rather than tweaking at the edges of an inhumane system that locks people in cages en masse, PIC abolition and transformative justice seek to build a new world where justice looks more like repair and healing than punishment; where safety is not secured via the caging of our neighbors, friends, and family; and where those who inflict harm on others are not harmed in the process of being accountable. Carceral responses to structural and relational harms, PIC abolitionists remind us, only increase the violence and harm in the world by imposing them on those who are incarcerated. A world in which people are caged is not one that is more just than one in which people live free and in communities of healing and support. PIC abolition and TJ really are "good news to the poor" who are most directly impacted by mass incarceration. They are especially good news to those who are structurally and disproportionately harmed by our criminal punishment systems: Black people, Latina/o/x/e people, Southeast Asian people, Native American and Indigenous people, transgender and gender-nonbinary people, disabled people, and poor and working-class white people.

Jimmy's Story

I do not remember when I was first introduced to the idea that policing and incarceration, especially as they are practiced in the United States today, were a system of mass oppression that should be resisted, but it is something that I've known since I was young. I heard themes like this in the hip-hop music that dominated the communities of my youth and in the streets of my neighborhood. In light of the political education I was getting from Public Enemy, Tupac Shakur, and others, I grew to be skeptical of criminal punishment systems early on. However, it was not until I read the autobiographies of Malcolm X, Nelson Mandela, and Angela Davis as a young adult that I was forced to face the depth of the racism, classism, and violence of contemporary punishment practices. Their stories invited me to think beyond prisons in ways mainstream political discourse did not.

Malcolm X was treated differently than his white co-conspirators in a series of burglaries because of racialized gender dynamics. Davis and Mandela were targeted for their politics of Black liberation. In prison they were mistreated, physically abused, and at risk of death. Each of them stared the evils of our current systems in the face and came out seeking radical transformations of their societies. What they sought was the abolition of white supremacy and racist political systems. For Davis, this has taken the shape of seeking the abolition of prisons and policing altogether.[1] She is the first person I ever encountered who expressed the idea that a world without prisons was possible and worth pursuing.

A world without prisons or police—what a radical thought! Indeed, it's almost impossible to imagine.[2] However, PIC abolitionists regularly remind me that abolition has happened many times before. The racialized enslavement of Africans and African-descended peoples was abolished in the United States. Apartheid was abolished in South Africa. British imperialism was defeated in India. The mass institutionalization of the disabled in the United States has ended.[3] Dictators and their political systems have been overthrown across history and in every part of the world. Religious traditions have transformed to be more inclusive and just. And these religious traditions and social movements have been mutually informed and influenced by each other in ways that have contributed to the liberatory potential of them all. It is possible for new worlds to be born if we have the courage and imagination to make it so. Indeed, as Jesus taught us, such new worlds can even be at the heart of the gospel.

Nelson Mandela, a political prisoner for twenty-seven years and a champion for democracy and human rights for most of his life, once wrote that "no one truly knows a nation until one has been inside its jails." He continued saying, "A nation should not be judged by how it treats its highest citizens, but its lowest ones."[4] By this measure PIC abolitionists insist that the United States is a nation that, like Babylon in biblical prophecy, will face a harsh judgment when it comes before God. The oppression, violence, and inhumanity of our current policing and prison systems are such that the only just, and the only faithful, response is to work toward the release of every prisoner and declare the year of the Lord's favor just as Jesus did when he preached his first sermon in Nazareth.

---

1. There is perhaps no more important book to the contemporary history of prison abolition than A. Y. Davis, *Are Prisons Obsolete?* See also the recently released A. Y. Davis et al., *Abolition. Feminism. Now.*

2. Davis makes this point succinctly when she says, "The prison is considered an inevitable and permanent feature of our social lives. . . . Prison abolitionists are dismissed as utopians and idealists whose ideas are at best unrealistic and impracticable, and, at worst, mystifying and foolish. This is a measure of how difficult it is to envision a social order that does not rely on the threat of sequestering people in dreadful places designed to separate them from their communities and families. The prison is considered so 'natural' that it is extremely hard to imagine life without it" (A. Y. Davis, *Are Prisons Obsolete?*, 9–10).

3. On the similarities, connections, and lessons to be learned from deinstitutionalization to PIC abolition, see Ben-Moshe, *Decarcerating Disability*.

4. Mandela, *Long Walk to Freedom*, 201.

Why Prison Abolition?

PIC abolition is grounded in several core commitments: (1) prisons, policing, and the ever-expanding administrative surveillance state are fundamentally unjust, and their resources would be better used to build robust social supports; (2) the promise that prisons and police make us safer is false; indeed they make many of our communities significantly less safe and actually increase the violence borne by many of the most oppressed in our society; (3) and the criminal punishment system as it exists targets poor, Black, Latino, Native American, disabled, queer, and Southeast Asian people in disproportionate ways that are fundamentally racist, classist, ableist, cisheteropatriarchal, and beyond reform.

In regard to the first commitment, Ruth Wilson Gilmore has argued that the ongoing expansion of the size and scope of the PIC is directly related to the social inequalities and problems created by post-industrial and late-capitalist society in the late twentieth and early twenty-first centuries. Many people in urban centers and rural communities have been made to be useless or discarded by a political-economic system focused on never-ending economic growth rather than on human and community flourishing. As industrial jobs are outsourced, in part by the weakening of labor unions, agriculture is monopolized, and business and political decisions are overly influenced by concern for maximizing the short-term profits of shareholders, people who are not already wealthy or able to flourish in a knowledge economy are discarded to communities with few social supports, jobs, or educational opportunities, and become over policed. This over policing functions to ensure that the people who live in communities filled with those who benefit from this system feel safe from and live far from those the system has made poor. One example of this is the ways that the building and filling of prisons have exploded in California since the 1970s.[5]

Gilmore helps us to see that the poor in urban centers, mostly people of color, and in rural areas, mostly white or Native American, are tied together via a racist system of over policing. As formerly industrial areas are abandoned, Black and Brown people are impoverished, their modes of survival are criminalized, and they are then policed and incarcerated at disproportionate rates. Similarly, as job opportunities dry up in rural areas, due to the same global political-economic trajectories, one viable option promised to them by politicians is the opportunity to build and then staff

---

5. See Gilmore, *Golden Gulag*.

prisons. So, the rural poor are promised financial wellness if they participate in the caging of the urban poor.[6]

The reality that rural prisons rarely increase the financial wellness of rural communities is often ignored. The fact that sending the urban poor to be caged far away from their families and communities of support often makes recidivism (i.e., the re-incarceration of formerly incarcerated people) increase is swept under the rug. Those who are incarcerated experience not only the punishment of being denied one's freedom; imprisonment also punishes by extracting people from the networks of love and community that could support their healing and restoration. By severing these bonds, imprisonment exacerbates the social conditions that often lead to future criminalized activity.[7]

In addition, the explosion of prisons and the budgets that keep them filled misdirects public funds away from the kinds of programs that might actually reduce harm. Rather, the ongoing failure of our prison and policing systems, evident in the fact that the United States is not safer or freer from violence than any country with comparable economic standing in the world, is used as justification for expanding the reach of this system on an almost annual basis. What we have, Gilmore says, is a PIC that is designed to hide the social, political, and economic failures of global neoliberalism by shuffling the poor out of sight from the majority of those who do not live in over-policed communities.[8] The PIC obscures rather than fixes the inherent shortcomings of the systems we have built. It makes invisible one of the most defining features of American life: our violence toward one another.[9]

The second core commitment of PIC abolition, that prisons do not make us safer but actually make many of us more vulnerable to violence, is evident as soon as we recognize the violence that is the modus operandi

---

6. As Gilmore says, "Prisons are partial geographical solutions to political economic crises, organized by the state, which is itself in crisis" (*Golden Gulag*, 26).

7. On the impacts of separation from family networks, and correlated increases in violent behavior and depression, see Loper et al., "Parenting Stress, Alliance." On the impacts of family connections on recidivism, see Folk et al., "Behind Bars but Connected." On the harmful impacts on the families of those who are incarcerated, see B. Myers et al., "Children of Incarcerated Mothers"; Hart-Johnson, *African American Women*.

8. Angela Davis makes a similar point when she says, "The prison therefore functions ideologically as an abstract site into which undesirables are deposited, relieving us of the responsibility of thinking about the real issues afflicting those communities from which prisoners are drawn in such disproportionate numbers. This is the ideological work that the prison performs—it relieves us of the responsibility of seriously engaging with the problems of our society, especially those produced by racism and, increasingly, global capitalism" (A. Y. Davis, *Are Prisons Obsolete?*, 16).

9. On the pervasiveness of violence in the United States, see McCarty, "Building Peace."

of the criminal punishment system. From the violations of privacy and due process that often are the experience of being policed; to the (sometimes deadly) force of arrest; to the often-emotional (and sometimes physical) abuse that is the investigation and trial process; to the caging of humans in inhuman prisons designed to punish mind, body, and soul, as well as sever social relationships, nearly every stage of the process from policing to incarceration entails high levels of violence. And, once one is incarcerated, it is culturally accepted that high rates of sexual violence, from fellow prisoners as well as prison staff; gang violence; racialized violence; and more will be regular occurrences for those who have been incarcerated.

In addition, the very act of locking humans in cages is itself dehumanizing and violent, and intentionally so.[10] In a society where the cultural imagination often equates justice with punishment and punishment with violence, it seems natural to many of us to assume that any harm caused, and crime committed, violent or nonviolent, deserves the same punishment: being locked away in a cage like an animal in a laboratory. To be taken from one's community, have free movement restricted, rights stripped away (like the right to vote or earn a liveable wage) are all violence. In addition, within prisons there are other forms of violence used as punishment for those who respond to the violence of the system with interpersonal violence. For example, solitary confinement, the practice of locking someone away by themselves without any other human contact, is one of the most damaging forms of violence as punishment that is regularly used. The psychological and physical torture that is such isolation violates core principles of what it means to be human: to be in relationship, community, and to be held in love. And, of course, the most obvious violence of our system is the ongoing use of the death penalty in many states and at the federal level. The state reserves the right to kill any of its citizens in the name of violence reduction.

All of this violence, abolitionists remind us, is enough to ground the rejection of the PIC. However, the injustice of such a system is even more evident when one takes into consideration whom this violence disproportionately falls upon: the poor, people of color, the disabled, and transgender people. In other words, those most oppressed and vulnerable to other forms of violence are also most often the victims of the violence of the PIC. Such a system is irredeemable. This is the third core commitment of PIC abolitionists.

---

10. "Dehumanization names the deliberate, as well as the mob-frenzied, ideological displacements central to any group's ability to annihilate another in the name of territory, wealth, ethnicity, religion. Dehumanization is also a necessary factor in the acceptance that millions of people (sometimes including oneself) should spend part or all of their lives in cages" (*Golden Gulag*, 243).

Seen in this light, the PIC is the kind of power and principality early Christians named as demonic and needing to be resisted. It brings the opposite of good news to today's poor. And it is the next stage in the ongoing evolution of humanity's rejection of God; from the cross through the executioner's axe and again through the lynching tree to the electric chair and lethal injection table. How can Christians want anything but to abolish a system that does to the poor what was done to the one we confess as Christ? As Jesus announced at the beginning of his ministry, the good news for those most vulnerable to this violence is their release from the grasp of such an evil system.

What Is Prison Abolition?

Prison abolition is composed of a variety of political practices, both formal and informal, that when seen as a whole take steps toward a world where everyone has enough (food, housing, clothes, health care, and more), where we see our safety as connected to the safety of others, and where we understand justice as the healing and repair of harm rather than merely as retributive punishment. To achieve this world we must dismantle and abolish the current systems that are imposing such great violence and injustice today and plant the seeds of new systems that can deliver on the undelivered promises of our current criminal punishment system. This work will take place over generations and will be varied across contexts. However, in each moment or place it is practiced, the work of abolition brings us closer to the horizon of a world where justice is present because prisons are absent.

In regard to the first of those sets of practices, those that dismantle and abolish the PIC, the work that is currently practiced includes political education, political protest, budget reallocation, and community control of public safety. We live in a world where most of us cannot imagine a world without prisons. However, prisons have not always existed, and neither have they always existed in the ways they do today. We know that a world without prisons is indeed possible because humans have lived in those worlds in other times and places. For people to build the imagination to know this reality, political education is required. Sometimes that looks like exposing the injustices and violences of the PIC. Other times it looks like inviting people to imagine a different way of being with one another. In all cases, political education involves both raising awareness about what is happening in the invisibilized world of the PIC and inviting people to imagine and practice new ways of responding to the harm we do to each other.

Beyond political education, sometimes the work of abolition is explicit political protest. Political protest is the organized, strategic, and intentional disruption of the status quo to highlight injustices often not seen by the mass public, build support for radical political change, and transform the systems that perpetuate the injustices at hand. In our historical imagination this often looks like the marches led by Dr. Martin Luther King Jr. in the 1950s and 1960s. This is not the only mode of protest in the abolitionist tool kit, however. Abolitionist protest also looks like Black Lives Matter uprisings after another unarmed Black person is killed by the police, queer and trans people rising up in response to ongoing over policing at Stonewall, and the strikes of laborers demanding living wages and safe working conditions.

Another area of focus for many PIC abolitionists is the reduction of the PIC on the way toward its eventual abolition. In particular, abolitionists often work to reduce police and prison budgets and redirect those funds to programs and policies that meet people's needs in ways that increase safety: education, basic needs like food and medical care, housing, jobs, and more. Related to this work, abolitionists also work to halt the construction of new prisons and insist on investment in other public safety measures like those mentioned above as well as community-led restorative approaches to responding to crime and harm. Rather than accepting the never-ending expansion of police departments, prisons, and their budgets, PIC abolitionists work to shrink the reach of the PIC and build other ways of meeting the presently unmet needs created by the neoliberal political-economic system we have created the last several decades.

Community control of public safety shows up in many forms in PIC abolition. One way that has manifested is in community- or citizen-run police oversight boards. Such boards provide public and transparent direction, oversight, and sometimes investigation into police conduct, especially cases of police misconduct such as excessive use of force. Due to a host of political factors, much of what police do goes unseen by the broader public. Oversight boards serve to make visible the real impacts of police on communities and to give power to citizens to have voice and influence on their everyday lives. Beyond formal community control of public safety and accountability like citizen review boards, many PIC abolitionists also engage in what has come to be called community accountability or transformative justice.

A related but distinct movement from PIC abolition, transformative justice also works to build a world in which there is no need for prisons to exist. Whereas PIC abolition can be tied to formal political processes and administrative organizations, transformative justice builds extra-political structures and systems that are led by oppressed communities to meet the safety and accountability needs that they identify as most important to them.

Transformative justice emerged from anti-violence organizing led by poor and working-class women of color, disabled women, and queer and trans people.[11] While a strong distinction between abolition and transformative justice as if the movements are unrelated is inaccurate, it is true that they have different histories and foci. It may be helpful to think of them both on a continuum of action from dismantling oppressive structures, changing existing systems to be more just, and building new systems that better reflect the values of abolition and community healing and accountability. Within this continuum, the abolitionist focus on dismantling existing institutions is inseparable from TJ's emphasis on building new structures.[12]

Johonna's Story

"My friend was sexually assaulted," he told me. "She doesn't want to involve the police." The person speaking to me supports Black communities in the work of healing and rebuilding after police brutality, particularly when police have killed their neighbors and family members. Thus, I knew that he was well acquainted with many of the reasons why his friend would not want to engage policing and the criminal legal system more broadly in response to the intimate violence she had experienced. As people of African descent who have lived in neighborhoods where harassment and abuse by police officers were common and where this abuse was visited upon people we love, he and I were intimately acquainted with what it means to experience police officers as an occupying force rather than a source of safety. Our lived experiences gave us deep insight on the need for viable community-driven strategies for safety, healing, and accountability in the wake of violence.

---

11. This initial insight was made practical when a group of feminist activists began working against gendered violence beyond carceral systems. See Chen et al., *Revolution Starts at Home*.

12. See Critical Resistance's Dismantle-Change-Build theory of change framework: "*Dismantle-Change-Build*, is CR's *'theory of change' framework* that empowers organizers to strategically chip away at the interlocking systems of policing, imprisonment, and surveillance (what we call the prison industrial complex, or PIC) and put abolition into practice. *We fight to dismantle* the PIC, including the caging, policing, practices, and larger systems that harm, control, and impoverish communities and greater society. *We strive to change* common sense, resource allocation, and practices (at all scales) away from harm, punishment, and control, and toward practices that empower communities and address harm and problems at their root cause. *As we dismantle and change, we build*: we build practices, skills, relationships and resources that address the needs of our communities. From interpersonal to local community to state and larger-scale, we demand that investments be made that are life-affirming and enable us thrive" (Critical Resistance, "How We Organize"; emphasis in original).

Transformative justice is a framework created by marginalized communities to create safety, justice, and healing without relying on prisons, policing, and the state at large, which encompasses government systems and institutions.[13] Moreover, transformative justice is a liberatory social movement to prevent and respond to intimate, interpersonal, and community violence using nonviolent collective action.

One moment when I became painfully aware of the need for what I later came to know as "transformative justice and community accountability" occurred during my early twenties in the small Midwestern town where I was attending college. It was the summertime, the day after I had moved into the first apartment I ever had had to myself, when my new next-door neighbor tried to rape me. After calling a friend to come and pick me up, I reported my assault to the police. The two officers who responded to my call told me that because the perpetrator of the assault, who lived right next door to me, did not leave any bruises, it would be difficult to prove the attempted assault in court, and little would result from pressing charges. Despite my feelings about what they shared, I later learned the content of their response was accurate. A 2021 NBC news article about the reasons why many sexual assault survivors are seeking responses beyond policing included the following statistics:

> Out of every 1,000 sexual assaults in the United States, only 230 are reported to the police, nine cases get referred to prosecutors, and five will result in a prison sentence, according to RAINN, the nation's largest anti-sexual violence organization. This means that more than three-quarters of sexual assaults go unreported to the police. And while there are many reasons why a survivor will choose not to report, the second most cited, after a fear of retaliation, was that survivors believed police wouldn't do anything to help.[14]

The police officers who responded to my experience of attempted rape did not offer to connect me with mental health counseling, resources for emergency housing, or resources that would help me address any of my other immediate needs in the aftermath of my assault. Instead, these needs were met by my friends, neighbors, mentors, and family members. For example, a graduate student I befriended at the university where I was studying provided me with immediate short-term housing; a mentor at the community organization where I volunteered opened her home to me for several weeks

---

13. Dixon, "Building Community Safety."
14. Wong, "'Defund the Police' Movement," para. 11. For the Rape, Abuse and Incest National Network's statistics, see RAINN, "Criminal Justice System."

and provided me with spiritual accompaniment and emotional support while I stayed with her and her family; and my father traveled from the city in the US South where he was living at the time to help me to move into a new apartment across town, which I secured later that summer. A few of the men that I knew from school joined my father and me in helping me to relocate. My experience highlights a key insight at the heart of the contemporary movement for transformative justice: while policing and prisons have never functioned as effective anti-violence strategies, the people closest to us provide our best hope for safety and healing.[15]

And yet, how many of us know how to effectively intervene when violence is happening around us? Months before my attempted rape, one of my close friends at college had been killed by her boyfriend. We had met during my first year and become close because of our shared interests and passions; we were both activists and poets who often railed against the violence of white supremacy and extolled the virtues of Blackness. When I returned to school after studying abroad at the start of my sophomore year of college, I did not see my friend around much, but I knew that she had a new romantic partner. I did not know that she was experiencing abuse at his hands, and it was only after her murder that other friends and I pieced together the various signs that we had witnessed or heard about as if they were patches of a quilt that we had hid even from ourselves, much less communicated to one another. Although I had grown up witnessing domestic violence in my own home, it was my friend's death that led me to long for the knowledge and skills that would enable me and the people in my life to effectively identify and interrupt physical abuse and other forms of interpersonal violence in our communities.

I recall times in graduate school that I heard yelling in the apartment next door that concerned me—particularly moments in which it sounded like what was a "domestic dispute" had escalated into a situation where physical injury could result. I think of these dilemmas in relation to the story Jesus told when he was asked to elaborate on what it meant to love one's "neighbor" (Luke 10: 29–37). As reflected in the parable Jesus narrates, love is an action of intervention to provide safety, support, and solidarity to those who have been violated and victimized. What would it look like for me to be a loving neighbor in those moments—to love myself, the person living next door who is being abused, and the person who is responsible for the abuse? What is a Christian ethical response to these very common forms of interpersonal violence?

---

15. See Mingus, "Pods and Pod Mapping Worksheet."

For many people, whether followers of Jesus or adherents of other faiths, an ethical response to these situations involves calling the police. But what if the person being abused is an undocumented immigrant who could be deported as a result of a phone call to "the authorities"? Or what if the victim-survivor is just as likely, if not more likely, to be harmed rather than helped by law enforcement officials because of white supremacy and other systems of oppression that often impact police responses? Consider the story of "Ms. H., an undocumented Latina woman sexually assaulted by a Los Angeles police officer responding to her 911 call for help when a man was beating her in her home."[16] Many of us are all too familiar with situations when police officers were called to help a loved one in distress, and the responding officers harmed or even killed the person that they were supposed to be helping. Alongside and intersecting with racially motivated police violence, "the risk of being killed during a police incident is 16 times greater for individuals with untreated mental illness than for other civilians approached or stopped by officers."[17] People who are lesbian, gay, bisexual, transgender, Two Spirit (LGBT/TS), and/or whose expression of gender identity falls outside of dominant norms and categories are also at greater risk for being harmed and abuse by police officers. These examples and stories attest that reliance on the police to intervene when interpersonal violence is happening is not the loving response many people think it is. In lieu of dependence on policing and the criminal legal system at large, transformative justice offers a nonviolent response to intimate and interpersonal forms of violence within our homes and communities that is also attentive to the contexts and contours of carceral violence committed by state actors and institutions.

What Is Transformative Justice?

The terms "transformative justice" and "community accountability" name a tradition of liberatory anti-violence movement building launched and led by women of color and gender-nonconforming people of color, many of whom are also rooted in and deeply informed by activist communities for LGBTQ justice and disability justice. As a grassroots social movement, transformative justice was birthed from the intersectional analysis and organizing of radical feminists of color active in feminist movements against domestic violence and sexual assault, as well as anti-racist movements to

---

16. Ritchie, "Law Enforcement Violence," 138.

17. Fuller et al., *Overlooked in the Undercounted*, 1; see also Office of Research and Public Affairs, *Overlooked in the Undercounted*.

end mass incarceration and police brutality. As visionary bridge builders, they linked these disparate movements by forging a holistic anti-violence agenda—an agenda that centered the experiences and needs of women of color who bore the brunt of the failure of social movements to recognize the simultaneity of the multiple forms of violence directed against and within their communities:

> There are many organizations that address violence directed at communities (e.g. police brutality, racism, economic exploitation, colonialism, and so on). There are also many organizations that address violence within our communities (e.g. sexual/domestic violence). But there are very few organizations that address violence on both fronts simultaneously. The challenge women of color face in combating personal and state violence is to develop strategies for ending violence that do assure safety for survivors of sexual/domestic violence and do not strengthen our oppressive criminal justice apparatus. Our approaches must always challenge the violence perpetrated by multinational capitalism and the state.[18]

This explanation of the genesis of approaches that came to be known under the lexicon of "transformative justice and community accountability" comes from Incite!, a US-based national network of radical feminists of color. When a group of feminists of color activists, community organizers, and scholars, including Beth Richie, Andrea Ritchie, and Julia Sudbury, formed the organization INCITE! Women of Color Against Violence, they also contributed to launching the contemporary movement for transformative justice and community accountability.[19]

"We seek to build movements that not only end violence," INCITE! wrote in a statement penned with the prison abolitionist organization Critical Resistance in 2001, "but also create a society based on radical freedom, mutual accountability, and passionate reciprocity. In this society, safety and security will not be premised on violence or the threat of violence; [they] will be based on a collective commitment to guaranteeing the survival and care of all peoples."[20] In expanding the options available to respond to violent harm beyond state entities such as law enforcement and social service agencies, the transformative justice movement offers Christians ethical

---

18. Incite! Women of Color Against Violence, *Color of Violence*, 2.

19. The organization formerly known as Incite! Women of Color Against Violence is now INCITE! Women, Gender Non-Conforming, and Trans People of Color Against Violence.

20. Critical Resistance and Incite! "Critical Resistance-Incite! Statement," 145.

vision and moral wisdom on what it means to love our neighbors and to pursue shalom, which refers to much more than "peace" but also to collective well-being and flourishing.

Goals of Transformative Justice

For therapist, writer, and educator Nathaniel Shara, transformative justice is primarily defined and distinguished by its aims: "Transformative justice seeks to provide people who experience harm with immediate safety, long-term healing and reparations, while demanding that people who have done harm take accountability; and mobilizing to shift oppressive social and systemic conditions."[21]

A first and primary goal is the safety and healing of people who have experienced violence. When this goal is met, survivors are believed and adequately supported by their communities when they come forward.[22] Ongoing harm is interrupted, and new incidences of violence are prevented. In the Gospels, Jesus is repeatedly described as not only "looking with compassion" but accompanying this gaze of compassion with concrete action to address the holistic needs of individuals and communities in need. These actions included feeding, healing, listening, and encouraging, as well as affirming the inherent worth and dignity of those whose humanity was systematically denied by the religious and political elites within his society. Such a holistic approach is also reflected in Jesus's "good Samaritan" parable. Carefully analyzing the intervening Samaritan's response to his "enemy's" experience of victimization, New Testament theologian Christopher Marshall concludes: "Just as love for God is to be all-encompassing, involving the whole of one's heart, soul, mind, and strength, so the Samaritan's love for the Jewish victim is depicted as engaging all the powers of his personality: his sight, his heart, his hands, his strength, his time, his possessions, and his intelligence."[23] The body of practical work emerging from the transformative justice movement on how to support safety and healing for people experiencing violence can guide Christians into such an all-encompassing engagement.

A second important goal is accountability and transformation for people who have abused and violated others.[24] Accountability means that if I have harmed someone, then I must recognize the harm, acknowledge

21. Zehr Institute, "Transformative Justice," 5:40.
22. generationFIVE, *Ending Child Sexual Abuse*, 45, 52. See also Survived and Punished, "S&P Analysis & Vision."
23. Marshall, *Compassionate Justice*, 119–20.
24. generationFIVE, *Ending Child Sexual Abuse*, 45, 52.

its impacts, make reparations, and work toward personal development and transformation with the support of others, so I do not hurt others again." Truth telling and accountability are two of the most neglected and underemphasized dimensions of agape, or unconditional love within Christian ecclesial communities and beyond. Speaking of the application of unconditional love in the face of violence, womanist theologian Melanie L. Harris writes, "There is a 'thorn in my flesh' about how this fierce love and compassion is actually lived out when it comes to holding an abuser or oppressor accountable—and 'loving them' in a justice sense, disallowing them to harm themselves or harm others."[25] For the foreword to *Love with Accountability*, a groundbreaking anthology on child sexual abuse within Black diasporic communities, activist and theological scholar Darnell Moore writes, "*Love WITH Accountability* is a reminder that reckon is, in fact, an act of love. Accountability is real love. It is radical love. And it is a just love that we need."[26] Transformative justice invites followers of Jesus into a practice of love with accountability.

A third goal in creating community safety is community response and accountability.[27] In fact, the term "community accountability" is often used alongside or synonymously with "transformative justice." This goal means that networks of people become equipped to respond to harm in ways that do not cause more harm. They know how to work together to provide support for survivors and other impacted people, encourage accountability among those who have caused harm, and transform problematic norms, without needing or involving the state. Mia Mingus, a founder of the Bay Area Transformative Justice Collective, envisions community safety systems that operate independently from police and government systems—"where we could get help from the people in our everyday lives."[28] Church communities and institutions have become infamous for inadequate and harmful responses to interpersonal violence such as child sexual abuse that occur within their contexts, as well as creating conditions that enable harm doers and punish survivors.[29] However, it does not have to be this way. The trans-

---

25. Harris, "Buddhist Resources for Womanist Reflection," 111.
26. Moore, "Foreword," 4.
27. generationFIVE, *Ending Child Sexual Abuse*, 45, 56.
28. Imarisha et al., "Fictions and Futures," final para.

29. The Catholic Church has often been in the public eye for protecting priests responsible for sexually abusing children. However, this pattern is not limited to the Catholic Church. At the time of this writing, for example, an independent investigation of sexual abuse in the Southern Baptist Church revealed that some members of the Southern Baptist Convention's Executive Committee responded to over two decades of reports of pastors and other church staff sexually abusing children "with resistance, stonewalling, and even outright hostility" (Guidepost Solutions, *Report*, 3).

formative justice movement offers concrete knowledge, skills, and resources for violence prevention, intervention, and response that can equip church communities to offer liberatory responses to interpersonal and intracommunal violence.

Finally, a fourth goal is to transform the community and shift the social conditions that create and perpetuate violence.[30] This goal pushes communities to engage in practices such as community organizing, which can transform institutions and norms that operate through "power-over" rather than "power-with" frameworks. In their place, communities begin to cultivate the everyday norms, practices, and relationships that lead to healthy and sustainable communities.[31] Reflecting on the story Jesus tells in Luke 10, Rev. Dr. Martin Luther King Jr. often implored his listeners to consider the conditions that enabled a man to be beaten and left to die on the side of the road and work to shift these conditions. For example, in his sermon "The One-Sided Approach of the Good Samaritan," King penned:

> Here was the weakness of the good Samaritan. He was concerned [*merely?*] with temporary reliff [*sic*], not with thorough reconstruction. He sought to sooth [*sic*] the effects of evil, without going back to uproot the causes. . . . But there is another aspect of Christian social responsibility which is just as compelling. It seeks to tear down unjust conditions and build anew instead of patching things up. It seeks to clear the Jerico [*sic*] road of its robbers as well as caring for the victims of robbery.[32]

"Clearing the road of its robbers" requires changing social, political, and economic policies and institutions that foster conditions where some people are so desperate for resources that they prey on others more vulnerable to get them. It also means uprooting hierarchical and oppressive systems of power, including white supremacy, capitalism, and heteropatriarchy, which give rise to predatory social relations, including acts of violence against people and communities deemed less valuable by these systems. Transformative justice thus provides a concrete expression for Christians' moral responsibility to shift the social conditions that create and perpetuate violence.

Transformative justice is intimately connected to a broader vision of a world without prisons, jails, and detention centers—a vision that is both critical and generative.[33] Abolitionist organization Critical Resistance offers

---

30. generationFIVE, *Ending Child Sexual Abuse*, 59–61. Zehr Institute, "Transformative Justice," 5:50–7:20.

31. See Kim, "Alternative Interventions to Intimate Violence."

32. M. L. King, "One-Sided Approach," 240.

33. Mingus, "Transformative Justice."

"Dismantle-Change-Build" as a three-part framework for understanding the multifaceted goals of abolition. It involves dismantling and changing existing systems, but also building new, non-retributive forms that are liberatory and transformative. The twinned pursuits of abolition and transformative justice are thus concrete avenues through which followers of Jesus might incarnate the good news of God's liberation and transformation.

Approaches to Transformative Justice

The aims of transformative justice are pursued through creative and holistic approaches that integrate concepts and methods from community organizing, peace building, nonviolent direct action, conflict transformation, and trauma healing. Many of the vibrant and multidimensional strategies associated with the transformative justice movement came out of projects and interventions led by and for communities experiencing multiple forms of violence. One example is the work of Creative Interventions, an intentionally short-term project founded in Oakland, California, with a mission to develop creative community-based strategies to intervene in and stop intimate violence, particularly domestic violence, without involving the state.[34] One co-founder of Creative Interventions, Mimi Kim, was a social worker responding to incidences of domestic violence within Asian immigrant communities. In her day-to-day work, Kim encountered many victim-survivors of intimate partner violence who were unwilling and/or unable to go to the police. However, many organizations linked their provision of services to survivors' affiliation with the criminal legal system. In order to expand the options available to survivors, Kim collaborated with a team of skilled community organizers committed to challenging gender-based violence and the prison-industrial complex simultaneously, including Rachel Herzing, a key leader and organizer in the California Bay Area chapter of Critical Resistance. Kim, Herzing, and members of their team began to support people who wanted to address the intimate violence they had experienced or witnessed without relying on state systems. Guided by facilitators from the team, survivors facing ongoing abuse identified people in their own personal networks who could likely help in the situation. A Creative Interventions team member met with her and those she identified to help them develop a plan for intervention. This was an organizing model—bringing people together to collectively envision and formulate objectives, strategies, actions; follow through; and build their capacity to carry out their own plan rather than turn to "paid professionals." Over the

---

34. See Kim, "Alternative Interventions to Violence."

two years of facilitating creative interventions to violence, the Creative Interventions team developed a compendium of tools and resources to help everyday people clarify what is going on when abuse is or may be occurring, develop collective goals, envision how safety can be established, map possibilities for individual and collective accountability, and create concrete follow-up plans. These resources are now made available for free as part of the Creative Interventions tool kit. In addition, Creative Interventions staff and volunteers collected stories of how everyday people have worked to interrupt interpersonal violence in their homes and communities, which were also archived at their website.[35]

Transformative justice approaches to addressing interpersonal violence committed by strangers were developed by the Audre Lorde Project, an organization of LGBTQ, gender-nonconforming, and intersex people of color in New York City who were experiencing a high rate of bias-motivated violence by people they did not know. They were often targeted for violent attacks because of their gender expression, sexual identity, and race, and they also experienced taunting and brutality by law enforcement officials, including at times when the police had been called to help them. As a result, the Audre Lorde Project launched Safe OUTside the System (SOS), a local campaign to increase safety for queer people of color. One of their efforts was to establish safe spaces in neighborhoods where they spent the most time. Neighborhood organizations and businesses were recruited to be "safe spaces" where people could go if they felt unsafe or were in danger of being attacked. Community members were also trained in bystander intervention so they could intervene in situations where someone who was a stranger to them was experiencing harm. The SOS Collective also organized the businesses and community-based organizations to commit to establishing spaces where harmful and oppressive behaviors did not occur—for example, by training them to nonviolently intervene when sexist, homophobic, transphobic, and racist comments and behaviors were heard or observed. Safe OUTside the System Collective members also led political education in those places and other public spaces so that community members could better understand the roots, impacts, and intersections of race, gender, class, disability, and sexual identity oppression. This work thus encompassed immediate intervention as well as prevention aimed at transforming the social and cultural conditions at the root of racist, homophobic, and sexist violence.

---

35. See https://www.creative-interventions.org.

Transformative Justice and Christian Social Ethics

By its very definition, the state has a monopoly on the use of violence and the legitimization of violence. Because the state is understood as the primary arbiter of violence, practitioners of transformative justice refuse to rely on a violent state to create safety, seek justice, and cultivate communities of care and connection. In this way, the framework of transformative justice is resonant with Anabaptist Christian theology, which posits nonviolence as an essential element of Christian social ethics, and position community commitment and pursuit of radical nonviolence at the heart of Christian discipleship. In the words of Anabaptist theologian J. Denny Weaver, "If the particular story of Jesus is the norm that gives the church its distinct character and shapes its communal practices and its life together, then peacemaking and the rejection of violence are incipient as the privileged manifestation of discipleship or of following the example of Jesus."[36] Rather than commit to nonviolence, violence has been made an idol in which people of all beliefs, including followers of Jesus, place their faith.[37] For Weaver writing in 2013, such an outsize faith in violence is manifest in "a huge but sacrosanct Pentagon budget, the war-related national holidays, the linking of defense contracts to industry and civilian employment across the country, [and] the defense of national violence by the majority of American Christians."[38] While this list primarily accounts for the vestiges of violence implicating the military-industrial complex, one can add to this list the manifestations of state violence by the prison-industrial complex, including forced sterilizations of incarcerated women, deportations of immigrant families, and billions of dollars pumped into the criminal legal system rather than education, food and hunger programs, medical care, affordable housing, and employment training.

Anabaptist Christians such as Howard Zehr and Lorraine Stuzman Amstutz have been visible and outspoken leaders in the movement for restorative justice (RJ), a related approach for addressing harm that emphasizes healing, repair, and accountability. While transformative justice shares much in common with its more well-known "cousin," RJ, "transformative justice is often distinguished from RJ by its explicit emphasis on both personal *and* social transformation, to which the term 'transformative' refers, as well as an emphasis on the collective pursuit of liberation, 'the process of breaking down all forms of oppression and creating a society that upholds

---

36. J. D. Weaver, *Nonviolent God*, 182.

37. J. D. Weaver, *Nonviolent God*, 183.

38. J. D. Weaver, *Nonviolent God*, 183. On this topic, see McCarty et al., *Business of War*.

the dignity, equity, and freedom of all people.'"[39] Rather than calling the police, social services, or other state institutions and agencies, transformative justice builds the capacities of individuals, families, and community members to not only intervene safely when violence and abuse are occurring, but also to respond in ways that are preventative. In addition, transformative justice makes visible the cultural, social, political, and economic conditions that make violence more likely to occur and emphasizes the need to shift those conditions and create new norms, values, and ways of being.

In 2021 Mennonite Church USA published *Defund the Police? An Abolition Curriculum* in response to calls from Anabaptist Christians for resources to help them "discuss and discern policing as another form of state-sanctioned violence."[40] Within the unit on transformative justice, the curriculum writing team offers that the violence of policing is not restricted to the work of individual police officers, but includes the retributive justice lived out within the context of friendship relationships, parenting and caregiving, and workplace contexts. In contrast, "transformative justice offers a set of tools and a way of imagining the world that draw us into the hopeful future of God's reign among us."[41]

Transformative justice is also consistent with Christian liberation theologies that emphasize "the relationship of the Christian faith to political praxis," to quote founding Black liberation theologian Rev. Dr. James Cone.[42] Transformative justice points to the ways in which systems of oppression, including white supremacy, heteropatriarchy, ableism, and religious oppression are root causes of direct and structural violence. Systems of oppression are by their very nature systems of value by which some groups are deemed worthy of dignity and respect, while others are devalued and violence against them is legitimized. Through the lens of liberation theologies, followers of Jesus are called to uproot systems of oppression as ungodly and idolatrous systems that deny the *imago Dei* in all creation, especially those whom dominant society has deemed "the least of these." Liberatory Christian ethics are "ethics from the margins," which call for ethical questions such as how to prevent and respond to violence, to be discerned by seeing

---

39. Zehr Institute, "Transformative Justice," 5:15. The definition of liberation comes from the organization Power U Center for Social Change, based in Miami. (Some traditions of RJ emphasize personal and social transformation as well as liberation, but these emphases are not shared across all traditions and proponents of RJ, as is the case within the contemporary transformative justice and community accountability movement.)

40. Florer-Bixler et al., *Defund the Police?*, "Introduction," para. 2.

41. Florer-Bixler et al., *Defund the Police?*, "Week 4: Transformative Justice," s.vv. "Video Introduction Transcript," para. 2.

42. Cone, "Relationship of Christian Faith."

and perceiving "from below."[43] Black feminist social ethicist Traci West has written that "Christian social ethics will remain inadequately formed without primary concern for socially and economically marginalized people that shapes both core notions for conceiving ethics as well as overarching goals for practicing it."[44] And, what does it mean to continually center those at the margins? INCITE!, one of the most influential organizations in the contemporary movement for transformative justice and community accountability, has explained, "When we shift the center of analysis, there is no permanent center of organizing. Rather, by constantly shifting to the center of communities that face intersecting forms of oppression, we gain a more comprehensive view of the strategies needed to end all forms of violence."[45]

Conclusion

Prison-industrial complex abolition and transformative justice are movements responding directly to the intractable, unjust, and racist violence of mass incarceration. From Jesus's declaration of the Year of Jubilee to his teaching in the parable about the prodigal son, we see Christian participation in these movements as faithful responses to the call of discipleship. And in the traditions of nonviolence, liberation, and social engagement found in radically different streams of the Christian traditions, from Anabaptist to liberation theologies, we find similar resonance. In a world filled with violence and injustice, working toward the abolition of our current criminal legal system and the transformation of retributive responses to relationships of mutual care and accountability is the work Christians are called to participate in.

"I came that you might have life, and life more abundantly," Jesus preached to his disciples (see John 10:10). Supporting communities of everyday people in identifying and drawing from the resources within their communities to address abuse and violation happening in their midst is an example of what it means to move from a scarcity mentality to one of abundance. The transformative justice movement offers prophetic gifts for seeing and thinking abundantly. Prison-industrial complex abolition and transformative justice also offer concrete strategies and practices through which followers of Jesus can embrace the ethics and principles at the center of Jesus's life and teaching, including solidarity, compassion, radical discipleship, the rejection of violence in all its forms, a belief in the dignity and worth of all of creation, and the transforming power of a healing and accountable love.

43. See De La Torre, *Doing Christian Ethics from Margins*.
44. West, *Disruptive Christian Ethics*, xvi.
45. Incite! Women of Color Against Violence, *Color of Violence*, 4.

Bibliography

Aberg-Rieger, Ariel. "'It Didn't Pump Itself.'" Bloomberg, Mar. 16, 2017. https://www.bloomberg.com/news/articles/2017-03-16/-it-didn-t-pump-itself.

ACLU and GHRC. *Captive Labor: Exploitation of Incarcerated Workers.* New York: American Civil Liberties Union and the University of Chicago Law School Global Human Rights Clinic. ACLU, 2022. https://www.aclu.org/wp-content/uploads/publications/2022-06-15-captivelaborresearchreport.pdf.

Adamson, Bryan L. "Debt Bondage: How Private Collection Agencies Keep the Formerly Incarcerated Tethered to the Criminal Justice System." *Northwestern Journal of Law and Social Policy* 15 (2020) 305–37.

Adler, Jeffrey S. "Less Crime, More Punishment: Violence, Race, and Criminal Justice in Early Twentieth-Century America." *Journal of American History* 102 (2015) 34–46.

Ahrens, Deborah M. "Retroactive Legality: Marijuana Convictions and Restorative Justice in an Era of Criminal Justice Reform." *Journal of Criminal Law and Criminology* 110 (2020) 379–440.

Ajunwa, Ifeoma. "The Modern Day Scarlet Letter." *Fordham Law Review* 83 (2015) 2999–3026.

Alexander, Michelle. *The New Jim Crow: Mass Incarceration in the Age of Colorblindness.* New York: New Press, 2010.

Alkon, Cynthia. "An Overlooked Key to Reversing Mass Incarceration: Reforming the Law to Reduce Prosecutorial Power in Plea Bargaining." *University of Maryland Law Journal of Race, Religion, Gender and Class* 15 (2015) 191–208.

Alliance for Higher Education in Prison. *National Directory.* Alliance for Higher Education in Prison, n.d. https://www.higheredinprison.org//national-directory.

Amasa-Annang, Jonny, and Gina Scutelnicu. "How Promising Is the Second Chance Act in Reducing Recidivism Among Male Ex-Offenders in Alabama, Georgia, and Mississippi?" *Journal of Public Management and Social Policy* 23 (2016) 22–37.

American Bar Association. "Rule 3.8: Special Responsibilities of a Prosecutor." American Bar Association, 2025. https://www.americanbar.org/groups/professional_responsibility/publications/model_rules_of_professional_conduct/rule_3_8_special_responsibilities_of_a_prosecutor/.

American Correctional Association. "Our History and Mission." ACA, Aug. 7, 2002. https://www.aca.org/ACA_Member/ACA/ACA_Member/AboutUs/AboutUs_Home.aspx?hkey=0c9cb058-e3d5-4bb0-ba7c-be29f9b34380.

American Correctional Association Congress of Correction. *Resolutions Adopted by the Annual Congress of the American Prison Association, New York, October, 20–24, 1919: Including the Declaration of Principles of the 1870 (Cincinnati) Congress Reaffirmed at the New York Meeting; Including Also the Names of Delegates in Attendance at the New York Meeting.* New York: New York Local Committee and the American Prison Association, 1919.

American Friends Service Committee. *Struggle for Justice: A Report on Crime and Punishment in America.* New York: Hill and Wang, 1971.

American Immigration Council. "Aggravated Felonies: An Overview." American Immigration Council, Mar. 2021. https://www.americanimmigrationcouncil.org/research/aggravated-felonies-overview.

Amuedo-Dorantes, Catalina, and Mary J. Lopez. "Immigration Policy, Immigrant Detention, and the U.S. Jail System." *Criminology and Public Policy* 21 (2022) 433–60.

Anderson, Michael G. "If You've Got the Money, I've Got the Time: The Benefits of Incentive Contracts with Private Prisons." *Buffalo Public Interest Law Journal* 34 (2016) 43–97.

Anselm of Canterbury. "Why God Became Man." In *A Scholastic Miscellany: Anselm to Ockham*, edited by Eugene R. Fairweather, 100–83. Library of Christian Classics. Philadelphia: Westminster, 1956.

Antenangeli, Leonardo, and Matthew R. Durose. *Recidivism of Prisoners Released in 24 States in 2008: A 10-Year Follow-Up Period (2008–2018).* Bureau of Justice Statistics, Sept. 8, 2021. NCJ 256094. https://bjs.ojp.gov/library/publications/recidivism-prisoners-released-24-states-2008-10-year-follow-period-2008-2018.

Appleman, Laura I. "Cashing In on Convicts: Privatization, Punishment, and the People." *Utah Law Review* 2018.3 (2018) 579–637.

Aquinas, Thomas. *Summa Theologica.* Translated by Fathers of the English Dominican Province. 5 vols. Allen, TX: Christian Classics, 1948.

———. *Summa Theologiae.* New Advent, 2017. From *The Summa Theologiæ of St. Thomas Aquinas*, translated by Fathers of the English Dominican Province, 2nd ed. (1920). https://www.newadvent.org/summa/.

Archibald, John. "Police in This Tiny Alabama Town Suck Drivers into Legal 'Black Hole.'" Al, Jan. 19, 2022; updated Jan. 20, 2022. https://www.al.com/news/2022/01/police-in-this-tiny-alabama-town-suck-drivers-into-legal-black-hole.html.

Arnold, Matthew. *Culture and Anarchy.* Edited by Jane Garnett. Oxford World's Classics. Oxford: Oxford University Press, 2006.

Arriaga, Felicia. "Understanding Crimmigration: Implications for Racial and Ethnic Minorities Within the United States." *Sociology Compass* 10 (2016) 805–12.

Ashe, Marie. "Prison-House of Prison-Houses: Incarceration in Theory and in Practice." *Rutgers Law Review* 53 (2001) 437–83.

Ashfaq, Abira. "Invisible Removal, Endless Detention, Limited Relief: A Taste of Immigration Court Representation for Detained Noncitizens." In *Keeping Out the Other: A Critical Introduction to Immigration Enforcement Today*, edited by David C. Brotherton and Philip Kretsedemas, 179–203. New York: Columbia University Press, 2008.

Atwell, Robert R. "From Augustine to Gregory the Great: An Evaluation of the Emergence of the Doctrine of Purgatory." *Journal of Ecclesiastical History* 38 (1987) 173–86.

Bibliography

Augustine, St. *The City of God*. Translated by Henry Bettenson. Penguin Classics. New York: Penguin, 1984.

———. *The Enchiridion on Faith, Hope, and Love*. Gateway. Chicago: Regenery, 1996.

Avio, Kenneth L. "On Private Prisons: An Economic Analysis of the Model Contract and Model Statute for Private Incarceration." *New England Journal on Criminal and Civil Confinement* 17 (1991) 265–300.

Aviram, Hadar. "Are Private Prisons to Blame for Mass Incarceration and Its Evils? Prison Conditions, Neoliberalism, and Public Choice." *Fordham Urban Law Journal* 42 (2014) 411–49.

Ayers, Edward L. *Vengeance and Justice: Crime and Punishment in the Nineteenth-Century American South*. Oxford: Oxford University Press, 1985.

Baker, Jeffrey R., and Allyson McKinney Timm. "Zero-Tolerance: The Trump Administration's Human Rights Violations Against Migrants on the Southern Border." *Drexel Law Review* 13 (2021) 581–661.

Baker, Kelly J. "The Artifacts of White Supremacy." Religion and Culture Forum, June 14, 2017. https://voices.uchicago.edu/religionculture/2017/06/14/813/.

Balto, Simon, and Max Felker-Kantor. "Police and Crime in the American City, 1800–2020." *Oxford Research Encyclopedia of American History*, May 18, 2022. https://doi.org/10.1093/acrefore/9780199329175.013.56.

Barram, Michael. "Economic and Social Reparations: The Jubilee as Biblical Formation for a More Just Future." *Word and World* 42 (2022) 77–86.

Barton, John, and John Muddiman, eds. *The Oxford Bible Commentary*. New York: Oxford University Press, 2013.

Bassett, Debra Lyn. "Ruralism." *Iowa Law Review* 88 (2003) 273–342.

Bazelon, Emily. *Charged: The New Movement to Transform American Prosecution and End Mass Incarceration*. New York: Random House, 2020.

Beale, Calvin L. "Prisons, Population, and Jobs in Nonmetro America." *Rural America/Rural Development Perspectives* 8 (1992) 16–19.

Beccaria, Cesare. *On Crimes and Punishments*. Translated by Henry Paolucci. New York: Pearson/Macmillan, 1963. First edition published 1764.

Beck, Allen J. "Race and Ethnicity of Violent Crime Offenders and Arrestees, 2018." Bureau of Justice Statistics, Jan. 2021. Edited by Edrienne Su. NCJ 255969. https://bjs.ojp.gov/content/pub/pdf/revcoa18.pdf.

Beckett, Katherine. "The Uses and Abuses of Police Discretion: Toward Harm Reduction Policing." *Harvard Law and Policy Review* 10 (2016) 77–100.

Beckett, Katherine, and Lindsey Beach. "The Place of Punishment in Twenty-First-Century America: Understanding the Persistence of Mass Incarceration." *Law and Social Inquiry* 46 (2021) 1–31.

Bellin, Jeffrey. "Reassessing Prosecutorial Power Through the Lens of Mass Incarceration." *Michigan Law Review* 116 (2018) 835–57.

Ben-Moshe, Liat. *Decarcerating Disability: Deinstitutionalization and Prison Abolition*. Minneapolis: University of Minnesota Press, 2020.

Berger, Dan, and Toussaint Losier. *Rethinking the American Prison Movement*. American Social and Political Movements of the 20th Century. New York: Routledge, 2018.

Bernstein, Alan E. *The Formation of Hell: Death and Retribution in the Ancient and Early Christian Worlds*. Ithaca: Cornell University Press, 1993.

———. *Hell and Its Rivals: Death and Retribution Among Christians, Jews, and Muslims in the Early Middle Ages*. Ithaca, NY: Cornell University Press, 2017.

Berry, William W. "Discretion Without Guidance: The Need to Give Meaning to §3553 After Booker and Its Progeny." *Connecticut Law Review* 40 (2008) 631–73.

———. "Eighth Amendment Presumptions: A Constitutional Framework for Curbing Mass Incarceration." *Southern California Law Review* 89 (2015) 67–102.

———. "Individualized Sentencing." *Washington and Lee Law Review* 76 (2019) 13–92.

Besser, Terry L., and Margaret M. Hanson. "Development of Last Resort: The Impact of New State Prisons on Small Town Economies in the United States." *Journal of Community Development Society* 35 (2004) 1–16.

Bhandar, Brenna, and Alberto Toscano, eds. "Editors' Introduction: Reports from Occupied Territory." In *Abolition Geography: Essays Towards Liberation*, by Ruth Wilson Gilmore, 1–22. London: Verso, 2022. Nook.

Bianchi, Herman. "The Biblical Vision of Justice." *New Perspectives on Crime and Justice* 2 (1984) 1–9.

Biden, Joseph R., Jr. "Executive Order on Reforming Our Incarceration System to Eliminate the Use of Privately Operated Criminal Detention Facilities." White House, Jan. 26, 2021. https://bidenwhitehouse.archives.gov/briefing-room/presidential-actions/2021/01/26/executive-order-reforming-our-incarceration-system-to-eliminate-the-use-of-privately-operated-criminal-detention-facilities/.

Birckhead, Tamar. "The New Peonage." *Washington and Lee Law Review* 72 (2015) 1595–678.

Blackard, Kirk. *Restoring Peace: Using Lessons from Prison to Mend Broken Relationships*. Houston: Bridges to Life, 2005.

Blackmon, Douglas A. *Slavery by Another Name: The Re-Enslavement of Black Americans from the Civil War to World War II*. New York: Anchor, 2008.

Blackwell, Christopher. "I Grew Up Believing I Was Dumb. A College Education Behind Bars Healed That Wound." Marshall Project, Apr. 15, 2022. https://www.themarshallproject.org/2022/04/15/i-grew-up-believing-i-was-dumb-a-college-education-behind-bars-healed-that-wound.

Blakemore, Erin. "How the GI Bill's Promise Was Denied to a Million Black WWII Veterans." History, June 21, 2019; updated June 21, 2023. https://www.history.com/news/gi-bill-black-wwii-veterans-benefits.

Boerner, David. "Sentencing Guidelines and Prosecutorial Discretion." *Judicature* 78 (1995) 196–200.

Bolter, Jessica, et al. *Four Years of Profound Change: Immigration Policy During the Trump Presidency*. Washington, DC: Migration Policy Institute, 2020. https://www.migrationpolicy.org/sites/default/files/publications/mpi-trump-at-4-report-final.pdf.

Bonnie, Richard J. "The Surprising Collapse of Marijuana Prohibition: What Now?" *University of California Davis Law Review* 50 (2016) 573–93.

Bounds, Elizabeth, et al. "Incarcerated Women's Understanding of a Good Life." IRB ID: CR001-IRB00100409. Collection of notes, last modified 2018.

Bounds, Elizabeth M. "What Must I Do to Be Saved? Punishment and Redemption Under Incarceration." *Political Theology* 23 (2022) 298–316.

Bowman, Hannah. "From Substitution to Solidarity: Toward an Abolitionist Atonement Theology." *Political Theology* 23 (2022) 362–80.

———. "How to Get Beyond Punitive Thinking in a Pandemic." *Sojourners*, Jan. 24, 2022. https://sojo.net/articles/how-get-beyond-punitive-thinking-pandemic.

———. "What Does the Bible Say About Prisons?" *Sojourners*, Mar. 2, 2022. https://sojo.net/articles/what-does-bible-verse-say-about-prisons.

Bowman, Scott W. "How Did We Get Here? Historical Considerations of Minority Imprisonment." In *Color Behind Bars: Racism in the U.S. Prison System*, edited by Scott W. Bowman, 1:1–5. Santa Barbara: Praeger, 2014.

Bradley, Anthony B. *Ending Overcriminalization and Mass Incarceration: Hope from Civil Society*. Cambridge: Cambridge University Press, 2018.

Branson-Potts, Hailey. "California's Prison Boom Saved This Town. Now, Plans to Close a Lockup Are Sparking Anger and Fear." *Los Angeles Times*, June 21, 2021. https://www.latimes.com/california/story/2021-06-21/newsom-plan-will-shut-rural-california-prison-lose-jobs-susanville.

Brickner, Michael, and Shakyra Diaz. "Prisons for Profit: Incarceration for Sale." *Human Rights*, July 1, 2011. https://www.americanbar.org/groups/crsj/publications/human_rights_magazine_home/human_rights_vol38_2011/human_rights_summer11/prisons_for_profit_incarceration_for_sale/.

Bridges to Life. "Fact Sheet." Bridges to Life, revised Sept. 2024. https://www.bridgestolife.org/fact-sheet.

———. "Program Impact." Bridges to Life, n.d. https://www.bridgestolife.org/program-impact.

Brockway, Zebulon Reed. *Fifty Years of Prison Service: An Autobiography*. New York: Charities Publication Committee, 1912.

Bronsteen, John, et al. "Retribution and the Experience of Punishment." *California Law Review* 98 (2010) 1463–96.

Bronsther, Jacob. "Long-Term Incarceration and the Moral Limits of Punishment." *Cardozo Law Review* 41 (2020) 2369–433.

Brooks, Gwendolyn. "The *Chicago Defender* Sends a Man to Little Rock." National Humanities Center Resource Toolbox, Fall 1957. From *The Bean Eaters* (New York: Harper & Brothers, 1960), 32–34. http://nationalhumanitiescenter.org/pds/maai3/protest/text11/brookschicagodefender.pdf.

Brotherton, David C., and Philip Kretsedemas. "An Annotated List of Immigration Laws." In *Keeping Out the Other: A Critical Introduction to Immigration Enforcement Today*, edited by David C. Brotherton and Philip Kretsedemas, 375–80. New York: Columbia University Press, 2008.

Brueggemann, Walter. *The Land: Place as Gift, Promise, and Challenge in Biblical Faith*. 2nd ed. Minneapolis: Fortress, 2002. Kindle.

Brungard, Ryan E. "Finally, Crack Sentencing Reform: Why It Should Be Retroactive." *Tulsa Law Review* 47 (2012) 745–73.

Buck, Richard. "The *Lex Talionis* and the Human Fetus." *Journal of Biblical Literature* 92 (1973) 319–20.

———. "Restorative Justice in the Hebrew Biblical Tradition." In *Redemption and Restoration: A Catholic Perspective on Restorative Justice*, edited by Trudy D. Conway et al., 88–97. Collegeville, MN: Liturgical, 2017.

Buffington, Jim, Jr. *Betrayed by Choices: A Family Story of Murder, Forgiveness, and Redemption*. N.p.: Self-published, 2023.

———, interview. *Seventy Times Seven*. Episode 11, "Forgiving Their Mother's Murderer." Shalom World, n.d. https://www.shalomworld.org/episode/forgiving-their-mothers-murderer.

Bunton, Derwyn. "Rising from Katrina's Ashes but Still in Crisis: Public Defense in New Orleans." *New England Journal of Public Policy* 32 (2020) 1–11.

Bush, George W. *The Department of Homeland Security*. DHS, June 2002. https://www.dhs.gov/sites/default/files/publications/book_0.pdf.

Butler, Paul. "One Hundred Years of Race and Crime." *Journal of Criminal Law and Criminology* 100 (2010) 1043–60.
California Department of Corrections and Rehabilitation. "CDCR Announces Deactivation of California Correctional Center in Susanville." CDCR, Apr. 13, 2021. https://www.cdcr.ca.gov/news/2021/04/13/cdcr-announces-deactivation-of-california-correctional-center-in-susanville/.
Câmara, Hélder. *Spiral of Violence*. Prayer and Practice. London: Sheed & Ward, 1971.
Caminero-Santangelo, Marta. "Responding to the Human Costs of US Immigration Policy: No More Deaths and the New Sanctuary Movement." *Latino Studies* 7 (2009) 112–22.
Carcasson, Martín. "Ending Welfare as We Know It: President Clinton and the Rhetorical Transformation of the Anti-Welfare Culture." *Rhetoric and Public Affairs* 9 (2006) 655–92.
Cassidy-Welch, Megan. *Imprisonment in the Medieval Religious Imagination, c. 1150–1400*. New York: Palgrave Macmillan, 2011.
Catholic Bishops of the United States. *Responsibility, Rehabilitation, and Restoration: A Catholic Perspective on Crime and Criminal Justice*. USCCB, Nov. 15, 2000. https://www.usccb.org/resources/responsibility-rehabilitation-and-restoration-catholic-perspective-crime-and-criminal.
CCA [Corrections Corporation of America]. *2014 Annual Report: Form 10-K*. CoreCivic, Dec. 31, 2014. https://ir.corecivic.com/static-files/01d82fd4-9aa6-41e5-b1ed-a5b76a3450ee.
Center on Budget and Policy Priorities. "Policy Basics: Temporary Assistance for Need Families." CBPP, updated Mar. 1, 2022. https://www.cbpp.org/research/family-income-support/temporary-assistance-for-needy-families.
Chase, Robert T. "Carceral Networks: Rethinking Region and Connecting Carceral Borders." In *Caging Borders and Carceral States: Incarcerations, Immigration Detentions, and Resistance*, edited by Robert T. Chase, 1–54. Chapel Hill: University of North Carolina Press, 2019.
Chen, Ching-In, et al., eds. *The Revolution Starts at Home: Confronting Intimate Violence Within Activist Communities*. Chico, CA: AK Press, 2011.
Chiao, Vincent. "Mass Incarceration and the Theory of Punishment." *Criminal Law and Philosophy* 11 (2015) 431–52.
Chicago Manual. "Black and White: A Matter of Capitalization." CMOS Shop Talk, June 22, 2020. https://cmosshoptalk.com/2020/06/22/black-and-white-a-matter-of-capitalization/.
Chishti, Muzaffar, and Kathleen Bush-Joseph. "Biden at the Two-Year Mark: Significant Immigration Actions Eclipsed by Record Border Numbers." Migration Policy Institute, Jan. 26, 2023. https://www.migrationpolicy.org/article/biden-two-years-immigration-record.
Chishti, Muzaffar, et al. "The Obama Record on Deportations: Deporter in Chief or Not?" Migration Policy Institute, Jan. 26, 2017. https://www.migrationpolicy.org/article/obama-record-deportations-deporter-chief-or-not.
Cho, Eunice Hyunhye. "More of the Same: Private Prison Corporations and Immigration Detention Under the Biden Administration." American Civil Liberties Union, Oct. 5, 2021. https://www.aclu.org/news/immigrants-rights/more-of-the-same-private-prison-corporations-and-immigration-detention-under-the-biden-administration.

Christian Churches Together. "Principles on Mass Incarceration." Reformed Church in America, Dec. 12, 2014. https://rca.org/wp-content/uploads/2015/06/CCT-Principles-on-Mass-Incarceration.pdf.

Civil Rights Digital Library. "Watts Riots." Civil Rights Digital Library, 1965. https://crdl.usg.edu/events/watts_riots/.

Clark, Elizabeth B. "'The Sacred Rights of the Weak': Pain, Sympathy, and the Culture of Individual Rights in Antebellum America." *Journal of American History* 82 (1995) 463–93.

Clear, Todd R. *Harm in American Penology: Offenders, Victims, and Their Communities*. SUNY Series in New Directions in Crime and Justice Studies. New York: SUNY Press, 1994.

Collinson, Stephen, and Lauren Fox. "Outrage Grows as Families Are Separated. Will Trump Change His Policy?" CNN, June 18, 2018. https://www.cnn.com/2018/06/18/politics/immigration-trump-congress-family-separation/index.html.

Colson Center for Christian Worldview, The, et al. "Justice Declaration: Take a Stand for Justice That Restores." Prison Fellowship, n.d. https://www.prisonfellowship.org/about/justicereform/landing-pages/justice-declaration/.

Committee on the Judiciary. *Federal Rules of Criminal Procedure: December 1, 2021*. Washington, DC: US Government, 2022. https://www.uscourts.gov/sites/default/files/federal_rules_of_criminal_procedure_dec_1_2021.pdf.

Cone, James H. *The Cross and the Lynching Tree*. Maryknoll, NY: Orbis, 2012.

———. "The Relationship of Christian Faith to Political Praxis." American RadioWorks, Mar. 12, 1980. http://americanradioworks.publicradio.org/features/blackspeech/jcone.html.

Congress. "H.R. 2061—Justice System Improvement Act of 1979." Congress, Oct. 12, 1979. https://www.congress.gov/bill/96th-congress/house-bill/2061.

———. "H.R. 3734—Personal Responsibility and Work Opportunity Reconciliation Act of 1996." Congress, Aug. 22, 1996. https://www.congress.gov/104/plaws/publ193/PLAW-104publ193.pdf.

———. "H.R. 5484—Anti-Drug Abuse Act of 1986." Congress, Oct. 27, 1986. https://www.congress.gov/bill/99th-congress/house-bill/5484/text.

———. "S. 1789—Fair Sentencing Act of 2010." Congress, Aug. 3, 2010. https://www.congress.gov/111/plaws/publ220/PLAW-111publ220.pdf.

CoreCivic. "Political and Lobbying Activity." CoreCivic, n.d. https://ir.corecivic.com/corporate-governance/political-lobbying-activity.

Coyle, Michael. "Race and Class Penalties in Crack Cocaine Sentencing." Prison Policy Initiative, n.d. https://static.prisonpolicy.org/scans/sp/RaceandClass.Sentencing.pdf.

Crayton, Anna, and Steven D. Neusteter. "The Current State of Correctional Education." *Prison Journal* 88 (2008) 1–19.

Critical Resistance. "How We Organize." Critical Resistance, n.d. https://criticalresistance.org/how-we-organize/.

Critical Resistance and Incite! "Critical Resistance-Incite! Statement on Gender Violence and the Prison-Industrial Complex." *Social Justice* 30 (2003) 141–50. http://www.jstor.org/stable/29768215.

Cummings, André, et al. "Private Prisons and the New Marketplace for Crime." *Wake Forest Journal of Law and Policy* 6 (2016) 407–40.

Curtis, Cara. "Fragmented Flourishing: Maternal Perspectives on the Good Life in an Unequal Social Landscape." PhD diss., Emory University, 2023.

Custer, Bradley D. "The History of Denying Federal Financial Aid to System-Impacted Students." *Journal of Student Financial Aid* 50 (2021) 1–20.

Dagan, David, and Steven M. Teles. *Prison Break: Why Conservatives Turned Against Mass Incarceration*. Studies in Postwar American Political Development. New York: Oxford University Press, 2016.

Dale, Elizabeth. *Criminal Justice in the United States, 1789–1939*. New Histories of American Law. New York: Cambridge University Press, 2011.

Davis, Angela J. "The Prosecutor's Ethical Duty to End Mass Incarceration." *Hofstra Law Review* 44 (2016) 1063–85.

Davis, Angela Y. *Are Prisons Obsolete?* New York: Seven Stories, 2003.

Davis, Angela Y., et al. *Abolition. Feminism. Now*. Chicago: Haymarket, 2022.

Davis, James F. *Lex Talionis in Early Judaism and the Exhortation of Jesus in Matthew 5.38–42*. Library of New Testament Studies. London: T&T Clark, 2005.

Davis, LaJuana. "Rock, Powder, Sentencing: Making Disparate Impact Evidence Relevant in Crack Cocaine Sentencing." *Journal of Gender, Race and Justice* 14 (2011) 375–404.

Davis, Lois M., et al. *How Effective Is Correctional Education, and Where Do We Go from Here? The Results of a Comprehensive Evaluation*. Santa Monica, CA: RAND Corp., 2013.

De La Torre, Miguel A. *Doing Christian Ethics from the Margins*. 2nd ed. Maryknoll, NY: Orbis, 2014.

Dervana, Lucian E., and Ellen S. Podgor. "'White Collar Crime': Still Hazy After All These Years." *Georgia Law Review* 50 (2016) 709–67.

Devers, Lindsey. *Plea and Charge Bargaining: Research Summary*. BJA, Jan. 24, 2011. Under contract GS-10F-0114L, order 2008-F_08151. https://bja.ojp.gov/sites/g/files/xyckuh186/files/media/document/pleabargainingresearchsummary.pdf.

Diamantis, Mihailis E. "White-Collar Showdown." *Iowa Law Review Online* 102 (2017) 320–34.

Dixon, Ejeris. "Building Community Safety: Practical Steps Toward Liberatory Transformation." *Truthout*, Aug. 25, 2015. https://truthout.org/articles/building-community-safety-practical-steps-toward-liberatory-transformation.

diZerega, Margaret, and George Chochos. "Postsecondary Education in Prison Is a Racial Equity Strategy." Vera Institute of Justice, July 14, 2020. https://www.vera.org/news/target-2020/postsecondary-education-in-prison-is-a-racial-equity-strategy.

Dolovich, Sharon. "State Punishment and Private Prisons." *Duke Law Journal* 55 (2005) 437–546.

Dorrien, Gary. *The Making of American Liberal Theology*. 3 vols. Louisville: Westminster John Knox, 2001–6.

Doty, Roxanne Lynne, and Elizabeth Shannon Wheatley. "Private Detention and the Immigration Industrial Complex." *International Political Sociology* 7 (2013) 426–43.

Douglas, Karen Manges, and Rogelio Sáenz. "The Criminalization of Immigrants and the Immigration-Industrial Complex." *Daedalus* 142 (2013) 199–227.

Douglas, Kelly Brown. "A Christian Call for Reparations." *Sojourners*, July 2020. https://sojo.net/magazine/july-2020/christian-call-case-slavery-reparations-kelly-brown-douglas.

———. *Stand Your Ground: Black Bodies and the Justice of God*. Maryknoll, NY: Orbis, 2015.

Dubler, Joshua, and Vincent W. Lloyd. *Break Every Yoke: Religion, Justice, and the Abolition of Prisons*. New York: Oxford University Press, 2019.

Du Bois, W. E. B. *Darkwater: Voices from Within the Veil*. New York: Harcourt, Brace & Co., 1920.

Dunbabin, Jean. *Captivity and Imprisonment in Medieval Europe, 1000–1300*. Medieval Culture and Society. New York: Palgrave Macmillan, 2002.

Durkheim, Émile. *Moral Education: A Study in the Theory and Application of the Sociology of Education*. Translated by Everett K. Wilson. New York: Free Press, 1973.

Dyszlewski, Nicole P., et al. "Mass Incarceration: An Annotated Bibliography." *Roger Williams University Law Review* 21 (2016) 471–518.

Edwards, Ezekiel, et al. *A Tale of Two Countries: Racially Targeted Arrests in the Era of Marijuana Reform*. New York: ACLU, 2020. https://www.aclu.org/report/tale-two-countries-racially-targeted-arrests-era-marijuana-reform.

———. *The War on Marijuana in Black and White: Billions of Dollars Wasted on Racially Biased Arrests*. New York: ACLU, 2013. https://assets.aclu.org/live/uploads/publications/1114413-mj-report-rfs-rel1.pdf.

Eisen, Lauren-Brooke. "Trump's First Year Has Been the Private Prison Industry's Best." Brennan Center for Justice, Jan. 15, 2018. https://www.brennancenter.org/our-work/analysis-opinion/trumps-first-year-has-been-private-prison-industrys-best.

Eisenhower, Dwight D. "President Dwight D. Eisenhower's Farewell Address (1961)." Milestone Documents, Jan. 17, 1961. https://www.archives.gov/milestone-documents/president-dwight-d-eisenhowers-farewell-address.

Equal Justice Initiative. *The Death Penalty in Alabama: Judge Override*. Montgomery: Equal Justice Initiative, 2011. https://eji.org/wp-content/uploads/2019/10/death-penalty-in-alabama-judge-override.pdf.

Erzen, Tanya. *God in Captivity: The Rise of Faith-Based Prison Ministries in the Age of Mass Incarceration*. Boston: Beacon, 2017.

Evangelical Lutheran Church in America. "A Social Statement on the Church and Criminal Justice: Hearing the Cries." ELCA Media Resources, Aug. 17, 2013. https://elcamediaresources.blob.core.windows.net/cdn/wp-content/uploads/Criminal_JusticeSS.pdf.

Fabens-Lassen, Ben. "A Cracked Remedy: The Anti-Drug Abuse Act of 1986 and the Retroactive Application of the Fair Sentencing Act of 2010." *Temple Law Review* 87 (2015) 645–92.

Federal Bureau of Prisons. "Memorandum on Use of Private Prisons Rescinded: Attorney General Sessions Rescinds Former Deputy Attorney General Yates Decision." Federal Bureau of Prisons, updated Feb. 24, 2017. https://www.bop.gov/resources/news/20170224_doj_memo.jsp.

Felker-Kantor, Max. *Policing Los Angeles: Race, Resistance, and the Rise of the LAPD*. Chapel Hill: University of North Carolina Press, 2018.

Fletcher, Jeannine Hill. *The Sin of White Supremacy: Christianity, Racism, and Religious Diversity in America*. Maryknoll, NY: Orbis, 2017.

Florer-Bixler, Melissa, et al. *Defund the Police? An Abolition Curriculum*. Mennonite Church USA, n.d. https://www.mennoniteusa.org/abolition-curriculum-intro/.

Folk, Johanna B., et al. "Behind Bars but Connected to Family: Evidence for the Benefits of Family Contact During Incarceration." *Journal of Family Psychology* 33 (2019) 453–64.

Forman, James, Jr. *Locking Up Our Own: Crime and Punishment in Black America*. New York: Farrar, Straus & Giroux, 2017.

———. "Racial Critiques of Mass Incarceration: Beyond the New Jim Crow." *New York University Law Review* 87 (2012) 21–69.

Fortner, Michael Javen. *Black Silent Majority: The Rockefeller Drug Laws and the Politics of Punishment*. Cambridge, MA: Harvard University Press, 2015.

Foucault, Michel. *Discipline and Punish: The Birth of the Prison*. Translated by Alan Sheridan. New York: Vintage, 1995.

Fredriksen, Paula. *When Christians Were Jews: The First Generation*. New Haven, CT: Yale University Press, 2018.

Freeland, Gregory. "Negotiating Place, Space and Borders: The New Sanctuary Movement." *Latino Studies* 8 (2010) 485–508.

Freire, Paulo. *Pedagogy of the Oppressed*. Translated by Myra Bergman Ramos. New York: Continuum, 1970.

French, Piper. "A Future for Susanville." *Bolts*, May 5, 2022. https://boltsmag.org/susanville-prison-closure/.

Friedman, Lawrence M. *Crime and Punishment in American History*. New York: Basic, 1993.

Fulcher, Patrice A. "Hustle and Flow: Prison Privatization Fueling the Prison Industrial Complex." *Washburn Law Journal* 51 (2012) 589–617.

Fuller, Doris A., et al. *Overlooked in the Undercounted: The Role of Mental Illness in Fatal Law Enforcement Encounters*. Treatment Advocacy Center, Dec. 2015. https://www.tac.org/reports_publications/overlooked-in-the-undercounted-the-role-of-mental-illness-in-fatal-law-enforcement-encounters/.

Ganucheau, Adam, et al. "The State Inked a Deal to House Parchman Inmates in a Private Prison. Is It Legal?" *Mississippi Today*, Jan. 9, 2020. https://mississippitoday.org/2020/01/09/the-state-inked-a-deal-to-house-parchman-inmates-in-a-private-prison-is-it-legal/.

Garcia, Alfredo. "The New Jim Crow: Churches Respond to Mass Incarceration." *ARC*, Aug. 13, 2013. https://arcmag.org/the-new-jim-crow-churches-respond-to-mass-incarceration/.

Garland, David. *Punishment and Modern Society: A Study in Social Theory*. Studies in Crime and Justice. Chicago: University of Chicago Press, 1993.

Garner, Steve. *Whiteness: An Introduction*. Routledge, 2007.

General Conference Mennonite Church. "Offender Ministries (General Conference Mennonite Church, 1977)." Global Anabaptist Wiki, Apr. 1977. https://anabaptistwiki.org/mediawiki/index.php?title=Offender_Ministries_(General_Conference_Mennonite_Church,_1977).

generationFIVE. *Ending Child Sexual Abuse: A Transformative Justice Handbook*. Generative Somatics, June 2017. https://generativesomatics.org/wp-content/uploads/2019/10/Transformative-Justice-Handbook.pdf.

Genter, Shaun, et al. "Prisons, Jobs, and Privatization: The Impact of Prisons on Employment Growth in Rural US Counties: 1997–2004." *Social Science Research* 42 (2013) 596–610.

Ghandnoosh, Nazgol. "Can We Wait 75 Years to Cut the Prison Population in Half?" Sentencing Project, Mar. 8, 2018. https://www.sentencingproject.org/policy-brief/can-we-wait-75-years-to-cut-the-prison-population-in-half/.

Ghoshray, Saby. "America the Prison Nation: Melding Humanistic Jurisprudence with a Value-Centric Incarceration Model." *New England Journal on Criminal and Civil Confinement* 34 (2008) 313–46.

Gilmore, Ruth Wilson. *Abolition Geography: Essays Towards Liberation*. Edited by Brenna Bhandar and Alberto Toscano. London: Verso, 2022. Nook.

———. *Golden Gulag: Prisons, Surplus, Crisis, and Opposition in Globalizing California*. American Crossroads. Berkeley: University of California Press, 2007.

———. "The Worrying State of the Anti-Prison Movement." *Social Justice*, Feb. 23, 2015. http://www.socialjusticejournal.org/the-worrying-state-of-the-anti-prison-movement/.

Golash-Boza, Tanya. "The Immigration Industrial Complex: Why We Enforce Immigration Policies Destined to Fail." *Sociology Compass* 3 (2009) 295–309.

Gold, Martin E. "The Privatization of Prisons." *Urban Lawyer* 28 (1996) 359–99.

Gómez, Laura E. "Race, Colonialism, and Criminal Law: Mexicans and the American Criminal Justice System in Territorial New Mexico." *Law and Society Review* 34 (2000) 1129–202.

Gorringe, Timothy. *God's Just Vengeance: Crime, Violence and the Rhetoric of Salvation*. Cambridge Studies in Ideology and Religion 9. Cambridge: Cambridge University Press, 1996.

Gorz, André. *Strategy for Labor: A Radical Proposal*. Boston: Beacon, 1964.

GovInfo. "Department of the Interior and Related Agencies Appropriations Act, 1985 [P.L. 98–473]." GovInfo, Oct. 12, 1984. https://www.gpo.gov/fdsys/pkg/STATUTE-98/pdf/STATUTE-98-Pg1837.pdf.

———. "District of Columbia Court Reform and Criminal Procedure Act of 1970 [P.L. 91–358]." GovInfo, July 29, 1970. https://www.govinfo.gov/content/pkg/STATUTE-84/pdf/STATUTE-84-Pg473.pdf.

———. "Elementary and Secondary Education Act of 1965 [as Amended Through P.L. 118-42, Enacted March 9, 2024]." GovInfo, n.d. https://www.govinfo.gov/content/pkg/COMPS-748/uslm/COMPS-748.xml.

———. "Higher Education Act of 1965 [P.L. 89–329; Approved November 8, 1965] [as Amended Through P.L. 118-45, Enacted December 11, 2024]." GovInfo, n.d. https://www.govinfo.gov/content/pkg/COMPS-765/pdf/COMPS-765.pdf.

———. "Law Enforcement Assistance Act of 1965 [P.L. 89–197]." GovInfo, Sept. 22, 1965. https://www.govinfo.gov/content/pkg/STATUTE-79/pdf/STATUTE-79-Pg828.pdf.

———. "Omnibus Crime Control and Safe Streets Act of 1968 [P.L. 90–351]." GovInfo, June 19, 1968. https://www.gpo.gov/fdsys/pkg/STATUTE-82/pdf/STATUTE-82-Pg197.pdf.

GovTrack. "H.R. 2461 (101st): National Defense Authorization Act for Fiscal Years 1990 and 1991." GovTrack, Nov. 29, 1989. https://www.govtrack.us/congress/bills/101/hr2461/text.

Graber, Jennifer. *The Furnace of Affliction: Prisons and Religion in Antebellum America*. Chapel Hill: University of North Carolina Press, 2011.

———. "Natives Need Prison: The Sanctification of Racialized Incarceration." Special Issue, *Carceral Intersections: Christianity and the Crisis of Mass Incarceration*. *Religions* 10 (2019). https://www.mdpi.com/2077-1444/10/2/87.

Green, Stuart P. "Moral Ambiguity in White Collar Criminal Law." *Notre Dame Journal of Law Ethics and Public Policy* 18 (2004) 501–19.

Gregory of Nyssa. "An Address on Religious Instruction." In *Christology of the Later Fathers*, edited by Edward R. Hardy, 268–326. Library of Christian Classics. Philadelphia: Westminster, 1954.

Griffin, Lissa, and Ellen Yaroshefsky. "Ministers of Justice and Mass Incarceration." *Georgetown Journal of Legal Ethics* 30 (2017) 301–35.

Griffith, Aaron. *God's Law and Order: The Politics of Punishment in Evangelical America*. Cambridge, MA: Harvard University Press, 2020.

———. "'The Real Victim of Lynch Law Is the *Government*': American Protestant Anti-Lynching Advocacy and the Making of Law and Order." Special Issue, *Carceral Intersections: Christianity and the Crisis of Mass Incarceration*. *Religions* 10 (2019). https://doi.org/10.3390/rel10020116.

Griffith, Lee. *The Fall of the Prison: Biblical Perspectives on Prison Abolition*. Grand Rapids: Eerdmans, 1993.

Guidepost Solutions LLC. *Report of the Independent Investigation: The Southern Baptist Convention Executive Committee's Response to Sexual Abuse Allegations and an Audit of the Procedures and Actions of the Credentials Committee*. Document Cloud, May 15, 2022. https://www.documentcloud.org/documents/22031737-final-guidepost-solutions-independent-investigation-report/.

Gunn, Carlton, and Myra Sun. "Sometimes the Cure Is Worse Than the Disease: The One-Way White-Collar Sentencing Ratchet." *Human Rights* 38 (2011) 9–12, 23.

Gutmann, Amy. "What Makes a University Education Worthwhile?" Penn Office of the President, Oct. 5, 2011. https://gutmann-archived.president.upenn.edu/meet-president/what-makes-university-education-worthwhile.

Hadden, Sally E. *Slave Patrols: Law and Violence in Virginia and the Carolinas*. Cambridge, MA: Harvard University Press, 2001.

Hager, Eli. "How Trump Made a Tiny Christian College the Nation's Biggest Prison Educator." Marshall Project, Dec. 17, 2020. https://www.themarshallproject.org/2020/12/17/this-tiny-christian-college-has-made-millions-on-prisoners-under-trump.

Halladay, Josh. "The Thirteenth Amendment, Prison Labor Wages, and Interrupting the Intergenerational Cycle of Subjugation." *Seattle University Law Review* 42 (2019) 937–63.

Hamilton, Neil D. "Rural Lands and Rural Livelihoods: Using Land and Natural Resources to Revitalize Rural America." *Drake Journal of Agricultural Law* 13 (2008) 179–206.

Harlow, Caroline Wolf. *Education and Correctional Populations*. BJS, Jan. 2003; revised Apr. 15, 2003. Bureau of Justice Statistics Special Report. NCJ 195670. https://bjs.ojp.gov/content/pub/pdf/ecp.pdf.

Harris, Melanie L. "Buddhist Resources for Womanist Reflection." *Buddhist-Christian Studies* 34 (2014) 107–14.

Hart-Johnson, Avon. *African American Women with Incarcerated Mates: The Psychological and Social Impact of Mass Incarceration*. Jefferson, NC: McFarland & Co., 2017.

Harvard University. "Radical Commitments [The Life and Legacy of Angela Davis], Session 3: Abolition (Radcliffe Institute)." YouTube, Nov. 26, 2019. https://www.youtube.com/watch?v=LpBSWx9peiM&list=PLTt9bwjR4BIczzzgUneQXntSFS4lQKroN&index=6.

Haugh, Todd. "Overcriminalization's New Harm Paradigm." *Vanderbilt Law Review* 68 (2015) 1191–241.

Haymarket Books. "Abolition, Cultural Freedom, Liberation." YouTube, Oct. 5, 2021. Hosted by Keeanga-Yamahtta Taylor, with guests Angela Y. Davis, Mike Davis, and Ruth Wilson Gilmore. https://www.youtube.com/watch?v=WLOoUuSnPzU.

Hays, Richard B. *The Moral Vision of the New Testament: A Contemporary Introduction to New Testament Ethics*. San Francisco: HarperSanFrancisco, 1996.

Henrichson, Christian, and Ruth Delaney. *The Price of Prisons: What Incarceration Costs Taxpayers*. Vera Institute of Justice, Jan. 2012; updated July 20, 2012. https://www.vera.org/downloads/publications/price-of-prisons-updated-version-021914.pdf.

Hernández, Kelly Lytle. *City of Inmates: Conquest, Rebellion, and the Rise of Human Caging in Los Angeles, 1771–1965*. Justice, Power, and Politics. Chapel Hill: University of North Carolina Press, 2017.

Herskind, Micah. "Some Reflections on Prison Abolition." Medium, Dec. 7, 2019. https://micahherskind.medium.com/some-reflections-on-prison-abolition-after-mumi-5197a4c3cf98.

Hertzig, Nancy A. *The School-to-Prison Pipeline: Education, Discipline, and Racialized Double Standards*. Santa Barbara: Praeger, 2016.

Hessick, Carissa Byrne. "The Myth of Common Law Crimes." *Virginia Law Review* 105 (2019) 965–1024.

———. *Punishment Without Trial: Why Plea Bargaining Is a Bad Deal*. New York: Abrams, 2021.

Hindus, Michael S. *Prison and Plantation: Crime, Justice, and Authority in Massachusetts and South Carolina, 1767–1878*. Studies in Legal History. Chapel Hill: University of North Carolina Press, 2012.

Hinton, Elizabeth. *America on Fire: The Untold History of Police Violence and Black Rebellion Since the 1960s*. New York: Liveright, 2021.

———. *From the War on Poverty to the War on Crime: The Making of Mass Incarceration in America*. Cambridge, MA: Harvard University Press, 2016.

Hinton, Elizabeth, and DeAnza Cook. "The Mass Criminalization of Black Americans: A Historical Overview." *Annual Review of Criminology* 4 (2021) 261–86.

Hirschberger, Jeanne. "'Imprisonment Is Expensive'—Breaking Down the Costs and Impacts Globally." Penal Reform, July 24, 2020. https://www.penalreform.org/blog/imprisonment-is-expensive-breaking-down-the-costs-and/.

Hollister, Annie. "Litigating ICE's 'Voluntary Work Program.'" OnLabor, Apr. 10, 2020. https://onlabor.org/litigating-ices-voluntary-work-program/.

Holmes, Stephen R. "Penal Substitution." In *T&T Clark Companion to Atonement*, edited by Adam J. Johnson, 295–314. Bloomsbury Companions. New York: Bloomsbury T&T Clark, 2017.

Horowitz, Helen Lefkowitz. "Balancing Hopes and Limits in the Liberal Arts College." ACLS, 2005. From *Liberal Arts Colleges in American Higher Education: Challenges and Opportunities*, 16–25. ACLS Occasional Paper 59. https://www.acls.org/wp-content/uploads/2021/11/Occasional_Paper_059_2005.pdf.

Human Rights Watch. "Incarcerated America." Human Rights Watch, Apr. 2003. https://www.hrw.org/legacy/backgrounder/usa/incarceration/us042903.pdf.

Hyle, Ken. "Annual Determination of Average Cost of Incarceration Fee (COIF)." *Federal Register*, Sept. 1, 2021. https://www.federalregister.gov/documents/2021/09/01/2021-18800/annual-determination-of-average-cost-of-incarceration-fee-coif.

Ifill, Gwen. "The 1992 Campaign: The Democrats; Clinton, in Houston Speech, Assails Bush on Crime Issue." *New York Times*, July 24, 1992. https://www.nytimes.com/1992/07/24/us/1992-campaign-democrats-clinton-houston-speech-assails-bush-crime-issue.html.

Ignatieff, Michael. *A Just Measure of Pain: The Penitentiary in the Industrial Revolution, 1750–1850*. New York: Pantheon, 1978.

Imarisha, Walidah, et al. "The Fictions and Futures of Transformative Justice: A Conversation with the Authors of *Octavia's Brood*." New Inquiry, Apr. 20, 2017. https://thenewinquiry.com/the-fictions-and-futures-of-transformative-justice/.

Immigration and Customs Enforcement. *Endgame: Office of Detention and Removal Strategic Plan, 2003–2012; Detention and Removal Strategy for a Secure Homeland*. Washington, DC: U.S. Department of Homeland Security, 2003. http://soli-deo-gloria.international/assets/endgame-usa.pdf.

Incite! Women of Color Against Violence, ed. *Color of Violence: The Incite! Anthology*. Cambridge, MA: South End, 2006.

Jacobson, Matthew Frye. *Whiteness of a Different Color: European Immigrants and the Alchemy of Race*. Cambridge, MA: Harvard University Press, 1999.

Jennings, Willie James. *Acts*. Belief: A Theological Commentary on the Bible. Louisville: Westminster John Knox, 2017.

———. *The Christian Imagination: Theology and the Origins of Race*. New Haven, CT: Yale University Press, 2010.

Jett, Brandon T. "'Many People "Colored" Have Come to the Homicide Office': Police Investigations of African American Homicides in Memphis, 1920–1945." In *Crime and Punishment in the Jim Crow South: The History of White Supremacy and Criminal Justice*, edited by Amy Louise Wood and Natalie J. Ring, 34–57. Urbana: University of Illinois Press, 2019.

Jobe, Sarah C. "Carceral Hermeneutics: Discovering the Bible in Prison and the Prison in the Bible." *Religions* 10 (2019) 101. https://doi.org/10.3390/rel10020101.

———. "Rethinking Responsibility: Moral Injury from War to Prison." *Political Theology* 23 (2022) 335–49.

Johnson, Lyndon B. "Annual Message to the Congress on the State of the Union." American Presidency Project, Jan. 8, 1964. https://www.presidency.ucsb.edu/documents/annual-message-the-congress-the-state-the-union-25.

Johnston, Norman. "Evolving Function: Early Use of Imprisonment as Punishment." *Prison Journal* 89 (2009) 10S–34S.

Jones, Robert P. *White Too Long: The Legacy of White Supremacy in American Christianity*. New York: Simon & Schuster, 2020.

Jouet, Mugambi. "Mass Incarceration Paradigm Shift? Convergence in an Age of Divergence." *Journal of Criminal Law and Criminology* 109 (2019) 703–68.

Kang-Brown, Jacob, et al. "People in Jail and Prison in 2021." Vera Institute of Justice, June 2021. https://www.vera.org/publications/people-in-jail-and-prison-in-spring-2021.

Kann, Mark E. *Punishment, Prisons, and Patriarchy: Liberty and Power in the Early American Republic*. New York: New York University Press, 2005.

Karakatsanis, Alec. "The Punishment Bureaucracy: How to Think About 'Criminal Justice Reform.'" *Yale Law Journal Forum* 128 (2019). https://www.yalelawjournal.org/forum/the-punishment-bureaucracy.

Keenan, James F., SJ. *The Works of Mercy: The Heart of Catholicism*. Lanham, MD: Rowman & Littlefield, 2008.

Kelly, Esteban Lance. "Philly Stands Up: Inside the Politics and Poetics of Transformative Justice and Community Accountability in Sexual Assault Situations." *Social Justice* 37 (2011–12) 44–57.

Kilty, Keith M., and Alfred Joseph. "Institutional Racism and Sentencing Disparities for Cocaine Possession." *Journal of Poverty* 3 (1999) 1–17.

Kim, Mimi. "Alternative Interventions to Intimate Violence: Defining Political and Pragmatic Challenges." In *Restorative Justice and Violence Against Women*, edited by James Ptacek, 193–217. Interpersonal Violence. Oxford: Oxford University Press, 2009.

———. "Alternative Interventions to Violence: Creative Interventions." *International Journal of Narrative Therapy and Community Work* 4 (2006) 45–52. https://dulwichcentre.com.au/wp-content/uploads/2021/12/Alternative-interventions-to-violence-Creative-interventions-M-Kim.pdf.

King, Martin Luther, Jr. "The One-Sided Approach of the Good Samaritan." Stanford University, Nov. 20, 1955. In *The Martin Luther King, Jr. Papers Project*, 239–40. http://okra.stanford.edu/transcription/document_images/Vol06Scans/20Nov1955TheOne-SidedApproachoftheGoodSamaritan.pdf.

King, Ryan S., and Marc Mauer. "The War on Marijuana: The Transformation of the War on Drugs in the 1990s." *Harm Reduction Journal* 3 (2006) 1–17.

Kotsko, Adam. "The Persistence of the Ransom Theory of the Atonement." In *T&T Clark Companion to Atonement*, edited by Adam J. Johnson, 277–93. Bloomsbury Companions. New York: Bloomsbury T&T Clark, 2017.

Krauss, Rebecca. "The Theory of Prosecutorial Discretion in Federal Law: Origins and Development." *Seton Hall Circuit Review* 6 (2009) 1–28.

Kretsedemas, Philip, and David C. Brotherton. "Open Markets and Militarized Borders? Immigration Enforcement Today." In *Keeping Out the Other: A Critical Introduction to Immigration Enforcement Today*, edited by David C. Brotherton and Philip Kretsedemas, 1–28. New York: Columbia University Press, 2008.

Küng, Hans. *Eternal Life? Life After Death as a Medical, Philosophical, and Theological Problem.* Translated by Edward Quinn. New York: Crossroad, 1996.

Kurzban, Ira J. "Democracy and Immigration." In *Keeping Out the Other: A Critical Introduction to Immigration Enforcement Today*, edited by David C. Brotherton and Philip Kretsedemas, 63–78. New York: Columbia University Press, 2008.

Kushner, Rachel. "Is Prison Necessary? Ruth Wilson Gilmore Might Change Your Mind." *New York Times*, Apr. 17, 2019. https://www.nytimes.com/2019/04/17/magazine/prison-abolition-ruth-wilson-gilmore.html.

Laferrière, Anik. "Peddlers of Paradise: The Sale of Indulgences and Confraternity by the English Austin Friars in the Fifteenth and Sixteenth Centuries." *Church History and Religious Culture* 97 (2017) 29–52.

Langan, Patrick A. "Racial Disparity in U.S. Drug Arrests." Bureau of Justice Statistics, Oct. 1, 1995. NCJ 174600. https://bjs.ojp.gov/library/publications/racial-disparity-us-drug-arrests.

Lapide, Pinchas. *The Sermon on the Mount: Utopia or Program for Action?* Maryknoll, NY: Orbis, 1986.

Lassiter, Matthew D., and the Policing and Social Justice HistoryLab. "The Creation of STRESS." University of Michigan Carceral State Project, 2021. In *Detroit Under Fire: Police Violence, Crime Politics, and the Struggle for Racial Justice in the Civil Rights Era.* https://policing.umhistorylabs.lsa.umich.edu/s/detroitunderfire/page/creation-of-stress.

Lauve, Ronald F. "Statement of Ronald F. Lauve, Senior Associate Director General Government Division, Before the Subcommittee on the Judiciary on Military Cooperation with Civilian Law Enforcement Agencies." United States Government Accountability Office, July 28, 1983. http://archive.gao.gov/d40t12/122004.pdf.

Lawson, Tamara F. "Human Dignity: The Clandestine Factor in Prosecutorial Discretion." *Intercultural Human Rights Law Review* 14 (2019) 193–200.

Lee, Stephen, and Sameer M. Ashar. "DACA, Government Lawyers, and Public Interest." *Fordham Law Review* 87 (2019) 1879–912.

Leonetti, Carrie. "Speaking of Prosecutors: Deceptively Descriptive on the Surface with a Heavy Normative Undertow." *Ohio State Journal of Criminal Law* 16 (2019) 453–62.

Levad, Amy. "Repairing the Breach: Faith-Based Community Organizing to Dismantle Mass Incarceration." *Religions* 10 (2019) 42.

Levin, Benjamin. "The Consensus Myth in Criminal Justice Reform." *Michigan Law Review* 117 (2018) 259–318.

———. "Criminal Law Exceptionalism." *Virginia Law Review* 108 (2022) 1381–448.

———. "Imagining the Progressive Prosecutor." *Minnesota Law Review* 105 (2021) 1415–51.

Levy, David. "Prison Education Across the U.S." Degree Choices, Nov. 4, 2021; updated July 3, 2022. https://web.archive.org/web/20221003123548/https://www.degreechoices.com/blog/prison-education-usa/.

Lichtenstein, Alex. *Twice the Work of Free Labor: The Political Economy of Convict Labor in the New South*. Haymarket Series. New York: Verso, 1996.

Liebmann, Marian. *Restorative Justice: How It Works*. London: Kingsley, 2007.

Lipman, David M. "Mississippi's Prison Experience." *Mississippi Law Journal* 45 (1974) 685–756.

Little, Ross. "Moral Sight and Ethical Praxis in the Prison Classroom." *Criminology and Criminal Justice* 0 (2023). https://doi.org/10.1177/17488958231197817.

Lloyd, Vincent, and Joshua Dubler. *Break Every Yoke: Religion, Justice, and the Abolition of Prisons*. New York: Oxford University Press, 2019.

Loper, Ann Booker, et al. "Parenting Stress, Alliance, Child Contact, and Adjustment of Imprisoned Mothers and Fathers." *Journal of Offender Rehabilitation* 48 (2009) 483–503.

Lopez, German. "These Maps Show the War on Drugs Is Mostly Fought in Poor Neighborhoods." *Vox*, Apr. 16, 2015. https://www.vox.com/2015/4/16/8431283/drug-war-poverty.

López, Ian Haney. *Dog Whistle Politics: How Coded Racial Appeals Have Reinvented Racism and Wrecked the Middle Class*. Repr., New York: Oxford University Press, 2015.

Lovato, Roberto. "Juan Crow in Georgia." *Nation*, May 8, 2008. https://www.thenation.com/article/archive/juan-crow-georgia/.

Luan, Livia. "Profiting from Enforcement: The Role of Private Prisons in U.S. Immigration Detention." Migration Policy Institute, May 2, 2018. https://www.migrationpolicy.org/article/profiting-enforcement-role-private-prisons-us-immigration-detention.

Luckey, John. *Prison Sketches*. New York: Carleton & Phillips, 1853.

Lujan, Carol Chiago, and Gordon Adams. "U.S. Colonization of Indian Justice Systems: A Brief History." *Wicazo Sa Review* 19 (2004) 9–23.

Lyman, Stanford M. "The Chinese Before the Courts: Ethnoracial Construction and Marginalization." *International Journal of Politics, Culture, and Society* 6 (1993) 443–62.

MacCormick, Austin H. *The Education of Adult Prisoners: A Survey and a Program*. New York: National Society of Penal Information, 1931.

Man, Simeon. "Anti-Asian Violence and US Imperialism." *Race and Class* 62 (2020) 24–33.

Mandela, Nelson. *Long Walk to Freedom: The Autobiography of Nelson Mandela*. New York: Back Bay, 1994.

Manion, Jen. *Liberty's Prisoners: Carceral Culture in Early America*. Early American Studies. Philadelphia: University of Pennsylvania Press, 2015.

Mann, Brian. "The Drug Laws That Changed How We Punish." NPR, Feb. 14, 2013. https://www.npr.org/2013/02/14/171822608/the-drug-laws-that-changed-how-we-punish.

Manual, Ian. *My Time Will Come: A Memoir of Crime, Punishment, Hope, and Redemption*. New York: Pantheon, 2021.

Marsden, George M. *Understanding Fundamentalism and Evangelicalism*. Grand Rapids: Eerdmans, 1990.

Markowitz, Peter L. "Prosecutorial Discretion Power at Its Zenith: The Power to Protect Liberty." *Boston University Law Review* 97 (2017) 489–549.

Marshall, Chris. *The Little Book of Biblical Justice: A Fresh Approach to the Bible's Teaching on Justice*. Little Books of Justice and Peacebuilding. Intercourse, PA: Good Books, 2005.

Marshall, Christopher D. *All Things Reconciled: Essays on Restorative Justice, Religious Violence, and the Interpretation of Scripture*. Eugene, OR: Cascade, 2018. Kindle.

———. *Beyond Retribution: A New Testament Vision for Justice, Crime, and Punishment*. Grand Rapids: Eerdmans, 2001.

———. *Compassionate Justice: An Interdisciplinary Dialogue with Two Gospel Parables on Law, Crime, and Restorative Justice*. Theopolitical Visions 15. Eugene, OR: Cascade, 2012.

Maruschak, Laura M., and Emily D. Buehler. *Census of State and Federal Adult Correctional Facilities, 2019—Statistical Tables*. Bureau of Justice Statistics, Nov. 2021. NCJ 301366. Census of State and Federal Correctional Facilities. https://bjs.ojp.gov/library/publications/census-state-and-federal-adult-correctional-facilities-2019-statistical-tables.

Martell, Loida I. "*La Nueva Encomienda*: The Church's Response to Undocumented Migrants as Mass Incarcerated." In *Thinking Theologically About Mass Incarceration: Biblical Foundations and Justice Imperatives*, edited by Antonios Kireopoulous et al., 161–93. National Council of the Churches of Christ in the USA Faith and Order Commission Theological Series. New York: Paulist, 2017.

Martinson, Robert. "What Works? Questions and Answers About Prison Reform." *National Affairs* 35 (1974) 22–54.

Mathews, Donald G. *At the Altar of Lynching: Burning Sam Hose in the American South*. Cambridge Studies on the American South. New York: Cambridge University Press, 2017.

McCants-Turner, Johonna. "Creating Safety for Ourselves." In *Colorizing Restorative Justice: Creating Safety for Ourselves*, edited by Edward C. Valandra (Waŋbli Wapȟáha Hokšíla), 291–321. Minneapolis: Living Justice, 2020.

McCarty, James W. "Building Peace in a Violent Nation: A Kingian Response to the Interconnected Violence of Racism, Materialism, and Militarism." In *The Business of War: Theological and Ethical Reflections on the Military-Industrial Complex*, edited by James W. McCarty et al., 179–92. Eugene, OR: Cascade, 2020.

McCarty, James W., et al., eds. *The Business of War: Theological and Ethical Reflections on the Military-Industrial Complex*. Eugene, OR: Cascade, 2020.

McDonald, Jennifer, and Dick M. Carpenter II. *Frustrating, Corrupt, Unfair: Civil Forfeiture in the Words of Its Victims*. Institute for Justice, Oct. 2021. https://ij.org/wp-content/uploads/2021/09/Frustrating-Corrupt-Unfair_Civil-Forfeiture-in-the-Words-of-Its-Victims-2.pdf.

McDowell, Robin, and Margie Mason. "Prisoners in the US Are Part of a Hidden Workforce Linked to Hundreds of Popular Food Brands." AP News, Jan. 29, 2024. https://apnews.com/article/prison-to-plate-inmate-labor-investigation-c6f0eb4747963283316e494eadf08c4e.

McLaughlin, Michael, et al. "The Economic Burden of Incarceration in the U.S." Prison Policy, Oct. 2016. Working Paper AJI072016. https://www.prisonpolicy.org/scans/iajre/the_economic_burden_of_incarceration_in_the_us.pdf.

Mikliszanski, J. K. "The Law of Retaliation and the Pentateuch." *Journal of Biblical Literature* 66 (1947) 295–303.

Miles, C. Austin. "In the Garden." Hymnary, 1912. https://hymnary.org/text/i_come_to_the_garden_alone.

Miller, Reuben Jonathan. *Halfway Home: Race, Punishment, and the Afterlife of Mass Incarceration*. New York: Little, Brown, & Co., 2021.

Miller, Teresa A. "Blurring the Boundaries Between Immigration and Crime Control After September 11th." *Boston College Third World Law Journal* 25 (2005) 81–123.

Mingus, Mia. "Pods and Pod Mapping Worksheet." Bay Area Transformative Justice Collective, June 2016. https://batjc.wordpress.com/pods-and-pod-mapping-worksheet.

———. "Transformative Justice: A Brief Description." Leaving Evidence, Jan. 9, 2019. https://leavingevidence.wordpress.com/2019/01/09/transformative-justice-a-brief-description/.

Mississippi Department of Corrections. "Mississippi State Penitentiary." Mississippi Department of Corrections, 2025. https://www.mdoc.ms.gov/facilities/missis sippi-state-penitentiary.

Moody, Josh. "A 5th Straight Semester of Enrollment Declines." *Inside Higher Ed*, May 25, 2022. https://www.insidehighered.com/news/2022/05/26/nsc-report-shows-total-enrollment-down-41-percent.

Moore, Darnell. "Foreword: Love Is a Reckoning." In *Love with Accountability: Digging Up the Roots of Child Sexual Abuse*, edited by Aishah Shahidah Simmons, 1–4. Chico, CA: AK Press, 2019.

Morín, Jason L., et al. "Cosponsoring and Cashing In: US House Members' Support for Punitive Immigration Policy and Financial Payoffs from the Private Prison Industry." *Business and Politics* 23 (2021) 492–509.

Morris, Norval, and David J. Rothman. *The Oxford History of the Prison: The Practice of Punishment in Western Society*. New York: Oxford University Press, 1995.

Moynihan, Daniel Patrick. "The Negro Family: The Case for National Action." U.S. Department of Labor, Mar. 1965. https://www.dol.gov/general/aboutdol/history/webid-moynihan.

Muhammad, Khalil Gibran. *The Condemnation of Blackness: Race, Crime, and the Making of Modern Urban America*. Cambridge, MA: Harvard University Press, 2010.

Mulch, Matthew. "Crime and Punishment in Private Prisons." *National Lawyers Guild Review* 66 (2009) 70–94.

Murakawa, Naomi. *The First Civil Right: How Liberals Built Prison America*. Studies in Postwar American Political Development. New York: Oxford University Press, 2014.

Myers, Barbara J., et al. "Children of Incarcerated Mothers." *Journal of Child and Family Studies* 8 (1999) 11–25.

Myers, Ched, and Elaine Enns. *New Testament Reflections on Restorative Justice and Peacemaking*. Vol. 1 of *Ambassadors of Reconciliation*. Maryknoll, NY: Orbis, 2009.

NAACP. "Criminal Justice Fact Sheet." NAACP, n.d. https://naacp.org/resources/criminal-justice-fact-sheet.

National Archives. "Executive Order 9066: Resulting in Japanese-American Incarceration (1942)." National Archives, n.d. https://www.archives.gov/milestone-documents/executive-order-9066.

———. "Medicare and Medicaid Act (1965)." National Archives, n.d. https://www.archives.gov/milestone-documents/medicare-and-medicaid-act.

National Archives Catalog. "Act of August 20, 1964 (Economic Opportunity Act of 1964), Public Law 88–452, 78 STAT 508, which mobilized the human and financial resources of the Nation to combat poverty in the United States." National Archives Catalog, Aug. 20, 1964. NAID 299896. https://catalog.archives.gov/id/299896.

National Association of Colleges and Employers. "What Is Career Readiness?" NACE, n.d. https://www.naceweb.org/career-readiness/competencies/career-readiness-defined/.

National Institute of Justice. "Recidivism." National Institute of Justice, n.d. https://nij.ojp.gov/topics/corrections/recidivism.

National Reentry Resource Center, The. "The Second Chance Act." CSG Justice Center, Apr. 2018. https://csgjusticecenter.org/wp-content/uploads/2020/02/July-2018_SCA_factsheet.pdf.

Nicklas, Tobias. "Ancient Christian Care for Prisoners: First and Second Centuries." *Acta Theologica* Supplement 23 (2016) 49–65. https://doi.org/10.4314/actat.v23i1s.3.

Niedermeier, Silvan. "Forced Confessions: Police Torture and the African American Struggle for Civil Rights in the 1930s and 1940s South." In *Crime and Punishment in the Jim Crow South: The History of White Supremacy and Criminal Justice*, edited by Amy Louise Wood and Natalie J. Ring, 58–78. Urbana: University of Illinois Press, 2019.

Nielsen, Marianne O. "Introduction to the Context of Native American Criminal Justice Involvement." In *Criminal Justice in Native America*, edited by Marianne O. Nielsen and Robert A. Silverman, 1–17. Tuscon: University of Arizona Press, 2009.

Noguchi, Yuki. "Unequal Outcomes: Most ICE Detainees Held in Rural Areas Where Deportation Risks Soar." NPR, Aug. 15, 2019. https://www.npr.org/2019/08/15/748764322/unequal-outcomes-most-ice-detainees-held-in-rural-areas-where-deportation-risks.

Nopper, Tamara K. "Why Black Immigrants Matter: Refocusing the Discussion on Racism and Immigration Enforcement." In *Keeping Out the Other: A Critical Introduction to Immigration Enforcement Today*, edited by David C. Brotherton and Philip Kretsedemas, 204–38. New York: Columbia University Press, 2008.

North Carolina Sentencing and Policy Advisory Commission. *Correctional Program Evaluation: Offenders Placed on Probation or Released from Prison, Fiscal Year 2019*. North Carolina Courts, Apr. 15, 2022. https://www.nccourts.gov/assets/documents/publications/SPAC-2022-Adult-Recidivism-Report-FY-2019.pdf.

Nowrasteh, Alex. "Obama's Mixed Legacy on Immigration." Cato Institute, Jan. 25, 2017. https://www.cato.org/publications/commentary/obamas-mixed-legacy-immigration.

NPR. "Read Martin Luther King Jr.'s 'I Have a Dream' Speech in Its Entirety." NPR, updated Jan. 16, 2023. https://www.npr.org/2010/01/18/122701268/i-have-a-dream-speech-in-its-entirety.

Oakford, Patrick, et al. *Investing in Futures: Economic and Fiscal Benefits of Postsecondary Education in Prison*. Vera Institute of Justice, Jan. 2019. https://vera-institute.files.svdcdn.com/production/downloads/publications/investing-in-futures.pdf.

Obama, Barack. "Remarks by the President in Address to the Nation on Immigration." Obama White House, Nov. 20, 2014. https://obamawhitehouse.archives.gov/the-press-office/2014/11/20/remarks-President-address-nation-immigration.

Office of Research and Public Affairs. *Overlooked in the Undercounted: The Role of Mental Illness in Fatal Law Enforcement Encounters*. Treatment Advocacy Center, Dec. 2015. https://www.treatmentadvocacycenter.org/storage/documents/overlooked-in-the-undercounted.pdf.

O'Hare, Kate Richards. *In Prison*. Farmington Hills, MI: Gale, 2010.

One Hundred Third Congress of the United States of America. "H.R. 3355—Violent Crime Control and Law Enforcement Act of 1994." GovInfo, Jan. 25, 1994. https://www.govinfo.gov/content/pkg/BILLS-103hr3355enr/pdf/BILLS-103hr3355enr.pdf.

Orozco, Anthony. "A Major Immigrant Detention Center Just Closed in Pa. but Plans for a New One Could Mean More Detainees Here Than Ever." *WHYY*, Nov. 3, 2021. https://whyy.org/articles/a-major-immigrant-detention-center-just-closed-in-pa-but-plans-for-new-a-one-could-mean-more-detainees-here-than-ever/.

Oshinsky, David M. *"Worse Than Slavery": Parchman Farm and the Ordeal of Jim Crow Justice*. New York: Free Press, 1996.

Paik, A. Naomi. "Abolitionist Futures and the US Sanctuary Movement." *Race and Class* 59 (2017) 3–25.

Palmer, Parker J. *The Courage to Teach: Exploring the Inner Landscape of a Teacher's Life*. San Francisco: Jossey-Bass, 1998.

Park, Andrew Sung. *From Hurt to Healing: A Theology of the Wounded*. Nashville: Abingdon, 2004.

Parker, Jeffrey S. "Developing Consensus Solutions to Overcriminalization Problems: The Way Ahead." *Journal of Law, Economics and Policy* 7 (2011) 725–44.

Patrick-Stamp, Leslie. "Numbers That Are Not New: African Americans in the Country's First Prison, 1790–1835." *Pennsylvania Magazine of History and Biography* 119 (1995) 95–128.

Payne, Sarah. "The Economic Impact of Prison Labor for Incarcerated Individuals and Taxpayers." *Princeton Legal Journal* 2 (2023) 14–21.

Peters, Edward M. "Prison Before the Prison: The Ancient and Medieval Worlds." In *The Oxford History of the Prison: The Practice of Punishment in Western Society*, edited by Norval Morris and David J. Rothman, 3–43. New York: Oxford University Press, 1995.

Pew Center on the States. *State of Recidivism: The Revolving Door of America's Prisons*. Washington, DC: Pew Charitable Trusts, 2011. https://www.pewtrusts.org/-/media/legacy/uploadedfiles/pcs_assets/2011/pewstateofrecidivismpdf.pdf.

Pfaff, John F. "The Incentives of Private Prisons." *Arizona State Law Journal* 52 (2020) 991–1019.

———. *Locked In: The True Causes of Mass Incarceration—and How to Achieve Real Reform*. New York: Basic, 2017.

Pisciotta, Alexander W. *Benevolent Repression: Social Control and the American Reformatory-Prison Movement*. New York: New York University Press, 1994.

Pizzi, William T. "Understanding Prosecutorial Discretion in the United States: The Limits of Comparative Criminal Procedure as an Instrument of Reform." *Ohio State Law Journal* 54 (1993) 1325–73.

Podgor, Ellen S. "The Challenge of White Collar Sentencing." *Journal of Criminal Law and Criminology* 97 (2007) 731–59.

———. "The Ethics and Professionalism of Prosecutors in Discretionary Decisions." *Fordham Law Review* 68 (2000) 1511–35.

Pohl, Christine D. *Making Room: Recovering Hospitality as a Christian Tradition*. Grand Rapids: Eerdmans, 1999.

Prison Fellowship. "Back to Basics: Equipping Prisoners to Take Responsibility." Prison Fellowship, Sept. 18, 2019. https://www.prisonfellowship.org/2019/09/back-to-basics-equipping-prisoners-to-take-responsibility/.

———. "Celebrating 101 Prison Fellowship Academy Sites with Our Top 10 Stories!" Prison Fellowship, Jan. 21, 2020. https://www.prisonfellowship.org/2020/01/101-prison-fellowship-academy-sites/.

———. "Good Citizenship Model." Prison Fellowship, n.d. https://www.prisonfellowship.org/research/good-citizenship-model/.

Prison Policy Initiative. "Reentry and Recidivism." Prison Policy Initiative, updated Dec. 20, 2024. https://www.prisonpolicy.org/research/recidivism_and_reentry/.

Prison Seminaries Foundation. "The Prison Seminary Model." Prison Seminaries Foundation, n.d. https://www.prisonseminaries.org/the-prison-seminary-model.

Pruitt, Paul M., Jr. "Convict Lease System and Peonage." In *The New Encyclopedia of Southern Culture*, edited by Charles Reagan Wilson et al., 24:49–53. Chapel Hill: University of North Carolina Press, 2013.

RAINN [Rape, Abuse and Incest National Network]. "The Criminal Justice System: Statistics." RAINN, n.d. https://rainn.org/statistics/criminal-justice-system.

Ray, Rashawn, and William A. Galston. "Did the 1994 Crime Bill Cause Mass Incarceration?" Brookings, Aug. 28, 2020. https://www.brookings.edu/blog/fixgov/2020/08/28/did-the-1994-crime-bill-cause-mass-incarceration/.

Recine, Jennifer S. "Examination of the White Collar Crime Penalty Enhancements in the Sarbanes-Oxley Act." *American Criminal Law Review* 39 (2002) 1535–70.

Richards, Jennifer Smith, and Jodi S. Cohen. "The Price Kids Pay: Schools and Police Punish Students with Costly Tickets for Minor Misbehavior." *Chicago Tribune*, Apr. 28, 2022.

Ringe, Sharon H. *Jesus, Liberation, and the Biblical Jubilee: Images for Ethics and Christology*. Philadelphia: Fortress, 1985.

Ringer, Christophe D. *Necropolitics: The Religious Crisis of Mass Incarceration in America*. Religion and Race. Lanham, MD: Lexington, 2021.

Ritchie, Andrea. "Law Enforcement Violence Against Women of Color." In *Color of Violence: The Incite! Anthology*, edited by Incite! Women of Color Against Violence, 138–56. Cambridge, MA: South End, 2006.

Ritter, Luke. "Immigration, Crime, and the Economic Origins of Political Nativism in the Antebellum West." *Journal of American Ethnic History* 39 (2020) 62–91.

Romero, Farida Jhabvala. "Immigrant Detainees Strike Over Working Conditions, California Regulators Investigate." KQED, June 22, 2022. https://www.kqed.org/news/11917597/immigrant-detainees-strike-over-working-conditions-california-regulators-investigate.

Robbins, Ira P. "The Legal Dimensions of Private Incarceration." *American University Law Review* 38 (1989) 531–854.

Robert, Nikia Smith. "Penitence, Plantation, and the Penitentiary: A Liberation Theology for Lockdown America." *Graduate Journal of Harvard Divinity School* 12 (2017) 41–69.

Rosenberg, Ben. "The Growth of Federal Common Law." *American Journal of Criminal Law* 29 (2002) 193–221.

Rosenfeld, Richard. "Overview and Reflections." Council on Criminal Justice, 2019. https://counciloncj.foleon.com/reports/crime-bill/overview-and-reflections.

Rothman, David J. "Perfecting the Prison, 1789–1865." In *The Oxford History of the Prison: The Practice of Punishment in Western Society*, edited by Norval Morris and David J. Rothman, 111–29. New York: Oxford University Press, 1997.

Rotman, Edgardo. "The Failure of Reform: United States, 1865–1965." *Crime and Justice* 12 (1990) 151–98.

Russell, Kelsey D. "Cruel and Unusual Construction: The Eighth Amendment as a Limit on Building Prisons on Toxic Waste Sites." *University of Pennsylvania Law Review* 165 (2017) 741–83.

Ruttenberg, Danya. *On Repentance and Repair: Making Amends in an Unapologetic World*. Boston: Beacon, 2022.

Ryan, Susan M. *The Grammar of Good Intentions: Race and the Antebellum Culture of Benevolence*. Ithaca: Cornell University Press, 2004.

Ryan, William. "D. Savage Discovery: The Moynihan Report." *Nation* 201 (1965) 380–84. http://www.columbia.edu/itc/hs/pubhealth/p9740/readings/william_ryan.pdf.

Ryo, Emily, and Ian Peacock. "A National Study of Immigration Detention in the United States." *Southern California Law Review* 92 (2018) 1–67.

Sabol, William J., and Thaddeus L. Johnson. "Impacts on Prison Populations." Council on Criminal Justice, 2019. https://counciloncj.foleon.com/reports/crime-bill/i-impacts-on-prison-populations.

Sage, John. "Foreword." In *Restoring Peace: Using Lessons from Prison to Mend Broken Relationships*, by Kirk Blackard, 1–4. Houston: Bridges to Life, 2005.

Salkeld, Brett. *Can Catholics and Evangelicals Agree About Purgatory and the Last Judgment?* New York: Paulist, 2011.

Sanneh, Kelefa. "Body Count: Engulfed by Crime, Many Blacks Once Agitated for More Police and Harsher Penalties." *New Yorker*, Sept. 14, 2015. https://www.newyorker.com/magazine/2015/09/14/body-count-a-critic-at-large-kelefa-sanneh.

Sawyer, Wendy, and Peter Wagner. "Mass Incarceration: The Whole Pie 2022." Prison Policy Initiative, Mar. 14, 2022. https://www.prisonpolicy.org/reports/pie2022.html#bigpicture.

Schanzenbacha, Max, and Michael L. Yaeger. "Prison Time, Fines, and Federal White-Collar Criminals: The Anatomy of a Racial Disparity." *Journal of Criminal Law and Criminology* 96 (2006) 757–93.

Schmidt, Benno C. "Principle and Prejudice: The Supreme Court and Race in the Progressive Era, Part 2: The Peonage Cases." *Columbia Law Review* 82 (1982) 646–718.

Schoenfeld, Heather. *Building the Prison State: Race and the Politics of Mass Incarceration*. Chicago Series in Law and Society. Chicago: University of Chicago Press, 2019.

———. "The Delayed Emergence of Penal Modernism in Florida." *Punishment and Society* 17 (2015) 258–84.

Schottroff, Luise. *The Parables of Jesus*. Translated by Linda M. Maloney. Minneapolis: Fortress, 2006.

Schriro, Dora. *Immigration Detention Overview and Recommendation*. Washington, DC: U.S. Department of Homeland Security, 2009.

Sentencing Project, The. "Report to the United Nations on Racial Disparities in the U.S. Criminal Justice System." Sentencing Project, Apr. 19, 2018. https://www.sentencingproject.org/publications/un-report-on-racial-disparities/.

Sered, Danielle. *Until We Reckon: Violence, Mass Incarceration, and a Road to Repair*. New York: New Press, 2019.

Sheikh, Irum. "Racializing, Criminalizing, and Silencing 9/11 Deportees." In *Keeping Out the Other: A Critical Introduction to Immigration Enforcement Today*, edited by David C. Brotherton and Philip Kretsedemas, 81–107. New York: Columbia University Press, 2008.

Siegel, Reva. "Why Equal Protection No Longer Protects: The Evolving Forms of Status-Enforcing State Action." *Stanford Law Review* 49 (1997) 1111–48.

Sigler, Mary. "Private Prisons, Public Functions, and the Meaning of Punishment." *Florida State University Law Review* 38 (2010) 149–78.

Simmons, Aishah Shahidah, ed. *Love with Accountability: Digging Up the Roots of Child Sexual Abuse*. Chico, CA: AK Press, 2019.

Simon, Jonathan. *Governing Through Crime: How the War on Crime Transformed American Democracy and Created a Culture of Fear*. Studies in Crime and Public Policy. New York: Oxford University Press, 2007.

Singh, Devin. "Sovereign Debt." *Journal of Religious Ethics* 46 (2018) 239–66.

———. "To Receive What Is Already Yours: Gifting and Common Goods." Keynote lecture delivered at "Signs of the Times: Christianity and Socialism" conference, Baylor University, Apr. 24, 2019.

Siskin, Allison. *Immigration-Related Detention: Current Legislative Issues*. Washington, DC: Congressional Research Service, 2012. https://irp.fas.org/crs/RL32369.pdf.

Sjoberg, Gideon. "The Corporate Control of Industry and Human Rights: The Case of Iraq." *Journal of Human Rights* 4 (2005) 95–101.

Skotnicki, Andrew. *Religion and the Development of the American Penal System*. Lanham, MD: University Press of America, 2000.

Slotkin, Richard. "Narratives of Negro Crime in New England, 1675–1800." *American Quarterly* 25 (1973) 3–31.

Smith, Christopher E. "Black Muslims and the Development of Prisoners' Rights." *Journal of Black Studies* 24 (1993) 131–46.

Smith, Stephen F. "Overcoming Overcriminalization." *Journal of Criminal Law and Criminology* 102 (2017) 537–91.

Soltis, Kathryn Getek, and Katie Walker Grimes. "Order, Reform, and Abolition: Changes in Catholic Theological Imagination on Prisons and Punishment." *Theological Studies* 82 (2021) 95–115.

Southern, R. W. *Saint Anselm: A Portrait in a Landscape*. Cambridge: Cambridge University Press, 1990.

Starr, Alexandra. "At Low Pay, Government Hires Immigrants Held at Detention Centers." NPR, July 23, 2015. https://www.npr.org/2015/07/23/425511981/at-low-pay-government-hires-immigrants-held-at-detention-centers.

Stevenson, Bryan. *Just Mercy: A Story of Justice and Redemption*. New York: Spiegel & Grau, 2014.

Stoddard, Brad. "'Slaves of the State': Christianity and Convict Labor in the Postbellum South." *Religions* 11 (2020). https://doi.org/10.3390/rel11120651.

Stumpf, Juliet P. "Civil Detention and Other Oxymorons." *Queen's Law Journal* 40 (2014) 55–98.

———. "The Crimmigration Crisis: Immigrants, Crime, and Sovereign Power." *American University Law Review* 56 (2006) 367–419.

Stuntz, William J. *The Collapse of American Criminal Justice*. Cambridge, MA: Harvard University Press, 2011.

Suddler, Carl. *Presumed Criminal: Black Youth and the Justice System in Postwar New York*. New York: New York University Press, 2019.

Survived and Punished. "S&P Analysis & Vision." Survived and Punished, n.d. https://survivedandpunished.org/analysis/.

Sweeney, Megan. "Reading and Reckoning in a Women's Prison." *Texas Studies in Literature and Language* 50 (2008) 304–28.

———. *Reading Is My Window: Books and the Art of Reading in Women's Prisons*. Chapel Hill: University of North Carolina Press, 2010.

Swift, Art. "Americans: 'Eye for an Eye' Top Reason for Death Penalty." Gallup, Oct. 23, 2014. https://news.gallup.com/poll/178799/americans-eye-eye-top-reason-death-penalty.aspx.

Tentler, Leslie Woodcock. *American Catholics: A History*. New Haven, CT: Yale University Press, 2020.

Thompson, Heather Ann. "Inner-City Violence in the Age of Mass Incarceration." *Atlantic*, Oct. 30, 2014. https://www.theatlantic.com/national/archive/2014/10/inner-city-violence-in-the-age-of-mass-incarceration/382154/.

Tonry, Michael. *Punishing Race: A Continuing American Dilemma*. Studies in Crime and Public Policy. New York: Oxford University Press, 2011.

———. *Sentencing Fragments: Penal Reform in America, 1975–2025*. Studies in Crime and Public Policy. New York: Oxford University Press, 2016.

Totenberg, Nina. "Race, Drugs and Sentencing at the Supreme Court." NPR, June 14, 2021. https://www.npr.org/2021/06/14/1006264385/race-drugs-and-sentencing-at-the-supreme-court.

Traisman, Ken. "Native Law: Law and Order Among Eighteenth-Century Cherokee, Great Plains, Central Prairie, and Woodland Indians." *American Indian Law Review* 9 (1981) 273–87.

Treatment Advocacy Center. "People with Untreated Mental Illness 16 Times More Likely to Be Killed by Law Enforcement." Treatment Advocacy Center, n.d. https://www.treatmentadvocacycenter.org/criminalization/.

Trocmé, André. *Jesus and the Nonviolent Revolution*. Rifton, NY: Plough, 2011.

Trujillo-Pagán, Nicole. "Emphasizing the 'Complex' in the 'Immigration Industrial Complex.'" *Critical Sociology* 40 (2014) 29–46.

Ubah, Chinedu. "Abolition of Pell Grants for Higher Education of Prisoners: Examining Antecedents and Consequences." *Journal of Offender Rehabilitation* 35 (2002) 73–85.

Ulen, Thomas S. "Skepticism About Deterrence." *Loyola University Chicago Law Journal* 46 (2014) 381–403.

United States Border Patrol. "Southwest Border Sectors: Total Illegal Alien Apprehensions by Fiscal Year (Oct. 1st Through Sept. 30th) [1960–2018]." U.S. Customs and Border Protection, Mar. 2019. https://www.cbp.gov/sites/default/files/assets/documents/2019-Mar/bp-southwest-border-sector-apps-fy1960-fy2018.pdf.

United States Sentencing Commission. "Annotated 2021 Chapter 1." USSC, 2021. https://www.ussc.gov/guidelines/guidelines-archive/annotated-2021-chapter-1.

Urbina, Ian. "Using Jailed Migrants as a Pool of Cheap Labor." *New York Times*, May 25, 2014.

U.S. Department of Justice. *The Clinton Administration's Law Enforcement Strategy: Combating Crime with Community Policing and Community Prosecution; Taking Back Our Neighborhoods One Block at a Time*. U.S. Department of Justice, Mar. 1999. https://www.justice.gov/archive/dag/pubdoc/crimestrategy.pdf.

U.S. Immigration and Customs Enforcement. "5.8 Voluntary Work Program." ICE, revised Dec. 2016. PBNDS 2011. https://www.ice.gov/doclib/detention-standards/2011/5-8.pdf.

———. "Fact Sheet." American Immigration Lawyers Association, Mar. 28, 2008. https://www.aila.org/aila-files/D8E34378-8566-41F9-ACAD-B0A1BE94A306/08032831.pdf?1697589844.

———. "ICE Releases FY2022 Annual Report." ICE, Dec. 30, 2022. https://www.ice.gov/news/releases/ice-releases-fy-2022-annual-report.

U.S. Sentencing Commission. *Preliminary Crack Cocaine Retroactivity Data Report*. USSC, Nov. 2010. https://www.ussc.gov/sites/default/files/pdf/research-and-publications/federal-sentencing-statistics/2007-crack-cocaine-amendment/20101214_USSC_Crack_Cocaine_Retroactivity_Data_Report.pdf.

———. *Report to the Congress: Impact of the Fair Sentencing Act of 2010*. USSC, Aug. 2015. https://www.ussc.gov/sites/default/files/pdf/news/congressional-testimony-and-reports/drug-topics/201507_RtC_Fair-Sentencing-Act.pdf.

Vera Institute of Justice. *Incarceration Trends in Florida*. Vera Institute of Justice, Dec. 2019. https://www.vera.org/downloads/pdfdownloads/state-incarceration-trends-florida.pdf.

Vesely-Flad, Rima. *Racial Purity and Dangerous Bodies: Moral Pollution, Black Lives, and the Struggle for Justice*. Minneapolis: Fortress, 2017.

———. "The Social Covenant and Mass Incarceration: Theologies of Race and Punishment." *Anglican Theological Review* 93 (2011) 541–62.

Vitiello, Michael. "Marijuana Legalization, Racial Disparity, and the Hope for Reform." *Lewis and Clark Law Review* 23 (2019) 789–821.

Wadhia, Shoba Sivaprasad. "Immigration Enforcement and the Future of Discretion." *Roger Williams University Law Review* 23 (2018) 353–68.

Walls, Jerry L. *Purgatory: The Logic of Total Transformation*. New York: Oxford University Press, 2012.

Walmsley, Roy. *World Prison Population List*. Prison Studies, 2018. 12th ed. https://www.prisonstudies.org/sites/default/files/resources/downloads/wppl_12.pdf.

Walzer, Michael. *Spheres of Justice: A Defense of Pluralism and Equality*. New York: Basic Books, 1983.

Weaver, Dorothy Jean. "Transforming Nonresistance: From *Lex Talionis* to 'Do Not Resist the Evil One.'" In *The Love of Enemy and Nonretaliation in the New Testament*, edited by Willard M. Swartley, 32–71. Studies in Peace and Scripture. Louisville: Westminster John Knox, 1992.

Weaver, J. Denny. *The Nonviolent God*. Grand Rapids: Eerdmans, 2013.

Weaver, Vesla M. "Frontlash: Race and the Development of Punitive Crime Policy." *Studies in American Political Development* 21 (2007) 230–65.

Weinberger, Evan. "Inmate Families Face Cash-Transfer Fees 'Just to Stay Connected.'" Bloomberg Law, Jan. 11, 2022. https://news.bloomberglaw.com/banking-law/inmate-families-face-cash-transfer-fees-just-to-stay-connected.

Weiner, Mark S. *Black Trials: Citizenship from the Beginnings of Slavery to the End of Caste*. New York: Knopf, 2004.

Weisberg, Robert. "Reality-Challenged Philosophies of Punishment." *Marquette Law Review* 95 (2012) 1203–52.

Weissmann, Andrew, and Joshua A. Block. "White Collar Defendants and White Collar Crimes." *Yale Law Journal* 116 (2007). http://yalelawjournal.org/forum/white-collar-defendants-and-white-collar-crimes.

Wellford, E. T. *Crime and Cure: A Review of This Lawless Age and the Mistrial of Christ*. Boston: Stratford Co., 1930.

———. *The Lynching of Jesus: A Review of the Legal Aspects of the Trial of Christ*. 2nd ed. Newport News, VA: Franklin, 1905.

Wells-Barnett, Ida B. *The Red Record: Tabulated Statistics and Alleged Causes of Lynching in the United States*. Gutenberg, 1895. https://www.gutenberg.org/files/14977/14977-h/14977-h.htm.

West, Traci C. *Disruptive Christian Ethics: When Racism and Women's Lives Matter*. Louisville: Westminster John Knox, 2006.

Western, Bruce, and Becky Pettit. "Incarceration and Social Inequality." *Dædalus* 139 (2010) 8–19.

White, Ahmed A. "Rule of Law and the Limits of Sovereignty: The Private Prison in Jurisprudential Perspective." *American Criminal Law Review* 38 (2001) 111–46.

White House, The. "Fact Sheet: Biden-Harris Administration Announces New Border Enforcement Actions." White House, Jan. 5, 2023. https://bidenwhitehouse.archives.gov/briefing-room/statements-releases/2023/01/05/fact-sheet-biden-harris-administration-announces-new-border-enforcement-actions/.

———. "Fact Sheet: President Bush Signs Second Chance Act of 2007." White House, Apr. 9, 2008. https://georgewbush-whitehouse.archives.gov/news/releases/2008/04/20080409-15.html.

———. "White House Faith-Based and Community Initiative." White House, n.d. https://georgewbush-whitehouse.archives.gov/government/fbci/president-initiative.html.

Wines, E. C. *The True Penitent Portrayed in a Practical Exposition of the Fifty-First Psalm: To Which Is Added the Doctrine of Repentance, as Declared in Acts XVII*. Philadelphia: Presbyterian Board of Education, 1864.

Wiseman, Samuel R. "Bail and Mass Incarceration." *Georgia Law Review* 53 (2018) 235–80.

Withers, Rachel. "George H. W. Bush's 'Willie Horton' Ad Will Always Be the Reference Point for Dog-Whistle Racism." *Vox*, Dec. 1, 2018. https://www.vox.com/2018/12/1/18121221/george-hw-bush-willie-horton-dog-whistle-politics.

Wofford, Taylor. "How America's Police Became an Army: The 1033 Program." *Newsweek*, Aug. 13, 2014. https://www.newsweek.com/how-americas-police-became-army-1033-program-264537.

Woodfox, Albert. *Solitary: A Biography*. New York: Grove, 2019.

Wong, Wilson. "'Defund the Police' Movement Could Offer Sexual Assault Survivors a Different Path for Justice, Experts Say." NBC, Aug. 2, 2020. https://www.nbcnews.com/news/us-news/defund-police-movement-could-offer-sexual-assault-survivors-different-path-n1235478.

Wright, Christopher J. H. "Theology of Jubilee: Biblical, Social and Ethical Perspectives." *Evangelical Review of Theology* 41 (2017) 6–18.

Wright, Kevin. "Pell Grants, Politics and the Penitentiary: Connections Between the Development of U.S. Higher Education and Prisoner Post-Secondary Programs." *Journal of Correctional Education* 52 (2001) 11–15.

Yates, Sally Q. "Phasing Out Our Use of Private Prisons." Archives: U.S. Department of Justice, Aug. 18, 2016; updated Mar. 3, 2017. https://www.justice.gov/archives/opa/blog/phasing-out-our-use-private-prisons.

Young, Elliott. *Forever Prisoners: How the United States Made the World's Largest Immigrant Detention System*. New York: Oxford University Press, 2021.

Yukich, Grace. "Constructing the Model Immigrant." *Social Problems* 60 (2013) 302–20.

Zehr, Howard. *Changing Lenses: Restorative Justice for Our Times*. 25th anniv. ed. Harrisonburg, VA: Herald, 2015.

———. *The Little Book of Restorative Justice*. Little Books of Justice and Peacebuilding. Intercourse, PA: Good Books, 2002.

Zehr Institute for Restorative Justice. "Webinar: Transformative Justice." Zehr Institute for Restorative Justice, Feb. 15, 2017. Hosted by Johonna Turner, with guests R. J. Maccani, Mia Mingus, Nathaniel Shara, and Ejeris Dixon. http://zehr-institute.org/webinars/transformative-justice/.